THE
SHAAR
PRESS

THE JUDAICA IMPRINT
FOR THOUGHTFUL PEOPLE

SARAH

A GIFT

A
SHAAR
PRESS
PUBLICATION

SHAPIRO

PASSED ALONG

A woman looks at the world around her

Several of the essays that appear in this volume were published, either in their present form or in abbreviated form, in the following publications: *The Jewish Observer, The Los Angeles Times, Olam, Horizons, The Jewish Woman's Journal, Soferet, The Jerusalem Post, Jewish Action, Am Echad Resources, Jewish World Review.com,* and *Aish.com.*

Published by **SHAAR PRESS**
Distributed by MESORAH PUBLICATIONS, LTD.
4401 Second Avenue / Brooklyn, N.Y 11232 / (718) 921-9000

Distributed in Israel by SIFRIATI / A. GITLER
6 Hayarkon Street / Bnei Brak 51127

Distributed in Europe by LEHMANNS
Unit E, Viking Industrial Park, Rolling Mill Road / Jarrow, Tyne and Wear, NE32 3DP/ England

Distributed in Australia and New Zealand by GOLDS WORLD OF JUDAICA
3-13 William Street / Balaclava, Melbourne 3183 / Victoria Australia

Distributed in South Africa by KOLLEL BOOKSHOP
Shop 8A Norwood Hypermarket / Norwood 2196, Johannesburg, South Africa

ISBN: 1-57819-489-X Hard Cover
ISBN: 1-57819-490-3 Paperback

Printed in the United States of America by Noble Book Press
Custom bound by Sefercraft, Inc. / 4401 Second Avenue / Brooklyn N.Y. 11232

In memory
of my parents,

Norman and Eleanor
Cousins

with reverence,
love and gratitude

ACKNOWLEDGMENTS

It is an honor and joy to express my gratitude to Rabbi Nosson Scherman and Shmuel Blitz of ArtScroll/Mesorah.

My thanks to Avrohom Biderman, for the extreme patience and care he exercised throughout its production.

My thanks to the editor Mrs. Judi Dick, for her extraordinary dedication to her craft and her ideals.

My thanks to Eli Kroen for enhancing my book with his magnificent cover, which is evidence of the time, patience and effort he put in on my behalf.

My thanks to Rabbi Nisson Wolpin, Editor of the Jewish Observer, for his support through the years; and to Nechama Carmel and Matis Greenblatt, Editor and Literary Editor of Jewish Action, whose encouragement and editorial advice were indispensable to the essay, "Circles in the Sand."

My thanks for the encouragement and inspiration provided through the years by Rav Nachman Bulman, and for the teachings of Rebbetzin Tzippora Heller.

Above all, I thank Hashem for my precious family — my husband Yaacov Tzvi and our beloved children, sons-in-law, and grandson, and for my beloved sisters.

May we and all *Klal Yisrael* merit His protection in these dangerous times.

TABLE OF CONTENTS

A Note
to the Reader

The reader is asked to bear in mind that many of the chapters which follow describe an individual's growth process, or a search of one kind or another. As with any journey, the traveler does not end up where he began. The reader is therefore advised not to take the starting points out of context.

In some of the essays, it may become apparent that the author has not tried to explain an experience but simply to describe it. As much as I might wish otherwise, daily life does not come with labels of explanation attached. If we hold up a mirror to the world around us, we will see reflected there — amidst lucid instances of Divine Providence — ambiguities and unanswered questions, as well.

It is on those occasions, when the meaning and purpose of difficult events is too complex for us to fathom, that we have our best opportunity to develop trust in Hashem's infinite kindness, and faith that one day, all will be understood.

Jerusalem

7 Adar 5762

One day I was walking along a Jerusalem street, consumed by my own thoughts and worries, when I looked up just in time to see a child whose T-shirt read, "Wish I Were Here."

Among all the passers-by, the child disappeared in a flash — as do our lives — but the message he bore is still with me.

How can we be here? Amidst all the sorrows and pressures, doubts and pains and worries, the present is veiled to our own sight. We tend to look back on childhood — whether it was happy or unhappy, idyllic or tragic — as an illuminated period of time in some kind of mythic land. But that's just because as children, our perceptions are undefended. No matter where it takes place, all childhoods unfold in the same miraculous spot.

This instant — which holds all the great, vast beauties of the world — is what we cannot afford to lose in the unceasing onrush of overwhelming events. "The past is history," goes a jingle I heard last year. "The future's a mystery. Right now is a gift, that's why they call it the present."

> *The Ibn Ezra put it this way:*
> *The past is nothing.*
> *The future is yet to be.*
> *The present is a blink.*
> *So why worry?*

To be here. It's the simplest of ambitions but the most elusive to fulfill. Years have intervened since that child passed me on the sidewalk, but I'm still in search of the path into that kingdom, the vast and wondrous kingdom of the present moment.

1

ON THE RETURN OF LOST OBJECTS

One of our children has a particular gift for finding things.

"Devorah, could you help me find the..."

"Devorah, by any chance have you seen..."

"Devorah, do you know where the..."

A proficiency for returning lost objects has never been lost on me, especially since I myself am differently blessed. It has always been my inclination less to keep track of things than to let go of them; less to locate objects, than to misplace them.

Today she said, "Are you missing one of your flower earrings? I think I saw it." She came back a few moments later, my silver rose in hand. It had been on a shelf next to the washing machine.

How lovely, to get back what one thought was gone! There's something about having a lost item restored that momentarily ties together all the loose strings of one's life.

And there's something about losing it that produces a particular and distinctive uneasiness. No matter how trivial a possession it may seem to be, its loss can be counted on to evoke a pervasive feeling of futility, however fleeting, and a disconcerting sense that all is not right in the world.

≈≈

However slight a lost object's apparent value, from either a sentimental or a monetary standpoint, the value of returning it to its owner remains — as is the case with any mitzvah — immeasurable and absolute.

In our neighborhood, like most Orthodox neighborhoods, the local bulletin boards usually carry a number of *HaShovas Aveidah* notices. "Found near Building 48, *knissah aleph*: ballpoint pen, call 532-1074." "Found outside supermarket during Chol HaMoed, coin purse with sum of money. To identify, call 581-0731." "Found in playground, piece of girl's jewelry. Call..."

One notice which recently caught my attention reported a pair of women's sunglasses found near Building 47, and ever since, I've been meaning to ask my *mechutenister* Ruthie if perhaps hers are missing. She had taken one of her children to Dr. Slater about that time, and the thought of being the one to help her find her glasses (if indeed hers are lost) elicits on my part an extremely pleasing sensation; it's a mitzvah not to be missed.

But the thought keeps slipping my mind, itself a lost object, and I forget to ask. The mitzvah eludes me.

Losing that opportunity is not insignificant. One of the children's books which we used to read aloud, through the years, told the story from the Gemara about R' Chanina ben Dosa. Under a tree near his home, R' Chanina found a sack of chickens which a wayfarer had mistakenly left behind. The traveler didn't return. Those chickens laid eggs, which, in turn, hatched and in time, the Rabbi's small hen-yard could no longer handle the growing poultry population, So he finally sold all the chickens, and with the money received, purchased a number of goats. Under the rabbi's diligent care, the goats, too, multiplied.

One day, years later, the same traveler passed by, and he suddenly recalled how he'd lost his bag on that very spot. Rav — was overjoyed to have located the chickens' rightful owner and handed over to him the herd of goats, whose value, of course, far surpassed the original item.

The story was teaching us not only that we are supposed to guard stringently against taking possession of anything not rightfully ours, and to pursue zealously the fulfillment of this Torah commandment, but also that a lost item's value and significance may not be readily apparent to the one who finds it; in fact, its true value may be something of which even the original owner himself may be unaware.

≈⸙≈

In my life, earrings are the items which most frequently disappear, then reappear, like objects washing in and out with the tide.

A pair of the silver roses is what my husband usually gets me for my birthday; he can count on the probability that at least one of them was lost during the previous year. He has been buying them almost annually from the same little old man, at the same little old jewelry store in Meah Shearim, in their successive stylistic variations.

On the plane to my father's funeral more than a decade ago, I was wearing an early pair of those roses. Sitting there devastated, my eyes streaming, too shattered to eat the meal, I suddenly noticed that one of them was missing.

"My earring!" The woman in the window seat looked up from her dinner tray. A child's face popped up over the head rest of the seat in front of me. "I've lost my earring!" Up I jumped and down I crouched to peer beneath my seat, and my neighbor's seat. All thoughts of losing my father had vanished. "Excuse me, I'm so sorry, would you mind looking under your seat for an —" I said to the people in the row behind mine, then to the man across the aisle, and the man behind the man.

This continued for a few frantic minutes, until rose the blessed cry, "Is this it?" It was the child who found it.

I put the earring back on and started crying again.

≈≈

My aunt gave me a pair of silver clip-ons last year in Los Angeles. I was really quite pleased with them and pressed them into immediate service, dropping the roses into the bottomless well of my purse. But at the airport a few hours later, I took one of them off while talking on a pay phone, and when the announcement came on that it was time to board, promptly finished talking, gathered together my stuff, and hurriedly took a place in line. Only when I'd taken my seat did my hand instinctively reach up to feel its absence on my ear.

I explained to the El Al stewardesses what had happened, got a security clearance, ran back out through the gate, rushed over to the phone, looked up, looked down, looked all around, but alas! Gone! How could it be? Could somebody have taken it that fast? And what good is an earring without its mate, unless the thief is partial to berets cocked jauntily to one side?

All year long the memory of that earring irked me, and I never mentioned it to Aunt Jeannie. If there's anything that could deftly evoke a feeling of futility as much as losing something, it must be finding out that the time and money you've spent on a gift has been carelessly squandered by an unworthy recipient.

So, that was the end of that, until just recently, when I zippered open an old telephone/address book/organizer in search of an important receipt, and out fell that earring upon the carpet. If I didn't know any better, I'd claim to have engineered the entire incident, just for the joy and surprise of its rediscovery.

≈≈

There was one occasion, in my experience, in which the loss of something expensive was utterly neutralized by the certainty that it was meant to be. In that case, I was glad it was never returned.

Once upon a time we had a Subaru station wagon. I was much enamored of that car, because every Friday, when our children were small, my husband used to take them for long rides on the dirt road behind our apartment building, along the ridge which is now the Jerusalem neighborhood of Ramat Shlomo.

He, on the other hand, was eager to sell. The cost of insurance and gas was ridiculous, our lives were such that we rarely could take trips, anyway, and on top of that, his yeshivah was right up the street, as was the supermarket.

But I was loath to give up the freedom of my Fridays.

One Thursday morning, as I was sweeping the living room floor, for reasons that never became apparent, an unannounced thought arose in my head: "Well, I guess we can sell the car now. We really don't need it."

I couldn't wait to give Yaacov the good news, but that night when he walked in, the expression on his face deterred me from speaking. Something was wrong. "I don't know where the car is," he said. Though it's unlikely this was actually the case, in my memory of the incident, he's scratching his head in a cartoon caricature of befuddlement. "I'm almost positive I left it down in the parking lot this morning, but it's not there. I walked back up to the yeshivah, to see if I drove it up there and forgot about it, but it's not there, either."

He stood there, confounded, then went to take another look in the parking lot. He walked up the hill to the yeshivah, checking the cars on either side to see if by some chance he'd parked it on the street and forgotten, then he came back down the hill again to check our building's parking lot. Back up, back down. Then he came home.

The car, of course, had been stolen, yet never before and never again would I know a finer *kapparah* (nor a bigger insurance payment).

⤳ ⤶

What are some of the many items I have loved and lost? The silver necklace my mother gave me when I was eighteen, that disappeared on the commuter train between New York and New Canaan. A little music box that played "Oh, What a Beautiful Morning!" which somehow fell — I know not how — out the car window into a snow bank, as my mother drove through a toll booth on the Merritt Parkway. A frayed, once-yellow comfort blanket which Devorah adored and trusted deeply, up until the age of two, when a babysitter left it behind on a playground. A beautiful shimmering-green raincoat that my sister Candis gave me. An envelope holding eight hundred dollars in cash, which disappeared in our apartment about five years ago; I still keep my eyes open; hope does not die. A child's invisible, clear plastic orthodontic retainer, which was left on a table and thrown out with the disposable tablecloth.

One loss that evokes a particularly poignant regret is the delicate Magen David on a silver chain, which my father gave me when I first started becoming observant.

Which brings to mind, though, the most valuable thing in my life that was ever lost, then found. It happened the first time I saw a woman light candles for Shabbos, then cover her eyes to address Hashem.

I'll never forget what it was like: the sense that something I'd been waiting for all my life, without being aware of it, had just been returned to me, and that *I* was being returned to *it*. Brought abruptly to life by those Hebrew words and the two flames, its reappearance revealed instantly that the darkness I'd always felt had been the shadow cast by its absence. It was brand new, and had always been mine. It was vastly larger than I, and deeply familiar. Everything within me was saying: *I see!*

For the first time, in the candlelight, I stepped into my own place between heaven and earth and with that, the whole universe with its stars and seas shifted, too, into proper alignment. *I was a Jew. A Jewish woman.* It was the place for which I had blindly hungered my whole life. All at once I was a small human being who knew that to be a small human being was no small thing.

I could speak to G-d.

If finding an earring brings some measure of pleasure, then imagine, if you can, the joy — the sheer joy, the gladdest joy, the joy that never ends — if the thing returned is your own self.

2

RABBI SCHEINBERG'S
LAUGHTER

If you ask me why he laughed, I'll say: your guess is as good as mine. Who am I to understand a tzaddik? At the time, I thought I must be missing something.

I was.

Then he laughed more, and I thought he must be seeing this question from some larger perspective.

He was.

A much larger perspective.

❧❧

We all know — or aspire to know — that all things come from G-d. But that Esther was given an allergy to cats is too ironic for words. To say she likes them is an understatement. She has felt an *affinity* for them ever since childhood. She feels their *pain.* Understands what they're *saying* when they purr.

So she does what she can, since she can't bring them home. And Jerusalem provides her with ample opportunities.

A cat in a religious Jerusalem neighborhood is a *persona non grata,* regarded with contempt. Reviled, disdained, and viewed with suspicion, the cat is shied away from and scorned, shooed away harshly if it dares come near. It scares us when we take out the garbage. Children stamp their feet to see it freeze in midmotion, shout to make it startle, throw stones to make it run.

The children think this is fun. And their parents don't mind, if the kids keep their distance. For the lowly cat reminds some of us pleasantly, if only half-consciously, of our own exalted position in Hashem's Creation — measurable in direct proportion to the separation between our species. In other words, holiness has nothing to do with cats. Felines in warm houses far away (whose owners do not know better) — felines such as these may well be kings and queens before the fire, sleek as panthers and petted and trusting and licking milk from their whiskers, but the cats of whom we speak — The parents say they're dirty, and that's the truth. Their eyes are infected; their eyes dart here and there. Their fur is matted and rangy; they carry diseases, slink along like thieves, hiss as if we're enemies, dash too close, like lightning in the night, arching their spines and drawing their claws. Who needs such animals?

We do our best to ignore them. We realize they keep down the rat population, and for this we're grateful.

When springtime comes and the kittens are born, the littlest humans respond. They bring out saucers of milk and stand there watching, lips parted in wonder.

This soon passes. The kittens become cats. The children get bigger.

❧ ❧

But we were talking about Esther.

She can't bear the sights and sounds of their starvation. Especially the kittens. Can't bear that meowing of hungry babies. So much meowing! So many kittens!

She's discussed it with Israel's Society for the Prevention of Cruelty to Animals. They say they're overwhelmed. They're doing the best they can, short of killing them all. They haven't the means to deal with the situation.

She started taking them scraps, out behind her building's garbage bin, where they congregate and prowl. She knew this wouldn't solve the larger problem, but what could she do? She heard them from her window.

After a while, they started recognizing her, and got used to her, relaxing bit by bit their brittle wariness of this human, and at last, after a number of weeks, would on occasion entwine themselves in her steps as she made her approach. But the neighbors complained, and with good reason. "You'll just increase the cat population. You think you're doing them a favor? They'll get used to being fed and it'll be harder for them to survive on their own. And they won't kill the rats anymore!"

One neighbor told her how the cats were coming fearlessly now into the entrance of the building. "I'm scared of them, if you want to know."

"Really?" said Esther. "But they're more scared of you than you could ever be of them."

Just then a gaunt, ill-looking kitten appeared at their feet, meowing piercingly, and the woman jumped. "You see! You just don't understand. You're being kind to them but cruel to me. And they bother my husband now when he goes out early to *daven*."

That was it. Esther stopped feeding them. But the cats didn't go away. Their numbers didn't diminish with time. That piteous meowing.

≈≈

She went to ask a *shaylah*.

"So," said Rabbi Chaim Pinchas Scheinberg, "can't you move away down the street a little? Feed the cats some place where it won't bother the neighbors?"

So that's what she did. Furthermore, she carried out the scraps each morning before dawn, so the sight of her with the food in hand wouldn't aggravate anyone.

Time passed.

A few weeks ago she got a call, this time from a friend who lives down the block — a *ba'alas chessed*, someone who had once gone out of her way to help Esther herself on an unrelated matter. "Look," the woman began, "I appreciate what you're trying to do. I know you're feeding the cats, and I think it's very admirable, really, but Esther, you're killing me."

Esther's heart jumped to her throat.

"The cats aren't scared anymore," the woman continued, "because of you. And since we're on the ground floor, we're the ones who bear the brunt of it. They jump right up onto our porch. I have to keep the windows and doors shut all the time — in this heat! — because if not, they come right into the living room! I found one sitting on my couch today and that's when I decided to ask you, Esther, please, please do something."

Esther went back to Rabbi Scheinberg.

The next day, I asked her how he had responded.

Now, I've never mentioned it to my friend, but I myself have scant love for cats, and can therefore identify with the neighbors' position. I had no doubt that under the circumstances, Rabbi Scheinberg would *pasken* that *shalom* comes first, and that in this case, she must forgo kindness to animals in favor of kindness to her fellow Jews.

But I was interested, anyway, in hearing precisely how he had framed it.

Esther said: "Rabbi Scheinberg said that the pain of the neighbors is more important than the pain of the cats."

"Well, that's what I expected."

"But then he said I should tell my neighbor that if she has *rachmanus* on Hashem's creatures, then Hashem will have *rachmanus* on her."

"Really? So Esther, what are you going to do?"

"I'll do what he says. But I have to admit, in a way I was disappointed, that this wasn't the end of the story. I think I was almost hoping to be let off the hook. It's hard getting up so early, going out there when it's still dark, trying to be quiet so nobody hears me. It makes me nervous. I hate sneaking and hiding. And I feel terrible, having my neighbors mad at me. I'm sorry to be upsetting them, they're such nice people. But now I don't know how I can ever stop. Especially the kittens. When I don't come, they're just out there meowing all the time. I feel responsible. Who else is going to do it? You know, one time a while ago my husband and I were going away on vacation but I was worried about the cats. So I went to Rabbi Scheinberg. I thought he'd say something like I should have *emunah* that *HaKadosh Baruch Hu* would take care of the cats and not to worry. But instead he said have a good time on your vacation and get someone else to feed the cats."

"You're kidding."

"No, and oh, there was something else yesterday. He said I should tell my neighbor she can have a *chelek* (share) of my mitzvah."

I asked if it was all right with her if I asked Rabbi Scheinberg about all of it myself, and a few moments later, the Rosh Yeshivah's phone was picked up.

On my end, I could just catch his far-off "Yes?" I could picture him there at his table, clad in his many layers of *tzitzis*, could see the Rebbetzin in her housecoat emerging from her kitchen, placing before him a plate of vegetables or fruit for his supper. I could see her telling him something, how he would nod ever so slightly in reply, and could see her returning to the kitchen to get him something else.

And for me, as always, understanding his quiet voice over the telephone would present me with a challenge.

I explained that I had heard about the problem which had arisen over feeding stray cats. "She told me what you said, Rabbi Scheinberg, and I'd just like to check that I understood correctly. Did you say that the pain of the neighbors is more important than the pain of the cats?

On the other end, ever so quietly: "It's true."

"But did you also say she should tell the neighbor that if she has *rachmanus* on Hashem's creatures, then Hashem will have *rachmanus* on her?"

"Yes."

"And did you say she can have a *chelek* of the mitzvah?"

He said something about *chelek* of the mitzvah.

"Is it all right if I quote you on that? Because I don't think people will believe it."

He gave what sounded like a laugh. Then he said something else, in which I caught the words *gemilus chessed*.

"Pardon me? Could —"

There was *rachmanus* again, and a long sentence that sounded as if it were coming from a thousand miles away. He was saying something about the time before *Mashiach*.

"Could the *Rosh Yeshivah* repeat that? I'm so sorry, I — "

Laughter again. Rabbi Scheinberg was laughing? Then on a buoyant stream, among some other words, came *mitzvah...* *Mashiach... rachmanus...* his voice reaching me like faint starlight, from a different realm altogether.

≈≈

When I came to him months later, with this story in hand, I asked if he would be so kind as to read it over. I wanted to try getting it published, and needed his permission.

"So read it to me," he said.

"Read it to you? You mean, out loud?"

He nodded.

When I got to the third paragraph, he gave a laugh. (What was going on here?) He called for the Rebbetzin, "Listen to this!"

I got as far as the second page, and she said: "You tell them!" She wagged her finger at me. "My father used to feed the cats in Jerusalem every single day! They used to follow him around, dozens of them! You tell them!"

Rabbi Scheinberg said, "It's true."

I asked if he could please say what was true.

He looked to the side and pointed to a large framed photograph "My father-in-law, Rav Yakov Yosef Herman. Every day." He chuckled and looked at the Rebbetzin. "There were a lot of them."

She smiled.

⤜⤏⤛

3

A HANDICAPPED LOOK AT DISABILITY

I was on 72nd Street, peering into the window of what had once been a kosher restaurant, when a stranger in a motorized wheelchair pulled up alongside and greeted me. "Hello? Can I help you?"

She was smiling up at me, and I recalled vaguely having noticed coming towards me along the sidewalk a wheel chair in which a woman wearing a hat was seated. Later on it would come back to me: how instinctively I had averted my eyes from Miriam. After all, aren't we taught from an early age not to stare at cripples? Isn't it embarrassing to face somebody like that, whose misfortunes are that much greater than your own?

I didn't know, then, how this woman was going to turn my notion of misfortune inside out; I didn't know that if insights acquired suddenly would only stay put, I could have rid myself in one evening of misconceptions that have crippled me over a lifetime.

I said I was looking for Famous Dairy, and she told me it had gone out of business years ago. "Do you have a place for dinner tonight?" she asked, when I told her I was visiting Manhattan by myself. It was late Friday afternoon. Shabbat would start in a few hours.

"We live right around the corner, " said the woman. "Come to us!"

⋙⋙

That night, upon entering what seemed at first sight a small, cramped apartment, I wondered how these people could live with so many papers and books stacked all around. Later on I would learn that since the muscle-function of Miriam's hands, arms, and lungs had been severely diminished by the polio she contracted at the age of 3, she can't afford to expend her limited physical strength and energy on unnecessary, demanding activities such as putting away what she will soon need to take out again. She is a writer, and her husband, Asher, has been blind from birth. The house is organized mostly for purposes of access.

As Miriam prepared her candles and mine for lighting, our conversation turned to what we had each been doing that afternoon. Suffice it to say that my own afternoon is long forgotten. Hers, however, I well remember.

Forgoing the expense of a taxi for a trip downtown to do an errand, Miriam had opted to go by bus. For some unknown reason, the bus driver had had to pull over in the middle of his route, announcing that another driver would arrive shortly to take his place. Those passengers who so desired could get transfers and disembark.

The bus emptied out. Miriam, for whom a brief wait was preferable to the trouble of getting off and on, and off again, asked if she could stay and await the second driver.

A few minutes turned into twenty, a half-hour into an hour and a half. She was alone on board. The doors were closed on the hot September day. The mechanism on the door for lowering wheelchairs to the street had to await the second driver's arrival.

I wanted to ask how she had endured the frustration, the exasperation, the stifling air, the sense of imprisonment. I wanted to ask if she had had anything to read. I couldn't. I was still pretending to be blind myself, and sought to conceal my horror at her predicament. If she had seethed at the unfairness, the inconvenience, the boredom, and the waste of her precious time, if she had felt maddeningly trapped, if she had gotten desperate at her helplessness, and infuriated by people's negligence, she didn't say. She had endured the wait, apparently, without banging on the windows and shattering them; without screaming for help; without going out of her mind.

The second driver had eventually arrived, and the bus continued on.

≈≈

It emerged in conversation that Asher directs a municipal program that teaches disabled people to use public transportation, and that Miriam's articles are published with some regularity in national women's magazines. Ten years earlier, doctors had told them that due to problems unrelated to either of their disabilities, having children would be impossible. Some of the doctors had advised that child-raising would have been out of the question in any case: A woman who can only stand, precariously balanced, a few minutes at a time — such a woman, they informed her, cannot responsibly consider bringing children into the world. A woman who has to spend a fair amount of time each day lying down, to recoup her strength, and whose atrophied hands and arms can't handle the usual maternal duties — such a woman, she was told, would in any case be unwise to insist on motherhood.

Asher and Miriam have two children, a boy of 5 and a girl, 7, and these children's demeanor quickly aroused some self-doubts on my part about my own mothering. I found myself summoning up the image of my own children at that age, trying to remember if they had been equally happy and uninhibited. These two definitely seemed at once more whimsical and more grounded than most, yet at the same time, perceptive and responsible beyond their years. I leaned over to murmur a comment to that effect to Miriam.

"That's a stereotyped image people have of the children of handicapped people," Miriam replied softly. "People think that the children of disabled people are in some ways deprived of their childhoods," she said, "by having to be helpful more than is considered normal."

I was embarrassed. Here I had thought she would be flattered, and instead, found I had come out with what evidently was an offensive cliché. Suddenly I got my first inkling, without being able to articulate it as yet, of a strange dichotomy in my reactions to all this: on one hand, there was my horror at these severe disabilities, and a need to ignore them; on the other, a tendency to perceive their difficulty as something enviably meaningful.

We didn't know each other yet, so I was reluctant to press the point. But I did inquire how she could deny that her children were unusually mature for their age, yet obviously not deprived of childhood, either. "Isn't it so," I asked, "that when you want them to understand something, or obey you, you have to converse with them instead of just forcing them to comply? Maybe that's the difference, and on account of that, they're more developed intellectually and emotionally?"

"True," she conceded. "I can't go over across the room and grab them and march them off to the bedroom. I have to rely on words."

Her husband spoke to the children attentively in a low, measured voice, as well, and the pleasure he was taking in them was palpable: an underlying enjoyment that was still evident when he was issuing reprimands. He seemed constantly buoyed by amusement at their antics, astute remarks, their irrepressible liveliness. Again, it was eating away at me: I consider myself a loving parent, and know that my children would agree, but is my appreciation for the sheer fact of their existence as palpable to them as the parental affection bestowed upon these two? Precisely on account of his limitations, Asher has to tune in completely to everything they say with the most focused manner of alertness, whereas so much of the time, the world draws me away.

I suspect now that had I expressed a comment such as this, Asher might have retorted wryly that like most of us, he's just on his best parental behavior when guests are around.

As the hours went by that Friday night, it became apparent that Miriam and Asher, functioning, together, approximated — for all practical purposes — two sighted, mobile parents. Nonetheless, to my mind, their parenting was greater than the sum of its parts. What do those children learn by having a mother and father for whom each and every trivial deed is a challenge, minute by minute; parents who are compelled to negotiate all of life's mundane demands less with physical agility than with ingenuity and will power; parents who can't afford the luxury of losing patience over life's stumbling blocks? Equipped as I am, thank G-d, with a normal body that takes me unthinkingly and quickly here, there, and everywhere, that has me running in and out of the kitchen twenty times during any meal — how often is my attention undivided? And as far as husband and wife were concerned, I imagined that the fact of Asher's never having seen his wife must only enhance his consciousness of all the nuances of meaning contained in her voice. Wouldn't most women say they want to be listened to that closely? I was getting jealous, jealous of these people who I had initially assumed were lacking so much. They *were* lacking, it couldn't be denied, much that American culture regards as essential to happiness. But two things they had obviously cultivated in abundance: love, and the belief that all events have their source in G-d.

When it came time for Shabbos songs and the four of them sat singing together, I ruminated dolefully.

Months later, I would tell Miriam that this is what I'd been thinking about that first night of our acquaintance, and she smiled indulgently. She said that they and their kids experience the clashes and conflicts of any family.

"All right, dear" I replied. "If you insist."

But to my mind, there was no denying the extraordinary environment of love prevailing in their home, one that must have arisen and grown out of the family members' ultra high level of mutual sensitivity. Miriam would say that such idealization of their lives is the flip side of pity. Either perspective is condescending. Asher would say, as he once did in an e-mail, that I'm viewing their disability as some sort of poetic metaphor. He would much rather be viewed as a person whose primary characteristic is not disability.

And I would say that on account of fear, and the embarrassed awkwardness about not knowing how to react, and out of a guilty sense of privilege about being sighted and mobile in their presence, most people are bound to perceive Miriam and Asher first and foremost, at least at the outset, through the lens of their disability.

By the Shabbos candlelight around their table, as the children listened to their mother's and father's harmonizing voices so keenly and subtly attuned one to the other, it seemed to me indisputable that this boy and girl could not help but absorb two truths I would most wish my own children to carry out of childhood: first, that love can transcend physical limitations. Secondly, that to whatever extent we identify with that which is eternal and intangible in ourselves, our divine images, to that extent are we human, and truly alive.

〰〰

A few years ago I read an article about someone who stopped one night to help a stranded motorist and got hit by a passing car. He lost the use of both legs. He quoted another quadreplegic as having said something along the lines of: "Quads [quadriplegics] want to be paras [paraplegics.] Paras want to be normals. And normals want to look like movie stars."

How thorough is our faith in bodily wholeness! How desperately we channel the human soul's natural drive to develop, to reach greatness, into the quest for physical perfection! Miriam, from age 3 on, had no choice but to develop a self-concept based on something other than her external self, and a self-image derived from something other than the imagined reflections of her face in other people's eyes. In her and her husband's home, where the physical level of existence could so easily exert a tyrannical grip over their lives, there is no good alternative other than to rise above it.

When I finally dared share some of my real questions with Miriam — the first person whom I've ever been able to ask what it's like to be disabled — I suggested tentatively, "Maybe you've had to extinguish so much of your egotistical self, in order to get along in the world, that that's why your singing voice is so beautiful." I paused, scared that once again she would think I wasn't seeing her realistically.

"Don't think," she said, "that my spirit always triumphs over the physical."

"But always having to depend on people for help," I continued, afraid of saying something ridiculous, "and the constant insult of having people look at you as some sort of separate species of human being — having to endure that humiliation —" I could sense her waiting indulgently. "So what remains of your personality is sort of like purified water."

She took this in for a moment. "Purified water?" There was a pause. " Sarah, please. I'm not an angel. I'm as egotistical as anyone."

I felt curiously relieved. Maybe she wasn't so different from me, after all.

And yet — Miriam doesn't hear her own voice as she sings at their table in the flickering candlelight. In that seemingly small, cramped apartment, she herself is neither small nor cramped. Together the two of them have built an essentially joyous existence for themselves, even though for Miriam taking a breath is hard, and sitting up is hard, and standing, and talking on the phone, and getting into the elevator and in and out of bed; even though brushing her teeth is hard, and picking up a fork, and typing on her computer, and getting to the synagogue on Shabbos morning.

Even though for Asher, the world is sheathed in what the rest of us can only imagine as darkness.

Sometimes nowadays, when I'm in the midst of one of my own life's various difficulties, I think of them. Is the hardship I'm experiencing overwhelming? Then this is my chance to acquire some of the nobility and dignity those two have developed. My husband once told me that one of the daily blessings recited in the morning prayers, "Blessed are You Who has provided me with all my needs," can be interpreted as follows: *Thank You for providing me with all that I need* — in other words, *with all that I lack.* For it's through dealing *with what I don't have* that I'm compelled to become the person I'm meant to be.

Would I ever trade places with Miriam? Never, not willingly. I would choose a normally functioning body over enlightenment any day. But I can try to put to good use whatever pains and limitations are sent my way, thereby providing my atrophied spiritual limbs with their necessary exercise.

At the very least, maybe I can accept one of this world's basic truths: *Life comes with hardships.*

None of us is exempt, and it is the difficulties that can force us to fly.

4

THE WRONG LINE

In Jerusalem, we don't converse. They're in their lives, we're in ours.

There's the Arab delivery boy, of course. I say, "Over here would be fine. Thank you." And a lot of them at Hadassah during visiting hours, in the hospital for who knows what personal catastrophe or for birth, as are we. The children are brought in frequently for cleft-palate, the result of generations of familial inbreeding. Grandparents, uncles, aunts, cousins, the women bearing baskets packed full as if for a picnic. I eye them, they look away quickly. They glance over, I stare straight ahead.

There's also the number 27 line, whose route ends up in their villages: many *kaffiyehs*, many black mustaches. Many black dresses to the floor, with the ancient embroidery across the front, and bags of fruit balancing atop draped heads. When moving among the Jews, their women travel in pairs.

⋙⋘

My daughter's U.S. passport expired. Our plan was to rise at six, arrive in the Arab sector of East Jerusalem — where the American Consulate is located — at seven, and be the first in line when the doors open, at eight.

We rise at eight; arrive at the American Consulate in East Jerusalem at nine; and at ten are still inching along the outside wall of the building, in a line that's a slow-crawling serpent in hot sun. My daughter wonders if this is the right line. She goes to ask the man posted outside the glass-enclosed, electronically-controlled entry way into the Consulate.

I watch her from the back as she approaches the black-mustached Palestinian official. He gives one shake of his head and hands her a paper, and in a few moments she is back at my side with a form to be filled out, the instructions say in capital letters, with black or blue ballpoint only. Rummaging through my purse for a pen, and some hard surface to write on, I bring up from the depths of loose coins and receipts, stray lipsticks and papers and eyeliners, a book entitled, *A Map of the World,* the as yet unread novel that my sister has just sent me from Massachusetts. It's a present for my birthday, my birthday on the Fourth of July. I'd like to be there with her now. I'd like to be there with Andrea right now on my wonderfully American birthday, sitting under the trees... some cool whispering New England trees — she with an iced decaf café-latte, I with my cappuccino, in our silence that's as good as conversation, at some wobbly little table on a wrought-iron stand.

Here in this Middle-Eastern oven of a morning, by this high sun-warmed stone wall with no shade in which to rest, can't time move for us at all?

New people are arriving behind us, and there's one woman back there who looks like an American right out of the Midwestern farm belt. In her early thirties, with double chins and pale, smooth brow, and a limp, skimpy blonde ponytail pulled back into a rubber band, physical dimensions overblown in the distinctive manner of many a Midwesterner in today's world. In bygone days, women of that grain were tough-skinned, no-nonsense pioneers. Today, they shop at the local thousand-acre mall and come home bearing take-out, to relax with their families over TV. What's she doing here?

My conscience gives me a pinch. What prompts me during un-occupied moments such as these to conjure up some stranger's imaginary secret weaknesses, this person who's never harmed me in any way? What is this gluttony? Out of what emptiness of my own do I take smug pleasure in fancying that I'm better, and bet-ter-off, than she?

She's turned the other way and I steal another look. There's a whining little girl at her side, who pulls at the woman's huge white shorts and oversize yellow T-shirt. But the girl's got dull black hair and olive skin; she couldn't be the blonde farm-woman's daughter. A tiny slip of a thing, around four, she gives off an air of being neglected. I get a glimpse of an angular, dark, bored, agitated little face. She's a Palestinian child.

She's clinging to one big pillar of leg. "Mama! Mama!" The woman, distracted, casually brushes her off and makes some complaint to the person next in line, who is a young man.

The young man is brooding and dusky, and, like the child, an Arab. Tall and slender as a vine, unspeaking as a shadow, he mutters some answer under his breath. Do he and the woman know each other? The girl twists away, defeated, and plops down crying, stub-born and thin, upon the baking sidewalk, whereupon the man scoops her up impatiently with one hand. The three of them are together? The experienced, proprietary way he handles her, and his simmering low-key frustration and authoritarian anger, are paternal. Yet his mustache is just a feathery wisp and his eyes are cast down with the self-concealing, keen self-consciousness of adolescence. Is he the husband? Or her son, gloomy and embarrassed by their mother's Kansas-style foreignness? He and she, like characters painted by different artists, in two different paintings, seem to inhabit incongruous worlds. Did the two of them meet during his visit to relatives in the United States, or perhaps when her church-sponsored chartered tour passed through the Holy Land? She makes some other annoyed comment — it must be English coming out of that Oklahoman face — and it becomes apparent that she has decided this is the wrong line. Off he glides obligingly through the crowd, and makes his way to the tinted glass cage. He inquires through its two-way microphone and reappears obediently a minute later, chastened and irritated, with the forms to be properly filled out.

The little girl's down on the sidewalk again, crying.

Behind the three of them in line stand two women in black *chadors.* One of the faces is impassive and the second indistinct, and behind them are other faces, waiting hopefully, as are we all, for America to please tilt her vast face toward us — and open her distant, beckoning arms.

A tall woman a few people ahead of us breaks abruptly out of her place in line. Rather surprisingly, she struts purposefully across the narrow street in her smart pair of slacks and platform heels, dragging deeply on a cigarette. What's she doing? On the sidewalk opposite all of us, alone in a rectangle of shade provided kindly by a high stone wall, she crouches down and for several minutes, head tilted back, drags deeply, deeply on the cigarette. We all seem to be her audience. She's forty-ish. Her lips are painted dark maroon and her long frizzy hair is dyed blonde. An Arab, I think, a rebellious one, a non-religious one. She tosses the cigarette stub, seems to smile at someone — I follow her gaze but see no one smiling back — and struts back out again into the roasting bright light, crossing back towards us to her place in line.

We all avert our eyes and pretend we haven't been watching. The two women in *chadors* move aside to make room, then the three of them start talking. When the tall blonde opens her mouth to speak, I can hear that she's not Palestinian, after all; she's Israeli.

Someone is saying something — to me, I realize — in English. "Is this the right line for visas?" It's an Arab woman right next to me, her face encircled by a gauzy white veil. Though I'd probably sensed someone in a *chador* at my side, I can't say I'd seen her.

She's got on that same dark maroon lipstick. Her *chador* is light grey. From the chin down it conceals her entirely, except for the hands.

"I don't know," I answer. "We're renewing a passport."

She's smiling a wide smile. Her teeth seem perfectly white. "They wouldn't let me renew my visa." Could it be? She's got an American accent. "They said I was here longer than six years so they don't know if they'll let me. I'm from here but I used to live in New York." Indeed, this is a Brooklyn accent. And in her voice are these things: she's young, bored, restless, friendly, curious... she wants to talk with an American.

"Where in New York?"

She names some area of the city that I've never heard of.

"So..." How much interest can I show? "You live here now?"

"My mother and father are there. I'm here with my husband. This is my mother-in-law and my little boy."

I turn my head to see to whom she's referring and find myself confronted by a short, squat, square-jawed woman in her 50's, also in a *chador*. This woman is holding in her arms a black-haired baby who's gazing at me with large dark eyes, and I give a cheerful greeting. *Whoops.* Mom's pretty grim. She gives zero response and looks off in another direction. The daughter-in-law and I resume our conversation.

"You live here?" she asks, smiling. "In Jerusalem?" The white teeth, the dark lipstick.

I say, "Yes. And this is my daughter."

She looks at Rachel and they exchange hellos, with a quick mutual recognition: they're the same age. It's hard to believe, talking in English like this with an Arab woman in an Islamic *chador*. I want to ask her so many things. Does she believe in terrorism as a means of acquiring a Palestinian State? What does she think of suicide bombings? My son is a paratrooper in

Lebanon fighting the Islamic Hezbullah. Is she a Hezbullah fan? Does she understand the Israeli viewpoint? Is she more hopeful now that Barak is in? Hopeful for what? Is she foolhardy enough to imagine that we'll give them Jerusalem? I say, "Do you like living here?"

The smile slopes downward. "I like America."

"You do? Why?"

"There's more freedom."

"Oh. So you're going back?"

"Oh yes." She nods with certainty. "I am. I don't mind all the people there, I like it. The Chinese, the blacks. I like everybody." Her eyes drift slightly. She's seeing something. "My husband's family, they don't understand me."

It has just struck me: this is a teenager, an American teenager. There's a trace in her voice of... who knows what...

"It sure is unusual for people like you and me to be talking to each other!" I say with a chummy chortle, as if I were just making light banter. Then I dare to look her in the eye.

Her dark eyes are shining. They're made up elaborately with violet eye shadow and liner. "Yeah," she agrees. Then, with a certain regret, like a kid being grounded, she says, "My family, my husband's family, they don't like Jews." In a flicker she looks me over. "How about you, you like it here?"

"I love it."

"So do I!" my daughter happily interjects.

The young woman's face falls a little. "You do?" Her eyes linger on Rachel a few more beats. One, two, three... Then she thinks something to herself and in the same instant seems imperceptibly to shrug it off. "Yeah... well, it's better for your side."

I want to ask: *What do you mean? Tell me what it's like.*

"In America, I don't have to wear this." She touches her veil. Then she gestures to the scarf on my head and smiles sympathetically. "You also have to wear one."

"Oh, but it's O.K., though. I like it."

"You do?" Her lips are parted, trying to fathom... "Well, yours isn't as hot as mine." She gestures again to her veil — how except for the face that it leaves revealed, it's wrapped entirely around head, forehead, and neck.

I'm about to say something to the effect that whether or not my scarf is cooler has nothing to do with why I like it. My scarf is an expression of... my belief.

"My husband doesn't understand what I want to go back there for," she is saying. "I met him there. We got married in New Jersey. He doesn't like it there." She brightens. "You want to see our wedding picture?"

She opens her handbag and withdraws a wallet, and from the wallet extracts a photograph, which she carefully hands over. I hold it up between my daughter and me, and try to conceal my spontaneous reaction... for the husband's eyes have leapt out at me. They grab me. Black, extremely wide open, and deadly serious. The eyebrows are two thick, black, straight lines, each of which slants upwards on either end, and they're echoed neatly by the mustache, the third thick black line.

That's a powerful pair of eyes you have there, sir. They seem to be telling me something.

How right you are, Jewish madam, so listen well. They say: 'Who goes there? What infidel dares spy on my wife and me upon our wedding day!'

At his side — all mirth and buoyant gaiety — is she, the bride. She's got a mass of glossy blue-black hair piled up unnaturally high, and all around her face fall luxuriant blue-black ringlets stylishly curling. Her head's thrown back slightly in joy. Such joy! Her lips are painted incandescent pink; we see the ruffled collar of an ornately brocaded wedding gown; and on each of those white satin shoulders... is a large dark male hand.

And each hand unambiguously declares: *This is mine.*

"Oh, that's lovely," I tell her. My daughter murmurs something.

The young woman takes back the portrait, gazes at it proudly, and happily declares: "My son is eight months old." I look around and spot him over on the side with the mother-in-law. The baby — quite still, quite serious in his grandmother's firm hold — responds to my smile with a level gaze.

"Wow, he's big for his age, isn't he?"

"Oh, I don't know." She shrugs modestly. "I want him to grow up in America. To go to school there." She pauses, and for a second, averts her eyes. "My husband is very strict."

Our line suddenly seems to be breaking up; there are some empty spaces and we all advance aggressively to fill the gaps. The Israeli woman with the blonde hair and cigarette turns around and says to me, in Hebrew: "Aren't you an American?"

I nod.

Her lower lip expertly directs some smoke off to the left. "They just said American citizens should go over there."

Before you can say "American Consulate," Rachel and I have lickety-split darted away together through the crowd.

In this new line, for those of us with United States passports, Rachel and I are once again at the end. I look around. That woman from Kansas... from Oklahoma... where is she? All these American faces; I feel obscurely pleased. All different kinds — Hebrew University Jews, modern Orthodox Jews... California, Borough Park, Chassidic — instantaneously we've gotten a little community together here. In normal life, our paths rarely cross. We'd hardly give each other the time of day. Here we're packed in so closely, we can hear each other breathing in the hot sun.

This brisk American line moves along nicely and in no time at all, Rachel and I are being zipped on through the glass cage. Our purses are checked for weapons, our Israeli IDs computer-verified, and the two of us are ushered through the metal detectors.

We step into a cool, lovely pool, all-enveloping, of air-conditioning, and just as my daughter leans over to whisper in my ear, "That husband was so scary, wasn't he?" a stray little thought — *did I say goodbye?* — has come along, and is gone.

◦◦◦

5

SOMETHING YOU
ALREADY KNOW

The world is divided into two kinds of people: those who are on diets and those who are not.

The world is divided into two kinds of people: the kind and the unkind.

The world is divided into two kinds of people: computer users and computer-phobics. Givers, takers. Haves, have-nots. Republicans, Democrats. Leaders, followers.

The world is divided into two kinds of people: those who divide the world into two kinds of people and those who do not. Those who do, perceive the world as being dominated by one or another theme, and reasonably conclude that the rest of mankind shares their preoccupation.

The world is divided into two kinds of people: those who fear getting older and those who do not. Those who think of themselves, above all, as bodies and those who think of themselves as souls. Those whose eyes are used for seeing, and those who look with eyes shut tight. Those who are astounded by the aggression of time, amazed that they themselves don't remain the same, who brace forever against what they believe must be the dark, and those who

> catch the joy as it flies,
> and live in eternity's sunrise.

When time was a flower blossoming slowly in the palm of my hand, how was I — the baby in the family — to know it wouldn't take a hundred years to reach middle age? With each step I take into deeper water, my definition of the term middle age has magically continued to shift, like an outgoing tide, farther and farther off toward the horizon.

For decades, I've been trying to keep each passing present momentary fragment under lock and key, to preserve it, to save myself from being swept away in time's maddeningly unstoppable tidal wave.

≈≈

This year, our first time ever, my husband and I experienced the incredible satisfaction of introducing two people who subsequently got married. "You've hit the bulls-eye!" the man exulted. "Thank you!" said the woman, as she handed us $500 in cash.

An unexpected side effect of our success (in spite of their speedy divorce) is that we've now gotten three calls asking for "the *shadchanim*, Mr. and Mrs. Shapiro." I got the third call this morning.

"Hello," she said, with what sounded like a Dutch accent. "My name is H., and I was given your name by C. I converted to Judaism seventeen years ago, during the final stages of my husband's illness. The conversion was an outgrowth of that absolute loss, and certain insights which it fostered, which — well, I don't need to go into it. Two of our children are married and working happily, and the third is going through what he has to go through. I am 51. I look quite a bit younger than that, however. Not that I've tried."

"That you tried?" I said. "Tried what?"

"To look younger than I am. I respect age too much to do that."

"You respect age?"

"Just that. I respect age."

"You do?"

"Oh, certainly. I would not trade what I have learned, nor the understanding that I have acquired, for a face without wrinkles or a firm this or smooth that. Age is an achievement. A crown."

I murmured an encouraging noise. I wanted her to go on.

"Because to get older," she said, "is to become part of the ultimate purpose. There is a purpose to all events, after all, you know. Each detail of our lives leads us toward a more complete flowering. To have the opportunity to grow older is a great — a great thing. It is a wonderful thing to learn through our individual trials, to become more wise, to open our eyes more and more to the greater reality. For there is a greater reality. There is a greater purpose than our individual trials, yet it is through these small personal trials that we become a part of G-d's goal in having created human beings in this world. And whether we know it or not, that is what each of us wants: to take part in this process. If we do not see that we are moving along towards G-d, which is what we really want, then all we see is that we are losing the self we possessed during earlier stages — which we usually had without even noticing it at the time. We are so afraid of the dying! Of the new wrinkle. All we see is: 'Look at this new gray hair! That gray hair!' That is a horrible trivialization of our role in the world." She paused. "Is this something that's on your mind, Mrs. Shapiro?"

"Sometimes," I said casually.

"Then forgive me for going on like this. Well, if any of it strikes a chord in you, I'm just saying something you already know."

While brushing my teeth this morning, I beheld in the mirror, lo and behold, a new wrinkle, previously undetected, and reserved a hall for a gala event.

At 7 o'clock sharp, the wrinkle stepped up to the podium. To the blasting of trombones and crashing of cymbals, the wrinkle, in its tux, proclaimed: "My human host," (I blushed) "is utterly *thrilled* to be progressing toward her *ultimate goal*! She's on the universal journey whose every second swells with *infinite meaning*! Whose course is unpredictable! Whose unknown destination will be eventually shared by *everyone in this room tonight!*"

The crowd went wild.

Then it was my turn. I modestly took a bow. "The world," I said into the microphone, "is divided into two kinds of people: the male and the female. 'So G-d created man in His own image, in the image of G-d He created him. The male and the female He created them.' "

A wave of impatience rippled through the audience.

"If that's something you already know, I mention it only because I thought maybe somebody out there would know of someone for my friend over here." I asked H. if she'd be so kind as to stand. "In the middle of her journey, H. is seeking a partner who — " I rummaged through my purse. "Oh, here it is. A nice Jewish fellow unfazed by the unknown, someone who will neither be terrorized by light years of despair, nor unduly discouraged by black holes of emptiness along the path. Should preferably know that the bitter is sweet and that darkness is just the flip side of light. Non-smokers only need apply." (H. gave a grateful nod in my direction.) "Have-nots welcome if they consider themselves haves. She's seeking a giver and a taker, but please, no IBM Compatibles. Someone in perpetual awe of the Creator, and who's supremely thankful, at this very moment, to be alive."

∽∾

6

MEANWHILE, WHILE WE SLEPT

Meanwhile, while we slept,
time was going by

though the view out the window is the same
as yesterday

the tree, and the mountain, and
the sky.

Meanwhile, the washing machine has finished its rinse cycle.
Like a locomotive hurtling through a mountain tunnel, banging and
Shaking on towards its quietness
At the end.

I have no gray hairs.
The baby didn't get bigger in the night.
Everything is all right.
I have time.

7

My Secret Internal Negotiations

My introduction to the Gaza-Jericho Peace Plan came not in Jerusalem, where I live, but in my parents' Los Angeles living room this past summer, where my chief contribution to world peace is to read sections A and B of the Sunday Times. It seemed that a Norwegian diplomat, of whom no one had ever heard, and an Israeli politician whose name sounded familiar but that I couldn't place, had engineered secret breakthrough negotiations with the PLO.

Like most Israelis, I'm skeptical about news reports of this kind, but in America I was subdued into silence by the unabashed enthusiasm of The New York Times, The CBS Evening News, and most of all, by my mother. She was thrilled. To tears. The prospect of peace in the Middle East was no less wonderful to her than the tearing down of the Berlin Wall a few years before, or the recent birth of democracy in Russia. In fact, it was far more so, because now her daughter and her family would be safe from war. "I wish Daddy could see this," she said, with more joy than sorrow.

Then El Al took me home, my insecurity about where all this would lead having cast a pall of low-key anxiety over the rest of my vacation.

A few weeks later, at a neighborhood newsstand, a banner headline in The Jerusalem Post announced the triumphant conclusion to the arduous preliminary negotiations. My mind instantly engaged in the quick little internal dance, back and forth, that it has danced so many times before. *"Shall I believe or should I beware, I want to believe, I must not be gullible."*

I forget now how that Post headline went, but once I'd made the split-second decision to believe rather than disbelieve, to indulge in hope rather than protect myself with fear, then my hoping heart lay open and my mother's tears filled my eyes, and I was joyous and incredulous. Israel is recognizing the PLO and the PLO recognizes Israel's right to secure borders! Maybe we really will have peace now! This is history being made right now, and I'm here to see it!

I paid three *shekels* forty to the dour man behind the counter. How could he not be smiling today? According to The Jerusalem Post, our forty years of national nervousness and terror were perhaps drawing to a close. No, make that two thousand years. As a matter of fact, make it three. So couldn't he at least look me in the eye and share unspoken mutual congratulations with a fellow citizen — as even strangers did during the Gulf War, when we'd emerge each morning from our homes, unscathed by the night's Scuds?

I emerged now from the newsstand, like some sort of dazed sleepwalker into the white light of August, holding the Post open before my eyes. Page after page of fragile hopes and hesitant skepticism. The words seem to waver and wobble in the heat and dazzling sun.

I entered the fruit and vegetable store, a lump of emotion lodged in my throat like a large purple grape. "Did you see this?" I asked Shlomo, one of the owners, setting the paper down before him. Shlomo was born in Morocco. He and his partner have Arabs working for them, and one of the things that has often made me happy as I walk up and down bagging my tomatoes and cucumbers, is the way these two Jews and their Arab employees sit around all day talking and joking, in Arabic, over their *café shachor.*

Shlomo glanced down at the photograph of Shimon Peres shaking hands with somebody in a *kaffiyeh,* then shoved the paper back toward me with a disgusted wave of the hand. "They're liars."

My eyes darted spontaneously around the store. Where were the Arabs?

Whatever expression had come over my face at that moment, Shlomo apparently found richly amusing. "You think peace has come, is that it?" His black eyes assessed me scornfully.

"I — "

"Huh? Is that what you think?" He grinned mockingly. "The lions and lambs are already lying down with each other?"

Thus did my very own peace process get its early momentum, with his smile. Shlomo was the first to shatter my luminous millennium.

≈⋙⋘≈

Two months have gone by.

A few days ago my mother called. We tried not to let it happen, but again, as usual, our conversation circled around to Gaza-Jericho. "Did you hear on the news that Arafat said he'd eventually get Jerusalem?"

"No, I didn't, but — "

"Well, read about it, Mommy! That's what they've been saying for years, that they're going to go step by step, and they're still saying it. They want us out of here completely, Mommy, preferably dead. It's part of their religion! The Jihad! You haven't read about that? Isn't it in the papers over there?"

"But Sarah, I'm sure that Rabin, who's experienced in this sort of thing, wouldn't have agreed to this if — "

I thought to myself: He agreed to it because the Arabs have won the *intifada*. He's been worn down by violence. But that was too depressing, so I just said, "He's tired, Mommy." So was I. "He just wanted to do *some*thing."

"Of course he wants to do something. That's the right thing to do. You've got to do something to stop these wars! Daddy would have said so, too, I think. You've got to try."

"Haven't you heard about the Jews who have been killed by Hamas the past few weeks?" I said. "They didn't report that over there? What's wrong with them? It wasn't on 'Sixty Minutes'?"

"I read about it, it's so terrible. I don't know what to say." My mother's voice broke. To someone who didn't know her, it would have been imperceptible. Why was I doing this to her? Did I think that if my mother were on my side, the whole world would fall into place? "But you know, Sarah... One of the things they say will happen after this autonomy thing gets set up is that those people will be controlled." She paused. There was a question in her hesitation. "I hope."

I wanted to burst out in my bitterness. Controlled? By whom? There are millions of Arab opponents to this plan. Even if Arafat wanted to follow through on it, he still has to please them. Unless he's ready to martyr himself for peace with the Jews.

I was about to ask my mother how she would feel if anything happened to anyone in our family. Then would she say we must try? But my better judgment prevailed.

"It's ironic, isn't it?" she continued in quiet bafflement. "How people on opposite sides can end up together. The people who feel as you do are in the same bed with Hamas."

Because my mother and I are beloved to each other, she heard the anger in my abrupt silence, and I heard her unspoken resolution to say no more. Somehow we had crossed over, again, into forbidden territory.

I asked if she could send some more vitamin C.

≈≈

I can't lean back on the confident sort of pronouncements that leaders of Israel, both political and religious, issued during the Gulf War, when virtually all of them said the country wasn't in danger. This time around, such statements have not been forthcoming, except from Peres and Rabin themselves.

Therefore I'm left largely to my own devices when it comes to believing that Hashem is taking perfect care of the world (and of my family in particular, I beg of Him). "Taking care" doesn't mean there won't be suffering. I have to perceive Israel's maddeningly increasing endangerment as meaningful, not random. I have to continue conducting my own private little negotiations — am I kidding myself? — between hope and fear.

It's that old, familiar impotence that I remember from childhood, and as in every crisis here through the years, I have to define that helplessness differently now. It's the only thing that gets us to lift up our eyes.

8

ON SWEEPING

"**I** too, dislike it," wrote Marianne Moore in her famous poem about poetry. "There are things that are important beyond all this fiddle."

Moore's line came to mind one day as I read a letter to the editor of The Jerusalem Post from a prominent Israeli professor and educator. The professor expressed her consternation that a recent photograph in the paper, of Suha Arafat (wife of Yasser Arafat) and Um Jihad (whose late husband was a celebrated terrorist), portrayed the two women in the act of "cleaning the streets of Gaza while men stood aside and watched." The letter-writer said that they should have been pictured in some political or governmental capacity, as their husbands would have been, and that the fact they had been photographed with brooms did not bode well for Palestinian women in the new Palestinian government. It reminded her of how Israeli MK Sara Doron, shortly after being put in charge of women's affairs, had "unfortunately appeared in the papers sweeping the streets of Tel Aviv."

I sipped thoughtfully from my morning cup of coffee and surveyed our living room. Definitely could use a good sweep. Perhaps even some *sponja*. Some spilled crayons over in the corner; someone would have to go over and pick them up. Breakfast dishes in the sink; I knew that when I got up and walked into the kitchen, those dishes would greet me.

Who should do all this cleaning up? I wasn't the one who ate off those dishes. And the crayons, for sure: they weren't my fault, either, though a more masterful mother would have trained her 7-year-old to pick up after herself before running out to the school bus.

Should I call my husband and ask him to come back from yeshivah? But last night he did all the dishes, and also remembered to take out the garbage this morning.

My mother would be a good candidate. There's no one else on earth more eager than she to lighten my load. She certainly cleaned up after me when I was growing up.

But she's in Los Angeles.

Maybe Mrs. Arafat? Should I give her a ring? Perhaps she has time to lend a Jewish housewife a hand?

No, chances are that Suha's probably busy cleaning up her own kitchen right now. I doubt she's convinced her husband to do it — though he was a bachelor for so long, anything is possible. Maybe she has a maid to do it for her. I wish we all had maids. And that our maids had maids.

In my mind's eye, I see that newspaper photograph of the two smiling Arab women with brooms in hand. Actually, I thought those were rakes they were holding. And if I recall correctly, the caption said that they were initiating a cleanup not of the Gaza streets but the Gaza beaches.

Not that it makes a difference. Cleaning is cleaning. A broom is a broom is a broom.

❧❧

Sometimes, however, a dish is not a dish. One Saturday night a few months ago, I visited a neighbor of mine who was undergoing chemotherapy. She opened the door with a weak smile and attempted a cheerful greeting.

Her lassitude alarmed me. "Bracha, what's wrong?"

"I'm just tired, *mammele*. And some people are coming over. I want to make them a little something, but I can't seem to get going."

Her sink was full of dishes. In a gesture that was out of character, I offered to do them for her, and to my surprise, she accepted — which was also out of character. That showed me how weak she felt.

I stood at the sink for the next half-hour doing my friend's dishes, and my heart became buoyant as a soap bubble. Seldom have I been carried on such a lovely flight of inner joy.

Why did washing that sinkful of dishes make me so happy? I realized that it was because I felt unambiguously useful. There was no question that I was doing something good, and important.

It felt so good to be joyful while doing Bracha's dishes, I wished I could feel that way every time I do my own. (Certainly Mrs. Arafat and Mrs. Jihad enjoyed sweeping Gaza Beach, before a large audience, more than wielding their own brooms at home.) How nice it would be right now if getting up and doing my breakfast dishes would fill me with the same blissful sense of mission that I experienced that night! In a few minutes, when I do start cleaning up, chances are that I'll get the place in order as fast as possible before going out to do the shopping. If the task of sweeping my floor has any genuine joy to offer, I probably won't notice.

⋙ ⋘

The author of the letter to the editor is indignant that the two women's potential roles in Palestinian society are being trivialized by symbols of wifely domesticity. She views the personal and the public realms as separate spheres of activity, apparently. By that definition, a mundane, small-scale, traditionally female activity cannot cross over into meaningful terrain. "If we must be involved in cleansing," she proposes in her letter, "then let it be in the removal of corruption and outdated stereotypes from politics."

But sweeping the Gaza beaches (which are said to be in serious need of cleaning) has something to recommend it. So would sweeping my kitchen floor (also much in need). If there's anything that could make me feel a minimal camaraderie with Suha Arafat and Um Jihad (in spite of their husbands), it's the down-to-earth and boring tasks of daily human living that we share. Nothing would have made my friend Bracha, who has since died, happier than getting up and attending to her own earthly chores.

I can think of no other genre of activity that restores emotional equilibrium and a sense of basic self-respect as fast, nothing that mends a mind as easily, as much as washing and drying, scrubbing and polishing, hemming, ironing, folding, sorting, arranging and putting away. And if it's inner peace you're after, it's sweeping that creates it best of all.

It seems to me no accident that our lives are inescapably constructed at their core of small, repetitious, apparently meaningless and uninspiring domestic duties. It seems no mere fluke that our existence is universally designed in such a way that we must constantly put back together what our living has undone. In the words of Marianne Moore, doing it

> with a perfect contempt for it, one discovers
> that there is in
> it after all, a place for the genuine.

9

WHEN STRANGERS MOURN

Every family has its own style of mourning, and its times and reasons. So does each nation. My thoughts this evening can wander around the cities of the world — Sarajevo, Port-au-Prince, Seoul — and to the American parents whose ten-year-old daughter was killed in a drive-by shooting yesterday, while they were vacationing in Italy — and try to imagine how various groups of people are feeling today.

In spite of cultural variations, however, the death of a loved one always turns the living person's eyes automatically towards the invisible, unknown realm into which the other one has vanished, and you see this influence of the infinite on the face of anyone in mourning.

In Israel, as stipulated by religious law, people "sit shivah" the first week after a family member's death. They aren't expected to make conversation with condolence callers. They don't listen to music, permit themselves the pleasure of parties, bathing, or alcohol. Freed from the normal social conventions, they sit on low chairs, or couches with the cushions removed, and just let their grief express itself, however that may be. These customs unburden the mourner of any sense of obligation to keep a stiff upper lip, to carry on bravely, to try to be happy in spite of the loss.

I paid a condolence visit yesterday to the Wachsman family, whose 19-year-old son Nachshon, a soldier, was kidnapped last week by Hamas terrorists and executed after a few days.

I can't claim the Wachsmans as acquaintances, though they did once live in our neighborhood. But when, amid all the silent people streaming in and out of their living room, I finally caught sight of Esther Wachsman, feet curled beneath her on their cushionless sofa, her face was startlingly familiar from the newspaper photographs.

We all knew her. She was the one who had said of the kidnappers, "They speak of the G-d of all of us."

Her husband's face was equally familiar. It was he who had asked that people not condemn Yitzchak Rabin for the unsuccessful rescue attempt, and who had said, "A father doesn't always say 'yes' to his children. This time G-d said 'no,' and to human beings, G-d's reasons are usually not apparent. But we still have faith in the G-d of mercy and justice."

When I went out into the day again, it was a sweet, magnificent autumn afternoon. A brush with death can bring about an awareness of life as being exquisitely precious, and this day was no exception. The sky was so blue, and on the bus ride home, the breeze through the open window was like a mother's cool hand on my face.

Opposite me sat a blond, Slavic-looking woman, about 50, chin uplifted with dignified self-containment. Though her hands were folded plainly in her lap, lips set stoically and face unmoving, after a few moments I noticed that tears were in her big, sky-blue eyes. It occurred to me that maybe she'd just been where I'd just been, and I leaned forward to ask, in an undertone: "Excuse me, are you coming from the Wachsmans' shivah?"

"Sixteen," she replied.

Suddenly, I noticed that the bus was silent, and realized, looking around, that everyone seemed to be listening to a news bulletin blaring out over the bus radio — the Hebrew too fast for my comprehension.

"Sixteen?" I said. "Sixteen what?"

"Sixteen died," she said impassively, eyes brimming. "In Tel Aviv, on Dizengoff Street. There has been a bomb."

It turned out to be more than sixteen, of course, and the dying more horrible than anyone on the bus then knew. At that point all I wanted was to get back home as fast as possible, and to be with my own family, safe inside our walls.

For families, like nations, all have their own style of fear, hope, and self-protection, as we try to chart a safe passage for ourselves through this brutally unpredictable world.

What remains are the manifold beauties of life, even as cruel events unfold day after day. To build one's belief, in the face of this pileup of suffering, that all events occur in accordance with an inscrutable plan.

10

A GIFT PASSED ALONG

To this day, when I see that man, I think of Ruth. Each and every time, I feel that aversion, and the instinctive desire to walk on by, so I stop, and take out five *shekels*.

"I know what it's like to be down and out." Those words come back to me.

She is a woman who has suffered. First and foremost as a child, at the hands of extraordinarily detached, negligent parents, who not only had no love of their own to offer, but — strangely enough — forbade her from finding friends among her peers. Then, there was a marriage — comfortable and not without affection — but which, in the context of the meaningless lifestyle in which it took place, left her feeling empty. Divorce prompted the search that ultimately resulted in her conversion to Judaism. Then, in a series of Orthodox communities, one after the other, she lived for decades as a semi-outsider. She also suffered from an annually recurring medical problem, which rendered her — in spite of her wealth of professional talent in various fields — periodically in need of *tzedakah*.

For how many years did she live with her old sense of being ostracized, in spite of efforts by scores of *frum* women to include her in their lives? Here she was, among the people whose Torah she had discovered, finally, in midlife, to be the first and only doctrine that satisfied her rigorous spiritual and intellectual hunger, yet she couldn't shake that feeling of being *different*. She *was* different — as she'd be the first to admit — an indefinable difference, perhaps, but undeniable. And feeling different, she was difficult. Prickly.

She did have many friends. They respected her for her dignity, and creativity, and her integrity, and valued her brilliance. They extended themselves consistently. They'd collect modest funds on her behalf to assist her through her series of illnesses, organized *bikur cholim* and grocery shopping when she couldn't get out of bed, arranged for Shabbos invitations and help with the rent. They constituted an informal circle around her, so to speak, a network of *chessed*. But most of them were primarily busy with their own families. Their time was genuinely limited, as was mine. She'd call for a chat and could hear their babies crying in the background, and their doorbells ringing. They had husbands, children, jobs, meals to cook, holidays to prepare for.

All that warmth… the dining room tables, and the singing, and candlelight…

What did she have? She had her rented rooms, one after the other, in various families' apartments. She had her half-shelf in their refrigerators, and people's invitations for Friday night dinner and Shabbos lunch. When she had come across Torah Judaism, she had said to herself: *Finally. The truth.* But among Torah Jews, she said to herself, *I'm not one of them.*

It had always made me feel dissatisfied — our inability, for whatever reasons, to embrace her as she needed to be embraced; had always felt guiltily contrite that as a group we had not yet succeeded in drawing her in. It seemed like a heaven-sent opportunity spurned. The commandment in regard to converts, to do *chessed* to the stranger in our midst, is stated in the Torah not once but a number of times. It is we who are in need of being kind, more than she who needs our kindness. Her *neshamah* had been with us when we received the Torah at *Har Sinai*. We believed that. So how could we allow cultural differences to hinder us in this, the cultural differences by which she herself was blocked? Why couldn't we just transcend in ourselves whatever we'd need to transcend?

On the other hand, how do you convince someone who has never experienced the love of family that she is a member of yours? How do you make her feel at home if to her, your home feels like foreign terrain? How do you convince someone who has grown up on another planet that she's one of you?

As a child, I was the only Jewish girl around, and had therefore been sensitized to that stranger on the fringe. I knew exactly what it was like: to feel excluded is the opposite of all that a child instinctively wants. But even if my entire hometown had turned out one day to greet me and welcome me in, I wouldn't have felt I was one of them. Because I wasn't. By nature I was different, intrinsically, and knew it. When as a young woman I discovered a Jewish way of life, a society based not on material well-being but spiritual well-being, it was something I hadn't known existed.

Unbelievably, now I was an insider!

But, like Ruth, I'd been formatted as an outsider.

One day, as a young, single woman living in an Orthodox community, it had struck me: *even if I were sitting in a room full of clones — clones of myself — I'd probably still feel different from all the others.* The sense of being alone and apart, a stranger in people's midst, had become engrained in my personality. When I moved to Israel, an entire country I could call my own, sometimes I'd be riding along in a bus full of Israelis and marvel: *All these people are Jewish.* But Group Member was not yet a program, apparently, that had been downloaded into my brain. I'd walk around the streets of Jerusalem as if I were wearing some kind of space helmet, with hazy kinesthetic images of my hometown — unbeknownst to me — imprinted wraparound style on the inside.

Not — when it came to Ruth — that my life experience made me capable of transcending myself any better than anyone else. So whenever I'd meet up with her, I'd end up doubting the genuineness of my own religiosity. In her presence, I perceived myself now as one of the lucky insiders: the well-meaning sort of person who, absorbed in her own happiness, doesn't necessarily forget about the people standing out in the cold, but who just can't find the time to extend herself on the practical level. What would have been helpful to Ruth was to offer her not only my words of friendship but my physical assistance, but these things I left to others. That I was busy with my life, like everyone else, was no fabrication, but perhaps if I had more deeply grasped my personal obligation, and put myself into the position of personally witnessing her needs, I would have found a way. My respect and goodwill were great, but empathy combined with action would have better proved I cared.

That was uncomfortable, seeing myself that way.

So, in her presence I'd find myself undergoing a little shift. I'd pick up her grievance. The chip on her shoulder would become my own. Why, I'd wonder, wasn't this wonderful woman sitting comfortably at the table? Why was she still outside, looking in through all our lighted windows? *People should jump up and open the door! They should offer her their chairs!*

❧ ❧

The two of us, Ruth and I, recently crossed paths on the Ben Yehudah Mall, after long being out of touch. The moment we met, I realized that just lately she'd been on my mind. Why *was* that? It took me a moment to rummage through my mental jungle of data.

Ruth had been in my thoughts, I realized, because of David.

David, in his mid-40's, is an eminently eligible man. A *talmid chacham,* according to his *rosh yeshivah*; a wonderful person, according to those who know him; and "tall, dark and handsome," to boot. So what's the problem?

The *dark* between tall and handsome.

David is an American black, but was brought up Jewish. "Most people don't know that," he told me with a wry smile. "They assume I'm new to this."

I had first heard about David from Bracha, a friend who used to invite him to join her family for Shabbos, and whom he later visited faithfully during her final illness, and who took care to be one of the ten men on the *minyan* when Bracha's husband would go out to her grave on Har HaMenuchot. After a few years, his name came up again, as one of those in a Jerusalem yeshivah who had been trying to help another, younger black American Jew, a teenage convert, to deal with the name-calling directed his way by Israeli children. In a meeting now with David about a *shidduch,* I made reference to that whole chain of events surrounding Matt, who had at last left Israel (he found a yeshivah in Long Island where he didn't have that problem) because of his emotional turmoil over the incessant taunting.

"Oh, well," said David, "that happened to me just now, on the way over here."

"Children jeered at you?"

"Sure."

"What'd they say?"

"Oh, monkey. *Kushi.* Things like that. Oh, but that's nothing new. I've come to expect it. It's a cultural thing. They're just not used to me."

I was aghast. "How do you —?"

He held up the earphones of a Walkman. "See this? I don't go anywhere in the city without them. *Gemara shiurim.* All the time. Block it out."

"But don't you think of leaving —?"

"It's not that different anywhere else. I've tried it out in America. New York, New Jersey, some other places. So I've come to terms with it. Unless children are taught otherwise, or exposed more often to people who look like me, the kids in a certain social sector are going to react to me like that. I'm a strange phenomenon here. And when they grow up they're going to secretly feel the same way. So, you have to be strong. That's all. And I'm strong. I've learned not to pay attention. Also, I know which neighborhoods to avoid. There are places I simply will not walk through because I know already what's going to happen there. The looks I get! Woooh!" He gave a low chuckle. "What I've learned is, this is their thing, not mine. *Shidduchim,* though, that's something. It's always the same old story, whenever I show up for an appointment with a *shadchan* — The poor fellow — or woman, as the case may be — well, they want to help, that's clear as day, but they don't know what to do with me! How many people do you think they come across who would be suitable? It is sort of interesting to me, seeing how they handle it when they get in touch — they always find some kind way of telling me. Usually that they don't have anyone 'in my age group.' They've been telling me that for the last fifteen years."

"David, how do you survive?"

"I stay focused on my learning. That's it."

"And — I guess — there's nowhere to run."

"Nowhere to run."

"So — aren't you tempted sometimes to just leave?"

"You mean the Orthodox world?"

"Right."

He shook his head. "I don't want anything else that's out there. Besides, where would I go? This is what I am. There's nowhere else I belong."

❧ ❧

Talking with Ruth on Ben Yehudah, I had already, as usual, undergone that subtle little re-alignment whereby I became one of the good guys — in other words, an outsider. In this involuntary, almost instantaneous shift, I'd find myself downplaying my bond with the society I loved, downplaying how totally I and my husband and family were identified with it. It was the world into which our children had been born, and in which they had happily grown. They have no familiarity whatsoever with the sense of otherness that I as a child had known — no familiarity whatsoever with the experience of living inside a divided self.

In the past, this had always seemed to facilitate our conversation adequately enough, but today, for some reason, she wasn't biting.

I was speaking agitatedly of David's experience. How eager I'd been to discuss this with someone, aside from Hashem Himself, to Whom I knew it would really matter, and now, of all people, I had run into Ruth. My indignation at the lack of genuine respect and understanding toward the stranger in our midst; the dilemma inherent in this self-contradictory fact, that the isolationism which has always sustained Orthodox societies down through the ages, and made possible our survival as a people, can in some cases undergo a change of direction and turn instead into what looked more like selfishness than self-preservation. My self-doubts as a member of this community — What I was feeling, I can say without pretension, was real grief. *This situation must change. But what can we do?*

Ruth was clearly taking all this in. But her eyes, somehow, were not reflecting my anger. They were empathetic eyes, totally empathetic, for sure, but also serene.

"You know, Sarah, this community is much better than others when it comes to taking in the stranger."

I was taken aback. How lovely to hear her say that! "You think so? Really?"

"Yes," she said gently. "This is a very good society. Much better than most. Lots of very good people. They're trying their best."

Oh, to hear these words on Ruth's lips, after all these years! I wanted her to go on talking, and she did, and I fell almost immediately into some kind of pleasant reverie. "So what you're saying," I said, "is that it's really just human nature we're up against." She nodded. "I guess we have to forgive ourselves the failings of eternal human nature. Even as we're trying to change. Instead of complaining about what people aren't giving, I guess we have to recognize how hard it is to give and work at becoming givers ourselves. Right, Ruth? No matter where we are, even in the best of all possible worlds, the *yetzer hara* will manifest itself one way or another. That's the struggle of being here, in *olam hazeh.*"

"Yes, " she said. "Human nature. It's always difficult."

We went on to discuss the universal human instinct to shy away from people who are culturally different, and the need to balance that impulse with our religious obligation to be kind to the stranger. On the other hand, the obligation to be kind to the stranger must be balanced with the community's overriding need for self-protection and self-preservation. And even as new arrivals can rightfully expect to be accepted unequivocally as family members by the community, they need simultaneously to develop humility before the depth of Judaism's ancient traditions.

Standing there in the middle of the incline of the busy pedestrian mall, the passersby were streaming past us, uphill and down, and the words of the morning prayer came to mind: *What are we? What is our life, what our kindness, what our righteousness... What is our strength?* My eyes opened a little: perhaps the shortcoming I had seen in others was precisely that which I couldn't acknowledge in myself.

At some point in our conversation, Ruth and I were interrupted. Out of the corner of my eye, I sensed who it was.

"What I've learned," she was saying, "is you just have to do what you can to somehow create your own brightness. To sort of illuminate your own little *dalet amos* — You know, we really don't understand how valuable the little things are, the little acts of kindness we can do. And when we do those apparently small mitzvos, the world gives it back to us. I believe that."

I'd never been this close to him before. I kept my face averted. Of all the beggars in Jerusalem, this was probably the one who aroused in me the most unpleasant feelings. I'd always managed to avoid him somehow, through the years. But this particular man — to face him elicited on my part a dim but intense unease; on some level, I knew I wasn't living up to the ideal. The ideal, after all, is to view giving *tzedakah* as a privilege. It's that basic Torah perspective: the beggar is giving us an opportunity to acquire eternal merit, which is of infinitely more value than any money we could give him.

I just kept looking into Ruth's eyes as she went on talking. But that insistent hand of his, rattling loosely and silently around in the periphery of my vision, thrusting itself into the space between us. How I disliked him!

Ruth, still speaking, seemed to be taking some money from her wallet. I couldn't just stand there. As I placed a coin upon his proffered, outstretched palm, it occurred to me that this was the first time I'd ever given him anything.

There on the upturned hand, when I looked, was a five-*shekel* coin, now joined by mine, a *shekel*.

He shuffled on past. "My goodness!" I exclaimed. "Five *shekels*, Ruth?" Her financial situation — I had no reason to think otherwise — was probably still precarious. "That's a lot! You gave him five *shekels*?"

"Oh, yes," she replied, with a tranquility that had apparently taken root sometime since our paths had last crossed. Ruth had always been a natural aristocrat, and bore herself accordingly. But this was something deeper, some fundamental peacefulness in her personality, composed in equal measure of humbleness and certainty. "Oh, yes. I identify completely with that man," she stated flatly, with a dancing little glint in her eyes. "I know what it is to be down and out."

≈≈

An hour later I was on Rechov Keren Kayemet. It was hot, around noon, and I was looking for number 36. I'd gone back and forth, up and down this street now several times.

Suddenly a woman was standing before me, saying something. I stopped. She was murmuring. It wasn't Hebrew, certainly not English. What was she saying? A kerchief was tied under her chin. She was in her 60's, probably, or an old-looking late-50's. She held out a little scrap of paper, on which was penciled something incomprehensible. It was Russian. She pointed vaguely up the street.

"You want to know how to get somewhere?" I asked, trying Hebrew, then English. No understanding. She was pointing again. I looked behind me. Oh, the bus stop. She must want directions.

Then she held out her hand, palm up.

"Oh!" I understood. "You want money for the bus?"

She understood. I understood. She nodded gratefully. I rummaged blindly in my purse for the fare and the coin that came up was five *shekels*.

I hesitated, then handed it over. It was from Ruth.

"Here!" I said. I was so happy all of a sudden, and before I knew it, the woman had leaned over and kissed me.

Fleeting as a breeze, and cool, that happy kiss planted for all time upon my face, and all at once I felt loved, by G-d.

11

IF YOUR SINS BE LIKE SCARLET

The threat of a major terrorist attack was splashed over the front page of yesterday morning's Jerusalem Post, and the whole city braced itself accordingly, as did we in our own household. But something else happened yesterday, too, that dissolved even the best-laid plans for a suicide bombing; or for that matter, any other plans, be they of Arab or of Jew. It transformed instantly the geopolitical reality of the Middle East, diverting not only yesterday's bloodshed, but just about anything else, as well: *Snow.*

Terrorism in Jerusalem, with or without a warning tip from our intelligence services, is not unusual. I am used to the cold uneasiness in the pit of my stomach, sending my children off to school when the buses have been explicitly targeted, and the little battle I have to fight with myself, to not keep them home. I'm accustomed to the guilt when I surrender to fear and order a taxi, castigating myself for the foolishness of imagining that one's fate can be avoided. I'm equally accustomed to the guilt of waving them cheerily goodbye, wondering how I could go on living if anything happened on account of such foolhardiness.

My children are different. They weren't raised in an American suburb during a Cold War that seemed to present only one danger, nuclear extinction: a possibility sufficiently abstract and far fetched that most of the time it could be forgotten. Like all Israeli children, they have grown up with daily, mundane confrontations with the possibility of death — on the way to school, or in school, or a mall, or walking along the street; and possess as a result a kind of bravery which to their mother is foreign, and a source of pride.

So, terrorist threats are not uncommon.

Snow, on the other hand, is rare. And snow that doesn't turn instantly to water on the ground, snow that can be packed into snowballs, and crafted into snowmen with carrots for noses, snow that falls not for a skimpy half-hour but steadily through the night, so you wake in the morning to an innocent world become white and trees turned to lace — that kind of snow in Jerusalem is unfamiliar, exceedingly so, as rare as peace itself.

It's an old joke in these parts: One snowflake makes its appearance in the Holy City and the whole society comes to a halt. We're just not equipped for it. Snow tires? There's no such thing. Snowplows? *Ein davar kazeh.* Buses stop running. Schools close. Municipal services all shut down. And this is in spite of or due to the fact that the last time it snowed in any meaningful fashion was about five years ago. Since then, whatever pitiful little flurries passed our way in the Promised Land were there one minute and gone the next, and whatever was under our feet turned to slush before you could count to ten. To one who was raised in Connecticut, where winter's bounty was unstinting, such snows would have been better left unsaid.

But this — this white blessing that began descending yesterday afternoon and was still going strong when we peeked out the windows amazed at 5 a.m., not only has it given us a chance to dig out our winter gloves from their burial places, deep in closet storage, and trudge out into the wonderland, but *it has kept all the children home.* No one's on the buses, for there are no buses. No one's downtown in vulnerable crowded places, for there are no crowded places. Everybody's either stuck at home looking out, or out getting wet. There's something about this kind of snowfall that brings out the 4-year-old in all of us. Netanyahu, with his two young boys, must surely not be immune. Arafat, whose daughter, if I'm not mistaken, must be about 3 by now: Is he pointing to the snow at this moment and telling her *Allah Akbar*?

That is the phrase, meaning "G-d is great," which is traditionally exclaimed by an Islamic suicide bomber at the moment of his attack, to seal his martyrdom and acquire for himself sure entry into heaven. The exclamation celebrates the Arab's successful perpetration of what he considers to be his holy mission: the killing of an infidel, in this case a Jew who by virtue of living here, by virtue of being alive, evokes in Esav's heart a deep and ancient chord of deadly insecurity.

No doubt there is somewhere in this country today a young man, hardly out of childhood himself, really, whose plans for the day have been thwarted, as for the rest of us. (For purposes such as these, it's the young and fervent ones whom Hamas and Hezbullah recruit, the young idealists, despairing of their predicament, eager for excitement and glory, like young men elsewhere.) Can he resist throwing a snowball? He, too, may be gazing out spellbound at the strange and overwhelmingly new world. He had thought to see heaven today, and there it is.

G-d is great, it's true, the Creator of all of us: He Who designs snowflakes, and humans who are enchanted by them, and Whose kindness endures forever. He will redeem Israel from her iniquities, as it is written in the Torah, "Come now, let us reason together, says Hashem; if your sins be like scarlet, they can become as white as snow."

12

A POT OF BEANS

I was up over the ocean in a flying bubble of see-thru Plexiglas, sharing a jumbo bag of potato chips with my old friend Lillian and gazing down upon the sun-glittering waves. Our bubble was rushing along through white feathery clouds that were parting for us as we soared on through. Her children and mine were being cared for in some other bubble by an ideal nanny with excellent references who was going to make them breakfast, lunch and dinner and put them to sleep in trundle beds, and our ideal husbands were off somewhere in office buildings making money to support their families, so the two of us had no worries to speak of, other than the Palestinian state, of course, and all the cooking for the upcoming holidays. I'd arranged for some exultant Baroque music to be piped in, so the skies were resounding now in glorious celebration, and had picked up two big comfy cushions at Home Depot the day before, along with a subtly meditative and complicated Persian carpet for the see-through floor. So Lily and I were having a lovely time when all of a sudden I remembered I had left a pot of beans on the stove.

I gave a little yelp.

"What's wrong?" said Lily.

"Oh, no."

"What's wrong? Tell me!"

"I left a pot of beans on the stove."

" A pot of beans?"

I nodded.

"Cooking?"

I nodded.

"You're kidding." She leaned over to turn down the volume. "So what does that mean? We have to go back?"

"I don't know."

"Yeah, I guess we have to go back. Was it on high?"

"I think so. I wanted it to come to a boil before I left the house, to get the *chulent* started."

She pressed her lips together, calculating. "And when did you leave the house?"

"9:30."

"So —" She pushed up the sleeve of her sweater to check. "9:30, 10:30. 11:47. Two hours and something. Yeah, so it's probably burning. Hey!" She reached for the cellular phone sticking out of my purse. "You can call Michael!"

"What, and ask him to leave work and drive all the way out to Brooklyn? Anyway, I can't reach him. It's lunchtime."

"So call his cell phone!"

"This is his cell phone," I said, pointing to the one in her hand. "I lost mine."

"So the children! Maybe their baby-sit — "

"Lily, you know where the children are."

"Oh. Right." We both spontaneously glanced around the sky, half-expecting, I suppose, to spot them. But they were probably over something Oriental by now, like Japan, or Korea.

"Lily. I'm sorry."

She dismissed me with one hand. "Oh, it's all right. Really."

I leaned my forehead against the Plexiglas. Far, far down, little white tongues of wave beyond wave beyond wave were turning over and over and up and down and up and down by the thousands, up to the sun and down to the shining blue sea, and the whole scene expanded beyond, way far out to the hazy horizon line. "After all we did to set this up. All our arrangements."

"Listen, that's life."

I looked now into her familiar brown eyes. There was the stray brown-gray tendril of hair curling around one edge of her scarf, and the smudged eyeliner, and pink lipstick. "Lily, you think maybe it's dangerous?"

"What, the pot?"

"Yes. You think it could explode? Is that what happens with something like this? And maybe set fire to the house, G-d forbid? You think so?" Of course I hoped for a no.

"Well, I — How would it set fire to the house, exactly? It's not a pressure cooker, is it?" I shook my head. "So, it probably won't start a fire. There might be a lot of smoke, though. And one of your neighbors will probably knock on the door and when nobody answers they'll call the fire department, and the firemen will probably break down the door to get in, and bring in their hoses, so your carpets — They'll probably get very dirty, and soaked. And the house will smell of smoke for a while."

"That pot. I always liked it. It was a wedding present from my Aunt Jeannie. She got it at Macy's."

"And you just had that carpet put in a little while ago, didn't you?"

"Yes. It was the color I always wanted. The carpet man called it Mediterranean Blue." We both fell into our own thoughts. "Like a little *siman* of *Eretz Yisrael*, right, Lily?"

"Well —"

"Yeah, I guess that's silly."

She shrugged.

"Lily, are you thinking how irresponsible I am?" No answer. "You are, aren't you?"

"No, I wouldn't say that."

"You're thinking I'm too self-absorbed and selfish."

"I am?"

"Yes. And that I'm a bad mother."

"Oh, really. Anything else? How about bad wife? Or just plain bad person?"

I pondered this. "Well, you're not thinking I'm bad, necessarily, but irresponsible. And it's true. Most people wouldn't do this kind of thing. Lily, are you laughing at me?"

Her eyes lost focus. She turned to gaze down at the dazzling ocean, extending in all directions under the midday sun. But for the low whispering of our bubble's flight, all was quietness.

Suddenly I became aware of The Four Seasons. It was still on, on the lowest volume: Vivaldi's busy, orderly, multicolored thread, unraveling in a highly organized pattern of certainty and purposefulness under the surface.

"You know what?" said Lily. "What this is, it's a learning experience. Next time you won't go out without checking the stove."

"You think so?" I considered this. "I'm not sure about that. I think I could do the same thing again."

Lily gave a low little grunt of a laugh. And all at once a tall brick wall within me crumbled mutely in a heap. I had done something bad. No psychological romanticizing in the world could do away with that fact. And I myself was bad, at least in some way. At the very least, seriously deficient. The house would be seriously messed up by the smoke, and who knows what else would be destroyed, and that expensive stainless-steel pot, it would be ruined, probably beyond repair, and worst possible scenario, the whole house would go up in flames, our main financial asset gone, home gutted, all possessions destroyed. Our lives would be uprooted like all those millions of refugees in the world from Bosnia and Sri Lanka and Chechnya and Somalia and all those other places whose names I couldn't recall. I'd never thought of ourselves as being in the same category as those homeless people. But on the other hand, none of us had been hurt. Thank G-d. And Michael and the children wouldn't be getting back home until evening, and by then the firemen would surely have gotten things basically under control, all hosed down and cooled off, and on account of this whole thing we would all undergo tremendous spiritual awakening and would have to go out for dinner tonight. That would be nice. I love going out for dinner. What a *kapparah*. Especially the carpet. A once-in-a-lifetime chance for personal growth and regeneration, big strides forward in *emunah* and reliance on *HaKadosh Baruch Hu*, a recognition of Hashem's *chessed* in everything and Divine providence, etc. Succos was coming up. No roof overhead, it would be for real this year. Michael would use some burnt-out pieces of wood from the foundation. We'd see the stars through the charred ceiling beams. It would be a letting go of the physical plane. Maybe we would even make *aliyah*.

"And you know what," Lily was saying, "no matter what, you're still loved, unconditionally."

"You do, Lily? That's so nice of you, sweetheart."

"I mean by G-d."

"Oh."

"That's just how Hashem loves all of us, even with all these things in us that are so — problematic. That's how we're designed, so we have to work through all of it. Through ourselves."

"Uh huh."

"Past ourselves."

"Uh hmm."

"It's what we've always wanted, that kind of love. Because it's without limit. You can depend on it. We yearn for love like that, and the thing is, we have it. It's not a fantasy, you know. G-d really, actually loves us. Completely."

Hurrah!

We stretched out on the cushions, turned the music up full blast, and stayed our whole allotted time in the Plexiglas bubble. We stared down at the sweet-faced splendor of the sea that sparkled back up at us from every point, and we stared up into the heavenly firmament soaring up majestically all around, until the vast blue invisible endlessness began to deepen and at last turned to twilight, and one by one appeared the small shining stars, and then all of a sudden there were thousands of them, everywhere, brilliant white diamonds in the huge darkness. I would throw open all the windows when I got home, if there were any left, and recycle the devastated pot. Then I'd resume my normal life as well as I could, given my personality.

When I arrived, I rushed to turn the key in the door and burst inside.

But nothing was burning, other than my heart.

13

PLAYING TUG OF WAR WITH SADDAM AGAIN

So, the time has come to play tug of war with Saddam again. How curiously familiar, this deadly game! And what sweet memories it evokes of the Gulf War gone by. There was our sealed room in which we huddled during his attacks, like every other Israeli family, packed in like sardines. Those bleach-soaked rags under the door, that my husband prepared precisely according to IDF specifications, and the cute little army kits with disposable needles in case we needed antidotes for chemical weapons. There were the long, pitiful strips of masking tape along the windows, diligently affixed, to seal out poisoned air. And the gas masks with their funny smell, that reminded me unfailingly, each and every time I donned mine, of rubber swimming goggles from my Connecticut childhood. Our children in *their* gas masks, looking like long-nosed wolf hounds, and the times I'd catch sight of the fear in their eyes through the plastic lenses —

Yes, the sealed rooms were a boon to family togetherness if ever there was one. (And it was only later that we learned that those masks would never have worked.) The sirens wailing outside in the night, the way they'd peak to a crescendo, drop, then spiral up again. The radio with its soft rock, to relax the population with its single listening ear, as the bombs made their way towards us, and the mellow-voiced army spokesman telling us, after each attack, where in Israel the Scuds had fallen.

Could it be, indeed, that Saddam's planning to treat us to another episode? If he only knew how his Scuds drew our disparate peoples together and healed, for a time, our society's wounds, he would never dream of doing it again.

There are differences, of course, this time around. First and foremost, now, it's a question of anthrax, not gas. Masking tape won't help. We have begun again, as we did in 1990, to acknowledge the creeping sense of danger. Could we really be at risk of biological warfare? Does Saddam's superb instinct for self-preservation not extend to the survival of his nation?

Tonight on the popular radio program *"Popolitica"* the host said that the Israeli Arabs are more scared than the Israelis are. Why is that? "I don't know," he replied. "Nobody knows anything."

There seems to be some sort of mechanism in the human spirit which self-activates when times are really frightening: We acquire a cutting comic edge. My British neighbor remarked that he has too many other things to worry about to fret about dying. Another neighbor informed me that the army has reinstalled the Patriot missiles which were used (to no avail, actually) during the Gulf War, and that the army spokesman described this as a routine procedure having nothing to do with Iraq. "That's when I got scared," she said, "when the army told us not to worry." This afternoon in the local supermarket, a woman remarked, "Look, the good news is that now Saddam's saying he won't attack Israel. He may have lied to his son-in-law" — that's the one he tricked into returning home so they could execute him when he arrived — "but to *us?* The Jews?" She smiled pleasantly. "Besides, even if we all end up dead, Albright says America will stand by us. Not to worry!"

I phoned Mazal, the 66-year-old Iraqi-Jewish woman who used to clean my house. On several occasions in the past when it's been difficult to assess the seriousness of a particular crisis, she has shown herself to be neither overly alarmist nor overly optimistic.

"Ach, *Sarale*," she said tiredly on the other end — she who as a girl came close to death by famine during Israel's War of Independence, she who as a 15-year-old had carried messages to young Menachem Begin when he was in hiding from the British, she who has witnessed a half-century's worth of terrorism, and sent her husband and sons to each of its wars and seen the nation's fortunes rise and fall and rise again. "All right, yes, I am worried. And I look at [Defense Minister] Mordechai's face on television and can see *he's* worried. But something will happen. Soon it will be Purim. Remember Purim seven years ago?"

How could I forget? It was on Purim morning, precisely as we read about the defeat of Haman in Queen Esther's time, that we got the amazing news: all of a sudden, Saddam had surrendered. "Remember," said Mazal, "how we tore open our sealed rooms? Remember how happy we all were? How we hadn't been expecting him to surrender, and couldn't believe our ears when it happened? *Ach*, we never know what's around the next corner. I believe," said Mazal, "Hashem will make something happen that will turn all this around."

14

CLASH ON THE AVENUE

One weekend during summer vacation, my daughters made Shabbos for my sister in California. The girls prepared some traditional dishes, made the blessings with her over the candles Friday night, and for one day — in honor of the Israeli cousins — Candis's family refrained from talking on the phone, traveling by car, or turning on and off lights.

On Sunday, the phone rang in Jerusalem. My sister's voice on the line from Oakland was uncharacteristically solemn. "It was so wonderful," she said quietly. "I've gotten a glimpse into what Shabbat can be."

Several months later, Candis and my octogenarian mother decided to visit us in Israel. Late Friday afternoon, heading out from the hotel by taxi for our apartment, with plenty of time before the onset of Shabbos, she tried to pronounce in Hebrew the directions I'd given her over the telephone. The Arab driver couldn't make heads or tails of the address, so he just took them to the only place whose name he understood — Rechov Shmuel HaNavi. After a lot of circling around, he was still driving here and there as twilight fell, searching for a street that didn't exist. And when the Shabbos sirens sounded, he pulled over onto Rechov Bar Ilan to ask a passerby for help.

Now, Candis had enjoyed many a Shabbat and holiday with various Orthodox friends in California, but up until this moment, this American sister of mine hadn't had extensive experience with Orthodox Jews in Israel, other than what she'd seen of my own family through the years. Nonetheless, she naturally had no trouble recognizing as Orthodox the group of angry young men in black who suddenly surrounded the taxi. She understood, too, of course, that explosive word these people were yelling, "Shabbos! Shabbos!"

As far as she and my mother could tell, they were about to be physically attacked.

Back home, we wondered. Fifteen minutes late, a half-hour late. Candlelighting came and went.

By the time we located the two of them an hour or so later, trying to find their way on a side street near our home, their blanched, stricken faces told us that something had happened.

What, indeed, had happened? A group of bored Israeli teenagers — lacking personal experience with nonreligious Jews from other cultures, and oblivious to the fact that their methods were violating grossly the very ideals they saw themselves as protecting — had sacrificed my sister's experience of Shabbos in Yerushalayim to their own exciting Friday-night agenda. To their minds, it was obvious that these western tourists were flouting their contempt for the holy Shabbos, so the women themselves deserved to be treated with contempt. The young men's behavior ensured that for the remainder of that visit, the primary emotion associated in my sister's mind with Shabbos would be fear. Her memory would carry the image of having been excluded from the religion — how was she to know that these teenagers were not representative of our community? — by religious Jews.

〜〜

Three weeks ago I was in my kitchen preparing *seudah shel-ishis*. We generally don't hear much of anything through our windows on Shabbos afternoon, other than children and birdsong. But as I stood there slicing cucumbers and tomatoes and setting out the gefilte fish, the hush was abruptly broken. Another demonstration against Sabbath traffic was going on over on Rechov Bar Ilan.

First came the whirring, clip-clippitting thunder of helicopters circling overhead, then the electronically trumpeted orders resounding over police bullhorns. I knew from experience that most of the police would be standing there warily, with clubs at their sides, but that some would be strutting around and pushing people roughly; some would use their clubs indiscriminately; some would rear up their horses to intimidate demonstrators and onlookers.

Next, my ears discerned the roaring of the counter-demonstrators' motorcycles: the left-wing Meretz supporters were zipping up and down Bar Ilan to demonstrate their opposition to closing the road. I could see them in my mind's eye as I had seen them in actuality, smiling with satisfaction under the loud torrent of "Shabbos! Shabbos!" that rained down upon them: it's not every day they get to be screamed at by hundreds of indignant *chareidim*. They would be exulting in this flagrant defiance of their religion's central hallmark — proudly advertising what they see as a jailbreak from Torah — right under the noses of those guys with long curling *peyos* and black coats.

Then came the ominous crescendo of ambulance sirens, and my insides percolated in anxiety and agitation. Nearly a year had gone by since the incident with my mother and sister, but my resentment toward that group of *chareidi* teenagers — and even more so at their parents, whoever they were, for not forcefully putting a stop to their sons' dangerously destructive antics — had by no means abated. This resentment, coupled with my fury at the Meretz people who were crudely provoking their Torah-observant brethren, ensured that my inner experience of Shabbos that week was as bereft of serenity as Rechov Bar Ilan.

What a society this is! I muttered with disgust. From left and from right, from religious and nonreligious, you get these violent macho types — young men, for the most part, pushy, intolerant, immature, insensitive — who are demeaning the ideals they claim to uphold. And both sides revel in the mutual hatred — all of them buoyed by a smug belief in their own superiority.

Let's go back to Connecticut!

The following Shabbos, Jerusalem's *gedolim* called for a legal, peaceful demonstration on Rechov Bar Ilan, and a crowd estimated by the police at 150,000 showed up to support a Sabbath closure. Distinguished *rabbanim*, among them Rav Shmuel Auerbach, danced and sang along the street, and since the thoroughfare was closed for the duration of the demonstration, this time there were no Meretz supporters driving up and down.

When the demonstration ended at the agreed-upon time and the streets were emptying out, a group numbering between one and two hundred — the raucous teenagers, as usual! — refused to leave, and engaged in a confrontation with the police. So naturally, it was not the serene crowd of 150,000 that appeared in The International Herald Tribune the next day. Religious Israelis were represented instead by the demonstrators who had ignored the calls to disperse. The photograph was accompanied by an article about the Orthodox Jews in Jerusalem who threw stones and overturned garbage bins to protest traffic on the Sabbath.

Over the following days, my intense irritation over all these events didn't dissipate significantly, but somehow, I never did get around to packing my bags. After all, squeezing twenty years' worth of stuff into our old suitcases calls for the sort of organizational skills with which I haven't been blessed.

So I was still in Jerusalem one night shortly thereafter when a class by Rebbetzin Tzipporah Heller was given in a neighbor's apartment. She happened to touch on the subject of nondivisiveness. "We're supposed to feel *achdus* with *Klal Yisrael*," she said at one point in the *shiur*, "but sometimes whole groups of individuals are wrong. How can you feel *achdus* with them? You start to hate someone because of your expectations. You hate because of your unwillingness to accept the variations among human beings, the differences of personality between one human being and another. But even in a confrontation between an absolute wrong and an absolute right, you don't have to demonize the other person."

I asked Rebbetzin Heller how I could feel *achdus* with the young men on Bar Ilan whose behavior creates such an incredible image which spreads *chillul Hashem* all over the world. And how could I not demonize those people driving up and down in their cars, who go out of their way to desecrate Shabbos and hinder other Jews' observance?

"If you want to deal with other human beings without demonizing them, you have to start out with a fundamental understanding that there are human beings who are different from you," she began. "We generally fail to fully appreciate the fact that people manifest wide variations of personality and perspective. So when looking at the various groups involved in the Bar Ilan struggle, first you have to grasp, and it's not easy, that just as you yourself will interpret reality according to your own unique standpoint, so will they. Then it becomes a matter of perceiving and responding to what you can identify with in the other person, even if you disagree absolutely with his position. Those young *chareidim* go out there, in part, on the same impulse that motivates males in other cultures to root for their team at football games. It gives them a chance to play good team, bad team. At the Olympics in Atlanta, the teenagers cheer for the USA. These kids are rooting for Shabbos. We share that with them. Yet the nature of their conviction brings about an inability to comprehend someone on the other side. Their personalities and backgrounds are such that they see other human beings in black and white, and certainly makes it difficult to persuasively convey their perspective.

"As for the Meretz people," she went on, "if you're interested in diminishing your own animosity, bear in mind that there are probably more pleasant ways to spend Saturday afternoon than driving up and down Bar Ilan. They could be at the beach."

"I don't think that's so," interjected one of the women at the *shiur*. "Publicly insulting the Torah seems to give them much more pleasure than sunbathing."

"Yes," said Rebbetzin Heller, "that's probably true. But this inner process of diminishing one's own hatred is a matter of finding the point of common ground, of the concealed virtue. It isn't a matter of condoning their anti-Torah philosophy, or of harboring tolerance toward their activism against Shabbos observance. It's not a matter of having a liberal attitude toward those who do everything possible to hinder *Yidddishkeit* in *Eretz Yisrael*. What is involved is a mental shift, an enlargement of our perspective, by which we can acknowledge that on some level, it takes a certain idealism for their greatest pleasure during their weekend leisure time to consist of devoting themselves passionately to an ideal, even if that ideal is animosity toward Judaism and observant Jews. Can you see this? That's why it's often the people most fiercely opposed to truth who end up being committed to it most profoundly. For such a person, ideals are real.

"And in case you don't believe it's really possible to feel *achdus* with someone whose beliefs are utterly opposed to your own, I'll tell you a story.

"Someone I know is one of those women who are perfect. We all know at least one person like this: her behavior is impeccable, her house is impeccable, and the way she dresses — You know the kind of stockings that cost 20 *shekels* a pair in Geulah? And you figure there must be somebody out there who buys them because the store does carry them? Well, this is the woman who buys them.

"When Labor ran the country, if you'll recall, they promised the community of Efrat that they would be able to expand the settlement onto one of the adjacent hills. The Arabs objected, claiming the land was theirs, so the government agreed to a different hill. When the Arabs once again objected, the government retracted this permit, as well, and the people of Efrat decided to lay claim to the land by going out to the hill and simply refusing to leave. It was a rough period. There was a great deal of physical confrontation between the army and the settlers; people were getting badly hurt. A lot of people were arrested; the soldiers were forcibly dragging men and women and children down off the hills.

"Now, this woman lives in Efrat and was present at the demonstration. A soldier approached, under orders to get her down off the hill along with everyone else. There she was, sitting like a queen with her dignified bearing on the rocky ground, in her elegant suit and hat, and her delicate shoes — and somehow, he balked. Something stopped him from using force. So he said, 'Geveret, you'll have to come with me now.' And she said, 'I'm not sure I should.'

"The soldier kind of smiled. 'Oh, really! You're not sure you should!'

"She nodded.

"'Isn't that nice! Well, take it from me, geveret, you should get down off this hill this minute, otherwise I'm going to have to use force. So if you'd just be so kind —'

"'I'm really not sure I should.'

"The soldier stood there amazed for a moment, then he said, 'Look, lady, how about this: You think it over a few minutes, all right? And you come to a decision about what you should do and then I'm coming back here and you and I are walking down this hill together. Understand?'

"The soldier went off, took care of some of the others, then returned. 'So!' he exclaimed. 'I trust you've arrived at a decision?'

"'Yes, I've thought about it.' The woman was speaking quietly.

"'Good! So off we go!'

"'What I've decided,' she said, 'is that I didn't come as far as I have and sacrifice all that I did in order to walk willingly down this hill.'

"He seemed to take this in. 'And you're sure this is the right decision?'

"'No, I'm not. But I want to ask you just one thing.' She looked him in the eye. 'Are you sure *you're* right?'

"The soldier stood there a moment, silent. And he said, 'No, I'm not.' Then he turned and walked away."

≈≈

Rebbetzin Heller continued: "There's a sequel to this story. That Shabbos, the soldiers who had carried out the evacuation were still stationed on the hill, ostensibly to guard the Jewish citizens from neighboring Arabs, but it was obvious that their actual purpose was to prevent the Jews from retaking the hill. On Shabbos morning, people in Efrat wanted to bring food to the soldiers, but they couldn't because there was no *eruv* on the hill. So they asked the officer in charge if the soldiers could leave their posts and come into their homes to eat. He refused to let his men go off duty. But the day was long and the soldiers got hungry. What happened was that the officer relented and all the soldiers — who had forcibly removed the people of Efrat from the hill in the days before — now joined them to eat and sing Shabbos *zemiros* together at *seudah shelishis*.

"There's another example," said Rebbetzen Heller, "that shows it's possible to be diametrically opposed to someone's position and yet communicate your belief in such a way that neither you nor the other person is dehumanized by the conflict between you.

"Years ago, Rav Amram Blau, who was head of the Neturei Karta, used to go every Friday night to the old Edison Theatre on Rechov Yeshayahu when it was still showing movies on Shabbos. Jerusalem's police had gotten used to him. They expected him there every Friday like clockwork. The people would be on line for the movie and Rav Blau would take hold of the bars on the cashier's window and grip them tightly and start shouting, "Shabbos! Shabbos!" at the top of his lungs.

"When Rav Blau was *niftar*, my husband went to his *levayah* and told me that policemen there were crying. Apparently there was something about the way Rav Blau related to the policemen that let them know he wasn't against them; he was against the desecration of Shabbos."

≈≈

When I got back home from Rebbetzin Heller's *shiur*, I pulled out from the bookshelf a volume I hadn't read for some time, *A Tzaddik in Our Time*, about the life of Rav Aryeh Levine. Rav Aryeh was known in Jerusalem as the rabbi of the prisoners, on account of the devoted care and loyalty he extended to the young Jewish inmates of the Russian Compound Prison, incarcerated during the British mandate for their pre-State underground activities. I was looking for an example of Rav Aryeh's manner with nonreligious Jews. Happily, the book was replete with such accounts. One of them begins by noting that anyone who knew Rav Aryeh remembers most vividly "his unique, affectionate handshake: He would hold the other person's hand and pat it, and it felt as though electric currents passed through the person's body, carrying the pure affection of the rabbi to every fiber of his spirit.

"One Sabbath morning, as Reb Aryeh was chatting as usual with the inmates of the prison in Jerusalem during his regular weekly visit, one prisoner came over and told him that he had taken an oath never to smoke cigarettes again on the Sabbath. When Reb Aryeh asked why, the man said, 'This morning, when you came over to me to wish me a good Sabbath, you took my hand and patted it, as usual, in your own gentle and affectionate way, with that heartening smile on your face. Dear Rabbi, at that moment my other hand held a lighted cigarette hidden behind my back, where you couldn't see it. I knew well enough that our religious law forbids smoking on the Sabbath, but that never meant anything to me. At that moment, though, I wanted most intensely that you should know nothing of my burning cigarette. I felt as if it were giving me blisters all over my body. One thought burned in my heart: Is it right that while the rabbi is holding my hand and giving new life to my spirit, my other hand should hold a lighted cigarette in direct violation of the Sabbath?'"

Another story describes how he was walking along to the synagogue late one Friday afternoon, "in the midst of the blazing summer heat," when he noticed "a long chain of customers lined up before a store that sold ice cream. Inside he could see the shopkeeper busy serving one person after another — with no thought of closing. Reb Aryeh stood still, debating in his mind. 'If I were that shopkeeper,' he thought, 'and all those people were in my store, could I withstand the temptation? Would I drive them all away and close up because the Sabbath was approaching?' He was not at all certain of the answer — There and then he entered the ice cream store, put his *shtreimel* carefully on a chair, and sat down calmly at a table. When he noticed him, the startled shopkeeper came over.

"'What can I say to you?' Reb Aryeh asked. 'You are certainly facing a great temptation. Nevertheless the Sabbath is the Sabbath.' Not a word more did he say, but rose from his seat, put on his *shtreimel* and left the store. When he was a bit of distance away, he turned around and looked back; and he saw the line of customers dissolving. The shopkeeper was closing his shutters and locking up. Some time later the shopkeeper happened to meet the rabbi. 'Do you know,' he said, 'those few words of yours struck home, to the depths of my heart? I realized that you knew and felt just what I was thinking and feeling, and yet you felt pain for the sake of the Sabbath. Then I thought in my heart: A Jew like that must not be made to suffer pain. So I overcame the temptation and sent those people away.'"

〰〰

Several weeks have gone by, and I'm angry all over again. A 14-year-old *chareidi* boy was recently imprisoned, incredibly, for three weeks' solitary confinement on an unsubstantiated charge of stone-throwing during a Bar Ilan demonstration. Police had no proof of his identity as the culprit, and the boy consistently denied having been the one who threw stones; he said he had been in a crowd of onlookers who ran off when they were rushed by the police. He tripped, so it was he who was caught. (The judge who sentenced him to prison, for endangering public safety, was herself stopped by police for speeding on a highway shortly thereafter. She was not arrested.) The boy's release from prison was made conditional upon his admitting to the crime. He held out for some time. Then he gave in and signed a confession, thus saving the court from an embarrassing admission of error.

This Shabbos, there will undoubtedly be another demonstration on Rechov Bar Ilan, with its intense clash between extravagantly disparate people. When the sound of the helicopters and the motorcycles and the bullhorns reaches me through my kitchen window as I prepare the third meal, I hope to overcome the temptation. I hope to interpret the event in such a way that my Shabbos is desecrated neither by my anger, nor by a sense of personal superiority. For the main problem facing us in this nation today is not assimilation and intermarriage and the breakdown of boundaries, as it is in America. The problem in *Eretz Yisrael*, at this moment in our history, is that we do not lack for hatred.

By the way, I will *not* be packing my bags to go back where I came from. I would never have the *zechus* of witnessing a passionate struggle over Shabbos in the suburbs of Connecticut.

15

THINKING OF BRACHA

One night I called Bracha to get an idea for dinner. "Oh, I have a delicious recipe and it's easy as pie. Dice up some onions and peppers." (She might have also said tomatoes.) "Saute it in a frying pan and then scramble it up with some eggs and *ummmm*! They'll love it."

I did as Bracha said, and it was much easier than pie. Not only that. *They ate it.*

It wasn't that I'd never made that dish before, but I think Bracha's confidence in its scrumptiousness must have affected the way I served it, and probably even the way I cooked it.

A lot of her confidence in the kitchen came from the fact that Bracha just loved cooking. Once, during one of her recovery periods following chemotherapy, she asked my father for advice about how to get her strength back. He said it was very important to do something she loved doing every day, and she said, "What I love most of all is cooking and keeping house."

Another factor in the intense pleasure she took in cooking and housekeeping was the dignity and significance she accorded those activities. "I've always made three meals a day," she once told me with obvious pride and satisfaction. "And I don't mean open a can, come and get it. I'm talking about first course, second course. Salad, a protein, two vegetables. Dessert. And as important as the food itself is the way it looks on the table. Put down mats or a tablecloth. Fold up the napkins. Make it pretty. It takes just a few minutes but what a difference it makes! It makes the food taste better."

In the same vein, she once said, "Make being in your home as nice as possible. Make it nice. Make it pleasant. Your family, your children, that's what's important in this world. That's what you really have, and even them you don't have. Nothing belongs to you, not even yourself. The only thing that belongs to you forever is your *emunah*. There's nothing else. If you don't have *emunah*, then it doesn't matter what you have — husband, house, family, friends, accomplishments — you have nothing. And if you do have it, it doesn't matter what you're lacking — you have everything."

A neighbor who occasionally borrowed things from her recalls that whether it was 50 *shekels* or a cup of flour, Bracha seemed happy each time she was asked to lend something. "Look," she'd say, "what's mine is yours."

One of the things that we, her neighbors and many friends, loved about her — and love still — was the way she was always simply herself, without pretense or falseness. Her reactions to life were often unpredictable but always totally in character. One particular memory that keeps coming back to me is the time she called up a little after 1 o'clock and asked what I was doing. Feeling bored and depressed, I said I was just making lunch and waiting for the children to come home from school.

"How nice." She sighed fondly. "You're making lunch. And waiting for the children to come home from school. Isn't that nice."

How much pleasure Bracha took in having energy and mobility — the ability *to do.* As I go about my various life chores, I try to bear in mind how one woman treasured the privilege of standing before a stove, sweeping a floor, taking out the garbage, putting in a load of laundry, folding towels, serving a meal, cleaning up afterwards.

As she used to say, "Enjoy it, *mammele,* it doesn't last forever."

16

TITCHADSHI

When on Friday afternoon I found myself not on the 27 bus heading home but on the number 7 going to Machane Yehudah, I felt like an onlooker wondering at my own self. Here I was setting off toward Rechov Yaffo when there was still so much left to do before candle-lighting: the cole-slaw, and the gefilte fish, and the cheesecake for Shabbos morning.

There wasn't any more shopping to get done; I couldn't use that excuse. So why in the world was I headed this way, rushing not in the direction of my own life but instead toward the *shuk* that I'd avoided these past ten years, the *shuk* I found distasteful not only for its history as a traditional target of terrorism but for its pushing and its crowds and its aggressive vendors' shouting? Last winter it had taken me two months to get back onto a bus again after a series of suicide bombings, and this time, here I was after two days, intent upon standing at the scene of the crime as if my life depended on it.

Traffic was heavy, the newspaper in my hands heavy in another way. A shot of a woman in her 60's: she appeared to have been blinded. A child in clothing wet with blood. A young wife screaming at her husband's funeral, head thrown back as if she'd been given a powerful kick under the chin.

One minute, two, three. We were entering the Machane Yehudah neighborhood now and people were everywhere, the place was packed, the place was a beehive of activity. We are indeed a defiant people, a stiff-necked people, for it seemed I wasn't the only one who insisted upon returning immediately to the scene of the crime. "I'm not going to stop living my life," said my daughter Mimi, *sabra* [native-born Israeli] that she is, when I didn't want her to take a bus to town. "That's what they want, isn't it, Mommy? To make us scared? To make us hide in our houses?"

❧ ❧

Mimi told me this story:

Her friend's brother has a best friend, 23 years old, who accompanied his mother to Machane Yehudah on Wednesday to help her shop for Shabbos. First they got some other shopping done, and then, outside the entrance to the *shuk*, he told her she could wait for him, with all the bags, there on Rechov Yaffo. He would go inside to get what she needed.

He entered the market. She stood there on the sidewalk. A minute went by. It was a quarter after 1.

Then came the tremendous, deafening explosion.

She screamed for her son and started running into the market. People were screaming and running out. She was pushing to get in. Police appeared, they wouldn't let her inside. She screamed. She was screaming.

They were not finding her son. They were not bringing him out to her. She screamed, screamed.

That day she and her husband and children went to the hospitals: Hadassah Ein Kerem, Hadassah Har HaTzofim, Bikur Cholim, Shaarei Zedek. She went to the morgue at Abu Kabir, looked at all the bodies.

No one had any information about their son.

It was not until 10 o'clock that night that her son was located on the operating table in one of the hospitals they'd already tried, his wounds having rendered him unidentifiable. The body had been penetrated by nails, which had been packed into the bomb to ensure maximum injury. He had multiple bone fractures and breaks, burns, and internal injuries. He was still unconscious.

I stand now at the entrance to the market, where that other woman stood screaming.

Do I dare step over — into this place? Have I the impudence, have I the almost obscene will, to tread upon a spot where the truest evil brought about truest suffering?

Yes, I dare.

≈≈

"How much is a candle?"

Here in the *shuk*, the woman behind the makeshift counter hardly looks over at me to reply. She is passing out memorial candles as fast as she can, but there are dozens of hands reaching out to her.

At her back, plastered in a row across the closed doorway to David Nasco's flower shop, several black-bordered notices of the owner's death stare out at me. Hundreds of memorial candles have been lit by passersby and are set down upon the earthen floor before the door. The teeny flames are flickering and burning in the afternoon sun. The sun's pouring down, in slanting columns of dust and light, through the blown-out roof of the marketplace overhead.

I, too, want to buy a *yahrtzeit* candle.

"It's free," she says, putting one of the small blue tins upon my palm. No sooner do I look around vaguely for a match than someone has passed me a box of matches. I cup my hand around the flame as it catches, kneel down, and place mine among all the hundreds. I would have liked to pay for it. I stand up. People are just standing around. They're quiet. In this little oasis of silence amidst the hubbub of the *shuk*, we who have happened to come by here at the same moment look at each other and look away, gaze down at all the little flames, with un-spoken questions stirring in the air between us. We read and reread the notices, wanting to distinguish him in our minds from the others. In my mind's eye, I see the picture in The Jerusalem Post of his sister at his funeral, her face in a grimace of screaming or of crying; she's being restrained by two other women who are crying.

How long to stand here like this, in limbo between death and duty? We who are alive, and standing at David Nasco's gate, we too, like candle flames, flicker uncertainly.

Then there's nothing more to do here. What can we do? One by one we move on, and others arrive.

I turn and go.

I want to buy something. What should I buy?

I don't need anything for Shabbos. I couldn't buy a candle. But I don't want to pass through here like a sightseer, not partaking. I want to belong, like everyone else.

A few stores down, there's a counter display of shoes. I stop, not expecting to find anything I like, then right there, looking right up at me, are the shoes I've always wanted. I pick them up in their white box and carry them out of the sun into the cooler dimness of the store. "Could I have these in 39?" I ask the saleswoman.

She nods and starts searching among piles of boxes. She searches and searches, as I watch. I look down at the shoe in my hand, turning it this way and that.

I wait. She searches.

Good! She's back at my side with a white box in hand, and she opens it up to show me — but those aren't the same ones! Similar, but so different. "Don't you have these in 39?"

"We have them in beige."

"Oh, no."

"We have them in blue."

I agree to look at them in blue, but the ones she brings out are bright, happy partying shoes, the color of neon. I don't like them. "No, no." I'm sad. I look at her beseechingly, searching for size 39, and find her instead, a Sephardic woman in her early 40's, with thoughtful brown eyes.

"How about 38?" she says.

"38? Oh, no, I don't think so. 38's too small." We're looking into each other's eyes. I say, "Were you here on Wednesday?"

She nods.

"Were you frightened?"

"Of course." She's not annoyed at me for asking such a question; she knows I just don't have the right words.

"But you're back."

She gestures as if to say, what else can I do? Her smile is as soft as her gaze.

"Did you know David Nasco?"

"Of course." Tears fill her eyes. Tears fill my eyes. "You know, he has young children."

We fall silent.

She says, "Why don't you just try the 38's and see if they fit? These, the ones you're holding."

I sit down, slip on the black shoes, stand up, take a few steps. I want so much to buy something. I want so much to buy these imitation leather shoes. "They're small," I tell her.

"Are you sure?"

"Oh, yes." I pause. "How much are they?"

"Seventy-five."

I'm a candle again, flickering uncertainly. Seventy-five *shekels* for shoes that don't fit?

She touches my hand lightly. "You can have them for fifty."

My old shoes are soon demoted, tied up in a plastic bag, and out the door I go in my new black mules, that are sturdy enough so I don't feel foolish, high enough so I feel quite tall. Out I step into the dazzling sunlight.

"Titchadshi!" she calls out after me. *Renew yourself!*

I'm strolling along now through the *shuk*, the past in its bag swinging gaily at my side. To my right, peppers and cucumbers and tomatoes. To my left, cashews and pecans and dishes from China. On the right, hazelnut pastries and melons and glassware. On the left, mangoes and pomelos, dried figs and raisins.

To my surprise, they're comfortable, these wonderful new shoes. Just as, year by year, my heart's getting bigger in order to live here, so do these shoes seem to have grown instantly to accommodate my need. But is it all right? To renew myself with a new garment today, here, in this place, on the very dust that just hours ago absorbed the blood of my brethren? It's the question that arises repeatedly for anyone living in this country: Should I permit myself joy, when the tragedy that occurred yesterday, or last week, or a month ago — the things from which we beg *HaKadosh Baruch Hu* to protect us, the protection we beg that our families should be worthy of — mirrors again and again and again the historic events that we commemorate at this particular time in the Jewish calendar, during the three weeks preceding Tishah B'Av.

I glance up overhead. In the particular section of the market through which I'm passing, where the second bomb went off, the roof isn't completely blown out — it's in shards — so the sun's pouring down shattered, in diamonds, and in broken triangles of shadow, and half-darkened fragments. There's tumult everywhere, shoppers bustle all around, vendors are calling. The passing faces are speaking wordlessly of the evil that has taken place and that this is why we're compelled to be here, but for a few split seconds, something odd happens to my senses. As if by some trick turning of the lens, the frantic scene is... altered. Some little children dash before my line of vision, but they seem to be running in slow motion. My feet pause.

There's noise, but it's far away.

The scene before me is one of lustrous stillness, suddenly, congruent with the one in front of my eyes, but so peaceful. It's a splendid realm illuminated sublimely from within, by an unimaginably tender — and infinite — love.

Then it's over, and the *shuk's* been restored to its normal self. Mangoes are mangoes, flames are flames, and I am a mother rushing back home, thinking of ironing and chicken soup, cheesecake and *sponja*, heading for the exit on Rechov Yaffo where that other woman stood so recently, screaming. We're here in this place of upheaval and conflict, where questions don't contain their answers and understanding is always undone.

But in all the commotion, a *nechamah* offers itself like a tiny light. The flames will be extinguished by wind or by time, but the soul in whose honor we lit them is inextinguishable.

17

SPEAKING OF
STUNNING ACCIDENTS

R' *Shimon ben Pazi pointed out a contradiction [between verses]. One verse says, "And G-d made the two great lights," and immediately the verse continues, "The greater light... and the lesser light." The moon said unto the Holy One, Blessed be He, "Sovereign of the Universe! Is it possible for two kings to wear one crown?" He answered, "Go then and diminish yourself." "Sovereign of the Universe!" cried the moon. "Because I have suggested that which is proper must I then make myself smaller?" (Chullin, 60b)*

"Russia Opens Fire on Islamic Rebels," "Nixon Quit 25 Years Ago, But the Tapes Play On," "For the Kosovars Lacking Homes, Not Enough Aid."

As the middle-eastern sun moves across the corner table in this downtown Jerusalem café, I survey the August 9th headlines of The International Herald Tribune, making my way leisurely from one to the other, and through the little hill of whipped cream atop my cappuccino. All things being equal, nothing in this coffee shop, nor in the busy plaza out the window down below, nor even in the tragedies that I will unfold, re-fold, and leave on the table when I go, are apt to shake me from the pleasant mindlessness that is the hallmark of my daily newspaper and coffee ritual.

One paragraph does jar me though, slightly, and I linger. In a piece entitled, "A Stunning Show by Sun and Moon," about the total eclipse due to occur on August 11th, Dana Sobel of The Washington Post writes: "Only Earth and the moon — and no other planets or satellites in the solar system — can figure in the ceremony of totality. By a stunning accident of cosmic gravity and geometry, these two bodies alone possess the precise size and distance relationships to periodically extinguish the central fire of the sun. The puny moon, only one-four-hundredths the sun's diameter, lies 400 times closer to Earth ..."

Glancing out the window to take this in, I find that the central fire is shining right in my eyes, and thus embark upon the elaborate business of moving one table over — rearranging purse, water glass, newspaper, narrow ceramic vase with its slightly wilting pink rose, the now empty coffee cup, and then myself.

Resume reading: "The puny moon, only one-four-hundredths the sun's diameter, lies 400 times closer to Earth. Thus the moon exactly matches the sun in apparent size in our skies, as though they were two halves of the same grapefruit."

Did they ever teach us that in science class? All I remember is Mrs. Warren in third grade, saying: "If the Earth were one inch closer to the sun, in one second it would burn to a crisp."

The waiter comes by to ask if I'd like another cup and I lose my place, then find it again: "... two halves of the same grapefruit. When the new moon dogs the sun across the daytime sky, it can sometimes step in front of that bigger, brighter heavenly body and obliterate it from our view. To some believers, this coincidence serves as proof of the existence of G-d."

I lean back in my chair.

... by stunning accident ... this coincidence ...

I look down at the people sipping cappuccinos at their tables, each table with its flower; each customer with his newspaper, and water glass. They, too, are leaning back. Leaning forward in conversation, skimming the headlines. The Israeli men survey the passers-by. Under the umbrellas they sit, protected from morning's growing heat, in the cool shade of a few potted trees, slender and young, in the full leaf of mid-summer.

Am I imagining things, or isn't that 400 to $\frac{1}{400}$ ratio a little over the top? But according to the reporter, who must know what she's talking about, it was one of the many conditions essential to life's emergence on this planet.

A lucky fluke, as well, I suppose, that there's such a thing as roses, and humans who for unknown reasons like having them on the table.

And that in summer when the trees are full, the shade's so convenient down there on the plaza.

≈ ≈

One afternoon after school, my daughter Elisheva and a friend were crossing the plaza when Shiri suddenly said she had to go straight home. "How come?" said Elisheva. "I thought we were going to get shoes today."

"But I feel so tired now, I want to go."

"But I don't want to look by myself. Can't you stay a few more minutes?"

"I'm sorry, I just can't. I'm so tired, I want to go home."

So Shiri went to her bus stop, and Elisheva, disappointed, had set off towards hers when she passed a shoe store. She stepped inside.

Then came the explosion.

She told us later it was so huge and deafening that it rocked the world.

Then there was silence.

The world had frozen. People were like statues.

Somewhere, a baby was crying.

Then all at once, chaos and screaming and Elisheva found herself outside. Before her stood a teenage girl, with a black nail sticking out of her face.

Then came another explosion.

People were running in all directions. Elisheva ran, not knowing which way to run, then she was back on the plaza where she and Shiri had parted, and at her feet lay a bloody abdomen with neither head nor legs. Someone was yelling that it was the body of the terrorist. Suddenly from within all the screaming something else, something familiar, was being screamed. "Elisheva! Elisheva!"

Shiri was running at her, they were falling into each other's arms. "I've been looking all over for you!" They were sobbing. "I couldn't find you anywhere!"

In that double suicide bombing, four people were killed. Some of the injured are still undergoing rehabilitation, among them the son of a woman I met last week at a *bris*. Someone else I know told me that one of the four who died was her doctor's 14-year-old daughter, who had been seated at an outdoor cafe.

So... if I were that girl's mother, would I say, If G-d's in charge, why couldn't He have made her sit one table over? Why not! Why couldn't she have just gotten up to leave a few minutes early? Why!

One inch closer... one inch farther away...

Can't you stay a few more minutes?

Of cosmic gravity and geometry, these two bodies...

A stunning accident, too, naturally (though in this case, one of those lucky ones) that next winter when the trees are bare, the people at the tables won't need shade — all leaves and coolness — but instead, the sun.

In any case, G-d made it onto the front page of The International Herald Tribune. That's surely proof of His existence.

18

SOME THOUGHTS ON THE BURNING FLAMES

One evening during Chol HaMoed Succos, at the *Simchas Beis HaSho'evah* celebration held annually at Neve Yerushalayim, a Jerusalem women's seminary, my daughters and I engaged in four or five hours of nonstop dancing. The boomingly loud music, provided as it is each year by a local women's band, was earsplitting, irresistible, rhythmic, sometimes sweet and yearning. The women and girls, mostly strangers to each other, came in all ages, and for those uninhibited hours hundreds of us danced and danced and danced as if nothing else in the world existed but our feet, and our songs, and our exhilaration.

On the bus ride home late that night, as my littlest girl fell asleep on my lap and my teenagers talked with their friends, I thought of a *Simchas Beis HaSho'evah* celebration twenty-five years earlier, when a young Jewish woman, harboring some tender hopes and fervent questions, entered a synagogue. By herself in New York City, she had heard that on this night there would be dancing going on here and she had looked forward to it all week. She couldn't wait to dance, she hoped to find a community that would embrace her, she wanted Jewish explanations for everything in her own life and on the planet. And last but not least, when she walked through those doors she wanted G-d Himself to be there waiting for her.

From the women's balcony of the 72nd Street Synagogue, I looked down upon the men dancing for a Jewish holiday I'd never heard of until that day. Fathers held children aloft on their shoulders as they circled around and around and around; small girls and boys dashed in and out of the delighted procession. These self-inclusive families were everywhere, it seemed. The music was fast and loud and catchy. Outside there was thunder and lightning and cold. In here it was warm, and bright.

I tapped my foot and looked around discreetly at the women occupying the tiered benches, and when I couldn't stand it any longer, sidled over to the sedate-looking lady seated a bit to my left. I had recently started recognizing these people's well-coiffed wigs; this woman had on a brown one, and a little round hat atop that. "Excuse me, can I ask you something?"

"Yes?" She turned her head partway. She appeared, I thought, to be some sort of European, in her early 30's: trim, no-nonsense, attractively even-featured, attired in a navy blue suit with a lacy white collar. I felt unkempt in comparison.

But it was the disorderliness of my ravenous heart that I was trying to hide.

"Excuse me, could you tell me —"

"Yes?"

"I'd like to know why the women aren't dancing with the men."

She stared with large hazel eyes. Her chin drew in. The pretty girl at her side, who I supposed was her daughter, around 12, with glossy auburn braids, leaned forward slightly and surveyed me with guarded curiosity. I felt like a wild-hearted monster com-

pared to these two. "The English," the woman said. "I am sorry, I do not know to speak Engl—"

I repeated the question, not trying this time to conceal the hard edge beneath my words.

One, two. A few moments stood between us, then: "You should speak to my husband. He is a rabbi. He will know how to answer you very good, he knows better to talk than I. Wait after downstairs and I will bring him."

Afterwards, in the wood-paneled anteroom, I waited. A cloakroom was on one side, an oaken stairway on the other. Girls and women and little children were all coming down the stairs with a lot of conversation and noise, men and boys and more little children were exiting out of some hallway to my right, everyone was getting their coats and wraps. Families re-united, the place gradually emptied out, and I was alone. Suddenly an opaque glass door opened up and a black-suited, bearded man with a large black yarmulka stepped forth. As the door shut behind him, I caught a fast glimpse of the brightly lit synagogue within.

He stood before me, wary. Was I scaring these people?

"Yes?" he declared. Also a European, it seemed, from some vague country like Belgium. "You want to know about the dancing?"

A sudden bitter irritation twisted inside me. This husband, this rabbi of hers, better prove women weren't second-class citizens, after all, in this whole getup. And heaven help him if he couldn't give me an answer, pronto.

"Right. I want to know why the women aren't allowed to dance with the men." My anger sounded to my own ears flat, cool, confident, the way I wanted it. "They should enjoy them-selves, too."

The man drew himself to his full height and looked down upon me with chin upraised. I know now that he was quickly cal-culating what could possibly be said in response. What would be of most benefit to this sad girl with the scared eyes? Is she from some Reform congregation? Is she one of those feminists? "The women do not need to dance because they are on a higher level than the men." He squinted a little, obviously trying to hit the mark correctly with this hostile, melancholy American Jewess. He hoped to. "Do angels need to dance?"

Something opened up within me, some channel. I wanted to believe...him? The anger melted for a moment in my desire, the desire which had brought me here to this painful place in the first place, where I felt impure and unworthy. Do angels need to dance? I tried to take it in. He's saying I don't need to dance, because I'm an angel.

But it was hard to keep my feet still.

Therefore, I'm unangelic?

I wish I were angelic.

Do angels need to dance ... It sounds like a compliment. It's surely a compliment. But not for me? Because I need to dance?

I wanted — something. I waited for more.

The rabbi, however, seemed to have completed what he had to say, and expected me, apparently, to go now.

Out I stepped into the wet Manhattan night, with his answer in my emptied heart.

Speeding along in this bus now, two decades down the road, a sorrow seized me for that child, almost as if she were a daughter to me rather than myself. I wished the well-meaning rabbi and his wife had told me that of course, separate dancing by women is permitted, and explained honestly why women can watch men as they dance but not vice versa. I wished they had convinced me that although no human being is pure, one day I would know what it is to feel angelic; that one day, I would even transcend the prison of my human limitations by restricting myself according to *halachah*. I wished that somehow they had known how to make me feel included, that cold and rainy night, rather than ostracized.

But how could such things reasonably be expected? Culturally speaking, their lives and mine were hardly taking place on the same planet. Just as mine hadn't prepared me in any fashion for them, theirs had in no way prepared them for relating to modern young American women. And in those years, there were no women's seminaries yet in Manhattan, designed to speak my language.

As familiar shadows of Jerusalem rushed by in the darkness, it struck me, though, that even if the rabbi and his wife had given me those frank replies, perhaps I wouldn't have had ears to hear. The whole notion of separation of men and women would probably have seemed to me so old-fashioned and oppressive and strange that I might have rejected uncompromised truth had it been proffered.

G-d Himself was waiting for me, however, just as I had hoped. A few weeks later, one of the couples in the neighborhood invited me to a Friday-night meal. When the woman lit two candles for Shabbat and covered her eyes, I found the sight so very beautiful, and was so touched that this was a Jewish ritual, part of my own heritage, that I sat right down, took out my drawing pad, and executed an exquisite charcoal line drawing of the candles and their burning flames.

She said nothing. I sat there blithely unaware that I was doing anything wrong, drew my picture until she distracted me with her baby (she saw that her guest was a newborn, too) and felt that perhaps this world could be mine, after all. I was on my way.

19

WE ARE WHAT WE SAY

When I as a teenager was searching for truth as only an assimilated Jewish teenager can, one of the self-improvement methods that I tried on for size was a systematic program of speech control offered by an organization called The Institute for Human Potential. Its stated goal was that adherents should "wake up" and become fully conscious human beings, rather than live out their lives as robots.

I signed up for a lecture whose teacher (he was Jewish, too, of course, as were most of the other students) took as his central premise this principle: Human beings live with the unconscious feeling of being "the worst in the world." The degree to which that feeling dominates his or her life will vary according to the extent, intensity, and manner that a person was put down in childhood. But wherever the individual falls on this continuum, he can end up spending his entire life trying to escape, however possible, from awareness of his unconscious feeling about himself. Either he'll try to do something that will make him feel good once and for all (it never works), to prove to himself and the world that he is lovable, after all. Or he'll do everything possible to just stay asleep.

This one seeks escape by winning the Nobel Prize, that one by becoming a garbage man. Many hope to feel better about themselves by getting married; others by getting divorced. Some feel parenthood will do the trick; others that it's a new house which will soothe that unease at the center. One person stays away from her feelings by watching television, or by getting a face-lift, another by going shopping, or by getting a Ph.D. In other words, the teacher proposed, unless a person is conscious of this essential negativity towards himself, almost anything he does with his life will constitute a flight from his own self. He or she can seek to remain blind forever, whether the escape expresses itself through "failure," through "success," or by simply "numbing out."

And what behavior is it, said the teacher, that best shields us from an awareness of this negativity toward our own selves, and therefore prevents us from undergoing the psychological and spiritual awakening that we seek?

The pervasive human impulse to put other people down.

To me at 19, put-downs didn't seem like such a big deal, and I found it odd to have such emphasis placed on eliminating something that, to my mind, was just a natural part of life. Nonetheless, as a diligent and earnest young seeker, I took it upon myself to adhere to the rules, and the chief rule was: "Don't let a put-down pass your lips."

Months went by, and something interesting started happening. This single abstention — inadequate as my sporadic practice of it proved to be — increasingly had the effect of casting a disconcertingly bright light onto all sorts of feelings within that had previously been hidden from my view. It seemed that this one gesture of self-restraint — that of denying myself the luxury of imposing my negativity upon others — was indeed, automatically, getting me in touch with the much deadlier criticalness that my mind was directing my own way. Stopping my lips from speaking against others threw me back onto my own self. As my use of speech became more disciplined, and my avoidance of putdowns started to become second-nature, I discerned with increasing clarity the voice within that found fault with my painful wanting, and my weakness, and fears, and neediness. It seemed that underneath it all, there was an emptiness at my core: a bottomless sense of inferiority before all of those whom I had previously made it my casual habit to diminish.

Terrible realizations, frightening. I wondered sometimes if I was making it all up in order to conform to the teacher's agenda. I wondered if my experience was being influenced by the dogma. But one thing I could not deny: It was easier to criticize someone else than to take a long look at myself. "Looking" at myself, in fact, was an amorphous business altogether, like gazing for one's reflection in a murky pond, whereas I had no problem at all spotting the faults of others. And recognizing someone else's failings involved a certain unacknowledged pleasure. What was that pleasure? Why did putting another person down give me an unarticulated, half-conscious sense of being one up, as if we were on some kind of invisible seesaw?

Let's say, for example, that there was a sharp, critical voice within castigating me for laziness. But the volume would be turned down low enough to allow me to go my merry way, and I'd cope with its muffled diatribe by dulling myself to its ongoing remarks. If, however, someone else came along who appeared to me as lazy, the same critical voice would instantly become audible.

Did it burn me up, so-and-so's selfishness? Or that one's insincerity? This one's small-mindedness, or irresponsibility, or vanity? Or the other one's lack of vanity? My critical responses were sure-fire indicators that I had come upon some inner weakness or bad feeling of my own of which I was unaware. By restraining that impulse to speak ill of others, the desire to criticize could be used, instead, as a sort of perpetually activated Geiger counter, one that could guide me through unexplored regions, towards long-buried radioactive feelings about myself.

Gradually I started to see how it works: Let the put-down cross your lips and presto, you've got a moment's reprieve from your own self.

≈≈ ≈≈

Not much time passed before G-d in His wisdom plucked me up out of the sunny West Coast and, to my surprise, set me down — where else? — in Orthodox Brooklyn.

The cultural milieu could not have been more different, except, to my mind, in one noticeable respect. Just as put-downs had been strictly forbidden during my memorable stint at the self-improvement class — whose forty or so students had waged a lonely, uphill battle against the socially accepted, casual denigration of one's fellows — here was an entire community that made *shemiras halashon* (literally: "guarding one's tongue") a pivotal, community-wide, institutionalized aspect of religious observance. The Torah, apparently, had forbidden gossip, slander, and derogatory speech quite some time ago — at Mount Sinai, actually — well before California's Human Potential Movement.

A book published just about the time I arrived in New York, *Guard Your Tongue*, by Rabbi Zelig Pliskin, set forth for the English-speaking public Judaism's laws governing this area of behavior. I learned that since human nature is such that we're all experts at rationalization and self-justification, goodwill is insufficient. The commitment to refrain from put-downs has to be buttressed by a subtle, comprehensive network of laws, which apply to all the infinitely varied situations that arise in daily life.

The nuances were intriguing. Sometimes, divulging negative information can be essential — for instance, when it comes to a prospective marriage partner, or a business deal. Under other circumstances, saying something positive about someone is the *wrong* thing to do — for example, when it's likely to arouse a listener's jealousy or skepticism.

I was taken aback by such savvy psychological realism in an ancient tradition which, tribally speaking, I could claim as my very own.

Aside from its vastly more comprehensive scope, however, there was an essential difference between what I'd learned in the self-study class, and Judaism's concept and practice of this discipline. As defined by Torah, the human being's inclination towards negativity, expressed destructively towards oneself and/or others, does not arise by fluke. It is not some error in our emotional constitution which can be permanently eradicated by this or that therapeutic program. Although the character and severity of any given individual's negative impulses are affected immeasurably and profoundly by his or her unique childhood experiences, the negative impulse itself is, in essence, an aspect of the eternal *yetzer hara*, and is part and parcel of our G-d-given humanity. Without it, we would be as animals, with no higher selves to strive for, and no inner conflict prompting us to strive.

Furthermore, as understood by the observant Jewish community which I had joined, the focus of *shemiras halashon* was not *me and my enlightenment*. At the center was G-d. What I came to see in Brooklyn was that as legitimate, noble and desirable as personal growth may be, and as effective a tool as guarding one's speech may be along the way to that goal, *shemiras halashon* goes beyond any particular individual's quest for personal liberation. To the extent that my mundane daily speech is morally sensitive, in private or in public, to that extent will it promote not only my own psychological well-being but the well-being of the group. In fact, it has an effect on the world beyond my reach, and to worlds beyond human perception.

I learned that the seemingly insignificant little words I utter have infinite significance in the eyes of our Creator. Refraining from putting people down, and from putting oneself down, is an aspect of our purpose here in the world: to arrive at the recognition that each and every one of us is a miraculous piece of Divine handiwork. To insult or disparage one of His creations is to disturb our own relationship with our Creator.

Decades passed. It's been years since I was picked up out of that community in Brooklyn and replanted once again, in Jerusalem, where the ancient traditions are far more deeply rooted than the tall old pine tree out my window. But I'm still surrounded, as I was back then, by Orthodox Jews of all ages who are conscious of the obligation to guard their speech. It's an environment in which, generally speaking, the idealism in this regard is as fervent and sincere as was mine, when as an innocent teenager I first started looking for truth.

There's a simple question which we can ask ourselves when in doubt as to whether a particular remark would be permitted: *Would the person I'm talking about be pleased or displeased were I saying it in his presence?* With a guideline as obvious and straightforward as that, why should it be necessary to review the laws of proper speech on a regular basis?

Another way of asking the same question is: why were we created with a feeling of weakness at our core?

That is indeed a mystery of the human soul. But the good news is this: If we felt complete rather than lacking, perfect rather than inadequate and at fault, we wouldn't feel the need for anything greater than ourselves. And if we didn't have to refrain from the desire to speak *lashon hara* — to resist the illusion that we enlarge ourselves by diminishing others — then we wouldn't have this perfectly designed opportunity to create our own characters daily.

The identifying characteristic of our species is our ability to speak, so it's no coincidence that only to the extent that we refine our use of it can we sense our intrinsic human dignity. Once we start curbing that inexplicable impulse to put people down, we find ourselves spending less time in the company of imbeciles, lowlifes, ingrates, and sadists, and surrounded more often, much to our surprise, by fallible, vulnerable, striving human beings who resemble — how uncanny! — none other than you and me.

20

Deep Pockets

No sooner did my husband walk through the door than he gave me the news. "The dentist says I have deep pockets."

An old tweed coat appeared in my mind's eye.

"At first I thought he meant I had a lot of unpaid bills," said Yaacov. "But he was talking about my gums. He says that little bits of food collect in there and create a space. Then bacteria develops and that makes the gums recede."

I nodded, taking this in.

"Then, if you don't take care of it, eventually you lose your teeth."

I bit my lower lip.

"The dentist says it's a sign of aging."

"Oh."

Yaacov looked into my eyes. "I think you should go, too."

"Good idea."

"You don't want to lose your teeth, do you?"

"Of course not!" I exclaimed, since of course I don't want to lose my teeth. Who would? I know that just as many problems go away with time, if you have the equanimity to ignore them, so do teeth.

"If you want," he said, "I can call up and make you an appointment."

"O.K., maybe, but Yaacov, you know what! When I did a load just now, the washing machine flooded! Should I call the repair guy or do you want to try to open up the filter?" For what Yaacov doesn't know is that I already know about deep pockets, and spaces where bacteria proliferate, and other things of that nature. He seems to have forgotten that I already have an excellent dentist, right here in Jerusalem.

≈≈

I first met Dr. Morton two years ago, when an old root canal got infected. As soon as I walked into his office and saw its state-of-the-art vertical blinds, I knew I was in good hands. That was just the beginning. From that initial emergency procedure I moved on to a tune-up of old, decrepit fillings, then to a cleaning, and then on to several educational sessions about dental hygiene and how to hold a toothbrush at the correct angle. I found that difficult to absorb, that I'd lived all this time without knowing how to hold a toothbrush.

For one year I made appointments and kept them. I felt, just as my husband feels now, that I had finally done what I should have done a long time ago, and that everyone else should be doing it, too. I was thankful to have been forced by circumstance to take care of this vital aspect of my own well-being. I recognized that my negligence in this area actually had its roots in a deep-seated lack of self-love, and that my having finally started attending to my teeth and gums was an act not only of dental health but mental health. I was taking personal responsibility, I was parenting myself.

The fact that it was a moral victory, though, had its flip side. The first time I missed an appointment, I felt like such a low-life that it was uncomfortable showing my face again in Dr. Morton's office. The first time I lay back in the reclining chair for a session with the hygienist and realized that I hadn't flossed my teeth since right before my last appointment, it felt not like a technical lapse but a character weakness. As the weeks and months went on, it wasn't so much my teeth that were on my mind but what Dr. Morton and his nurses, assistants and secretaries thought of me. I began manifesting Freudian slips of forgetfulness. For example, the secretary would say Tuesday the 9th and I was sure she'd said Wednesday the 17th.

Eventually, a curious psychological reversal set in. Failure to return their calls took on new meaning: such behavior exhibited not a weakness in my personality but a stand against dental coercion. My self-esteem was no longer reinforced by making appointments and keeping them, but by calmly resisting the secretary's intrusion into my personal space. Finally, when one day I received one of her calls to remind me of the next day's appointment, I replied assertively that unfortunately, my schedule was full for the next three months.

To my surprise, she stopped calling.

That was about six months ago.

Doesn't she care anymore how I'm holding my toothbrush? Does Dr. Morton ever wonder about my deep pockets?

My sister lives in California, where health practitioners make it their business to be aware and sensitive. She told me of the following exchange between her and her dentist:

Candis: "Dr. Lewis, do I really have to floss my teeth every day?"

Dr. Lewis: "No, dear, only the ones you want to keep."

Dr. Morton, if you are reading these lines, know that I'm waiting for your call. But in the future (if you and I are to have a future), I can only be approached with the kind of tact manifested by this Dr. Lewis. Susceptible as I am to disabling guilt-feelings, I must get my injections of admonishment *casually, without any suggestion of disapproval,* and at such an indirect angle that they won't inadvertently activate my natural self-defense-response. Gradually I'll come to realize that you're telling me to floss and brush not for your sake, or my husband's sake, or even for the good of mankind.

It would be for me.

My very own mouth.

Jorge Luis Borges, the Argentinian novelist and essayist, wrote that when young, he had realized that some bad things and some good things would happen to him in the course of his life, but in the long run, all of it would be converted into words. Particularly the bad things, "since happiness doesn't need to be transformed."

Taking my cue from Mr. Borges, I realized that my teeth fall into the category of things that need to be written about. So I came up with this poem:

Teeth, teeth, go away,

Come again some other day.

I wish I may, I wish I might

Keep the teeth I have tonight.

When I finished that stanza I liked it so much that I went on to compose another, but the last word kept on ending up "teeth," and I couldn't find a suitable rhyme. "Heath," as in "Heath Bar," the chocolate and toffee candy I used to like as a child, was inappropriate for obvious reasons. "Bequeath," also, was wrong, summoning up, as it does, associations with "bequeathing one's body to science."

"Death," an intriguing semi-rhyme in the style of Emily Dickinson, occurred to me, too, but of course that solution would never do, since that's the word at the crux of this whole subject in the first place. The loss of teeth, at least in one's dreams, can symbolize our mortality. I've heard that there's a *Gemara* to that effect. Aging, physical deterioration, progression towards one's ultimate destiny... All these underlying issues are pried from the unconscious, as if with a nurse's cold stainless steel cleaning scalpel, whenever one comes within ten yards of a dentist's office.

So, all I have to do is come to terms with my larger existential predicament. Then Dr. Morton can empty out all my pockets.

21

THE MAN ON
THE MOON

When all those fresh and innocent eggs tumbled down
onto Rechov Yaffo and broke yellow and shining in
the sun, a nonsensical notion crossed my mind: *Just
think of all the cheesecakes. Who'd ever want to use
such good eggs to kill us?*

I'd been making my way through a purposeful, noisy, rushing
crowd, precoccupied by my own thoughts, when the air filled everywhere with a booming bullhorn's disembodied baritone, and the
street that had been clogged with cars, and taxis elbowing in-and-
out of traffic, and by big Egged buses and minivans and trucks
spouting exhaust, opened all at once into a cleared expanse, a gray
rectangle of empty street about the size of a tennis court. We who
were standing along the perimeters were abruptly herded back behind imaginary ropes, and, with the ordinary mix of impatience and
resignation, stopped in our tracks to watch the familiar scene unfold.

Except for the bullhorns, and the distant, muffled cacophony of car horns farther down near the center of town, where they were just now running into our traffic jam, we were standing in silence, at the edge of an otherworldly realm.

A few birds darted mutely overhead.

"Back! Get back!"

I'm peering between heads, standing on tiptoe, craning my neck to get a glimpse of the spaceman. I worm my way up for a front-row spot, till I have a view of the unpopulated lunar surface. A line of policemen, their backs to the moonscape, are facing us, the crowd.

The faceless spaceman, as remote from us as if he were on Mars, plods dutifully, laboriously forward. Hindered by his unwieldy costume, with the clumsy robotic stiffness of a properly attired astronaut, he is proceeding on a diagonal across our line of vision — with this difference, however, between Rechov Yaffo and the moon: here the attentive audience is right on site, restless, eyeing his every move.

He's on a mission, heading in a determined straight line to — where? We press forward to see.

The unseen bullhorn is blasting, "Back! Get back!"

We press forward. We've been put through these paces before, of course, on countless occasions through the years. But even after so much terror we are not lacking completely in the curiosity of children. *Will there be an explosion?*

Litter's blowing about lazily here and there. I sidle over to the nearest policeman. "What's happening?"

When he spins around to respond with a pleasantly polite expression, he turns into a boy, hardly older than my teenage son. He points over his shoulder. "We're checking that package, *geveret.*"

I follow the line of his gesture. At first I see nothing, then my eyes arrive at a large white cardboard box perched upon the sidewalk. It looks like a bakery box and is tied with white string, but one flap's sticking up awry. It's the kind of box that holds cinnamon rolls.

My stomach yawns. (A cappuccino, please. With whipped cream, a cinnamon stick, and one large croissant.)

Our officer has his hands full. He couldn't have been long on this job, for he seems sincerely taken aback by the stubbornness of various men who keep trying to slip by him through the invisible ropes, men intent upon going their own way, men who would have us know that they've got more important things on their minds than life and death. I, meanwhile, have turned my attention back to the spaceman, who during my moments of distraction has not just been sitting around doing nothing; he has rigged up what looks like some kind of clothesline, or fishing line, one end of which he is now clipping onto the white box. Now he lumbers over to another spot, a few feet away, then he kneels down and attaches it to some other object, which resembles four or five cardboard trays of eggs stacked one atop the other, and is probably the computerized controls which will detonate the terrorists' explosive device over there in the white box.

I calculate my present distance from the pastries and take stock. Would shrapnel get this far? What if it's a nuclear bomb, in which case surely a few feet this way or that wouldn't make much difference. They say that could happen now, you know, we all fear it; terrorists could get hold of some plutonium, G-d forbid, and really do a number on the human race. Thus, in the twinkling of an eye, could they get rid not only of the infidels but of themselves, too: all of mankind's collective problems and distress, and all our joys, too. In fact, the deserted, desolate scene before me, with its lonely garbage drifting about mildly in the warm breeze, brings to mind *On The Beach*, that I read for eighth-grade English class, in which a neutron bomb during World War III renders the planet free of living things, yet leaves behind, intact, the skyscrapers and farms, the highways and byways, London's Big Ben and Egypt's pyramids, Kansas

City's deserted department stores and acres of Brazilian slums, and the Eiffel Tower, and many millions of suburban streets, with their methodically blinking traffic lights, flashing green to amber to red.

Shouldn't we in this crowd be edging back, not ahead, running as far away as possible from this malevolent scene, instead of insisting upon our inalienable right to witness it for ourselves?

Suddenly, the bullhorn is furious. "GET OUT!"

I look around. Seeing nothing, I inquire of our policeman, who explains that a few feet away from the cardboard box is a bakery, and that inside there are some people who have ignored the blasted police orders, waiting disobediently for the scare to pass. To my slight surprise, I can make out, through the semi-dark doorway, one of the guilty ones, leaning back nonchalantly, like a shadow, against a bakery counter, as yet unaware that the electronic voice is addressing itself to him. He's chatting and smoking with his co-conspirators.

"OUT OF THE STORE!" the loudspeaker's baritone is booming. "GET OUT! OUT!"

Suddenly two policemen rush across the deserted wasteland and burst through into the bakery.

Three or four seconds pass.

Two men emerge.

What a noble show of casual insouciance they put on, these middle-aged Israelis sauntering along the sidewalk to join the rest of us. It's a given that men of their generation were probably soldiers in the War of Independence, The Six Day War, The Yom Kippur War, Lebanon. Far be it from them to give a nod to danger, or to fear. *Our enemies won't scare us in our own home!* their faces are saying. *We won't give them that honor, or that satisfaction. We will not surrender to psychological warfare.*

The police are now engaged in wheedling us, haranguing, pleading, ordering, cajoling. "Get back! Get back!" But we, like the bakery bandits, are eager to get on with business as usual. *How dare you to try to save my life when I'm getting ready for*

Shabbos! The Sabbath Queen is on her way! You know as well as I that all this is just a scare, and if not just a scare, that there's nowhere to hide. Wherever we run, it will be into G-d's inescapable embrace. It used to be that each of us thought: "It'll never happen to me." Now it's the other way around. No longer is one place safer than another. No matter that countless bombs have been dismantled in precisely this fashion. No matter that just weeks, days, hours separate us from the evil that rained down upon this street, bringing untold suffering beyond description. It is this, our daily existence in this land, that they despise, and we so prize. It's Friday! We've got shopping to do!

⤸⤹

The spaceman is lumbering off now in a different direction. He stops, as if having second thoughts, then turns stiffly around to take another look. His big, blunt, silvery mittens hold one end of the clothesline, the other end of which is attached to the computer. *This is it, folks, our moment of truth.* The long line snakes and twitches along the ground. *Maybe now we'll get that big bang the scientists are always talking about!*

The white cardboard box is tugged along the sidewalk towards the curb.

It wobbles, and totters, then falls over onto the street.

All's quiet.

You see that? I told you so! Nothing!

A bird sings.

A child's voice: *"Ima, ma koreh?"*

The spaceman appears to have accomplished his task, and we who are known as innocent passersby start moving forward. *Come on now, everybody, let's get moving!*

But wait! The big, echoing voice sounds angry again. It's reprimanding us. Now what have we done?

Can't you see something else is going on, you stiff-necked people? Making assumptions prematurely, chafing childishly at the bit! Sure enough, when I look again across the moon's gray surface to the spot where the cardboard box has just given up the ghost, it's that odd mound of something or other which is now being dragged along the ground. Why would the space-man be *schlepping* their delicate hi-tech contraption around like that?

At first it slides warily, then faster, a little faster, more… and then… we hold our breath. Quick, one sharp tug! The whole thing jerks upright onto one side, for a split second stands magically upright, as if by its own volition, and then…

Kerplat!

Straight from Mother Hen, back on the kibbutz poultry farm. Good thing she doesn't know.

The eggs are all a mess upon the ground, the white box is snatched up by the spaceman and tossed into a garbage can, one mitten pulls off the other; a long-fingered brown hand appears — a gold wedding band catches the sun — the hand pulls off the oblong helmet, and the spaceman becomes … another young man, with curly dark hair and large dark eyes, and delicate Ethiopian cheekbones. He draws a spacesuit sleeve across a glistening forehead.

Now? There's a murmur of hesitation. *Won't you let your people go?*

Go! says the loudspeaker. *Go!* And in one second, nay, less than a second, the cars come alive, the mess of eggs is run over by a truck, and a car, and another car and a taxi. The horns are honking, the buses are revving their huge motors, and we, the Jews, are bursting our bonds.

We are alive!

Again! Bursting our bonds and we want to get back, chastened, to life, to life, to life.

22

BOTH SIDES NOW

I've looked at life from both sides now
From win and lose
and still somehow
It's life's illusions I recall
I really don't know life
at all.

— popular song from the '70s

Articles about Lebanon's internal politics used to bore me. Not anymore.

Falling asleep was never a problem. Now I engage every night in my own little war of attrition along the border.

I used to ignore the call-waiting signal. Now I take that incoming call faster than a speeding bullet.

IDF casualties were extremely sad to read about, but thank G-d, at least we weren't directly involved. Not to be callous, but this was other people's problems, brought on by their own failures, their own mistaken ways. People who were our fellow Jews, of course, but not religious. Religious but not Orthodox. Orthodox but not *our* Orthodox. Our Orthodox but Israelis. Americans, but nobody we knew.

My son always told me the truth. Now he says, "No, no, it's quite quiet here."

"No Hezbullah bombs today, Dan?" Hezbullah is the devoutly anti-Israeli Islamic fundamentalist group, based in southern Lebanon, whose terrorist incursions into Israel, and katushya rocket attacks over the border, are the reason for this country's military presence in the so-called "security zone."

"A few," he answers, "but not close."

"You saw them explode?"

"Yeah, yeah. Down the hill, though. I told you, we're up quite high here."

"But weren't they aimed at your base? You said it's not dangerous where you are."

"Right, because of the Druse. I told you, they can't hit the villages. "

"So who were they aiming at, then?"

At this point, there's yelling in the background. "O.K., look, I'll call Monday. Oh, not Monday. We're moving bases. Maybe Tuesday."

"Where are you moving to?"

"Mommy, I have to go."

"Somewhere more dangerous?"

"No, no, less dangerous."

"Why are they yelling like that, Danny? Is something happening?"

"No, no, don't worry, everything's O.K. I'll speak to you Tuesday."

Once upon a time when our son was still in yeshivah, I left the question of withdrawal from Lebanon to the Netanyahu government. When our son was drafted and, contrary to what we'd always expected, decided to serve, I noticed that my politics underwent a curious change, i.e. disappeared. I started hoping that maybe by the time he was inducted, the left would get voted back in and get us out of Lebanon — though they'd never gotten us out before.

When he was inducted and we were still in the security zone, I said, "Can't you try out for something less dangerous than paratroopers?"

He said, "Mommy, if I'm going into the army, I might as well do something good."

When I prayed he not make it into paratroopers and he was then accepted, I said, *All right, Hashem, he's all Yours.*

When his year of training ended, it didn't occur to me it would happen so fast. His voice got oddly low-key, his calls more infrequent, there was a lot of static on the line. Then his mobile phone stopped working altogether. But I believed him when he said he was just "up north." Talk about denial! I'm a baby-boomer baby. I believe in truth, the whole truth, and nothing but the truth. But let my baby lie to me now and I'll happily keep my eyes shut tight.

Dan tells me that his base is surrounded by Arab Druse and Christian villages, whose residents' biggest fear is that of an IDF pullout. "We talk a lot with them," he tells me. "They're nice people They're so scared the IDF is going to leave. That then they'd be at Hezbullah's mercy."

He tells me about the Druse children, and that the IDF made a summer camp for them.

There was an article about those children in The Jerusalem Post. I skipped it.

An Israeli soldier, age twenty, was killed last week by a roadside bomb. Dan's nineteen. I say, "Did it happen close to your base?"

"No, no, not so close."

"Did you know him?"

"Yes."

"But it wasn't close to where you are?"

"No, no. We saw the explosion, but I didn't see it happen."

Oh my, alas and alack, to have been a baby-boomer in the American suburbs! To be born and bred in that place at that time was to become intent upon *self-actualization, truth, and finding one's identity*. To believe in *personal growth and consciousness-raising* as the highest goal.

Now I've got a sense of identity such as I never dreamed possible. Personal growth, baby, coming out of the ears.

Both sides now, all sides now ... enough. Oh G-d, to just let me fall asleep again.

23

IN THE DARKNESS

He was seven, or eight.
We were out on the porch and I said, "Look at all those stars!"

He looked at the stars.

I said, "You know, there are millions more stars up there
than we're able to see."

His upturned face, in the light coming through the living room
curtains,
               was still.
He of the bicycle, and the ballgame, he of the skateboard flying

stood
still, face uplifted in the darkness.

I heard a plane somewhere, and cars over on the highway.
Some blinking lights were moving across the Big Dipper.
"So why did Hashem make so many stars if we can't see them?"
he said.

My heart
stirred.

"I don't know."
I didn't know.

"I know!" he said.

My eyes asked why. *Why?*

"So that we'd ask why!"

24

A WATCH AMIDST
THE GALAXIES

Last year while on a trip to the States, Mrs.Lazerus spotted a very nice watch at K-Mart.

It wasn't what she was looking for, exactly. Its face — while simple and ungimmicky — was *too* simple and ungimmicky, simple to the point of plainness. And the face was a little too big, and round. She had been thinking of getting one of those very feminine-looking watches with rectangular faces — a chic, narrow, rectangular face on a slender band, whose quiet self-restraint would express not just practicality but the quality conveyed by the phrase, used frequently in advertisements: "*understated elegance.*"

Furthermore, the watchband on this K-Mart watch was overly utilitarian, and lacked that little intangible dash of *je ne sais quoi* whereby the functional crosses over into the classic.

On the other hand, however, there was nothing really wrong with it. And during her long search for an exquisite watch, one she could live with happily, she had seen a lot of really terrible timepieces. Gaudy, overstated ones that tried too hard to catch your attention; corny ones that tried to look old-fashioned; ridiculously futuristic ones trying to look state-of-the-art, but that just ended up being juvenile and inauthentic. Watches that strove to make bold, uncompromising statements, or worst of all, watches that aimed rather pitifully for that indescribable quality of *understated elegance* and missed.

In its favor, the watch she found at K-Mart was silver, and thus matched the rest of her jewelry. All her jewelry is silver. She doesn't look good in gold. Also, Mrs. Lazerus was in a big hurry. Their frantic week of vacation was coming to an end and they'd be going back home to *Eretz Yisrael* the following day. And furthermore, there was the $19.99 price tag to consider, which would have been less of an inducement had two of the Lazerus children not been accompanying her. This was an opportunity to show them how modest their mother's tastes were, and on what a self-effacing scale her self-indulgence. Of course, she had no particular need to be admired by her children; it wasn't for her sake but theirs that such considerations even entered her mind. But if, for purposes of *chinuch*, she wanted to present them with a good role model, it was self-evident that this purchase would be a very smart move.

She bought it.

And from there on, it was all downhill.

≈≈

Well, maybe not *all* downhill, but it was certainly not uphill. Or maybe what I mean to say is that it was indeed uphill, as in *"uphill climb."*

What happened was that no sooner had K-Mart's electronic doors parted for their exit, and the two Lazerus pre-teens had set in chatting excitedly about their new bathing suits as their procession of three crossed the parking lot, than Mrs. Lazerus realized that her children were giving little thought if any to their mother's humble tastes. As she turned the key in the rental car, she was already wondering if perhaps her *mesiras nefesh* had not been unnecessarily extreme, and by the time she backed out of the parking spot and pulled into traffic, she was getting a sinking feeling that it would be she and she alone, when it all came down to it, who would have to live with that watch. She had a profound, if fleeting, realization that ultimately, we each have to walk through the valley alone.

Sure enough, during the next few hours as they finished up their last-minute shopping at Sears, Macy's, Radio Shack, Borders Book Store, Home Depot, and Staples, it gradually became apparent that the new watch was subtle not only to the point of understatement but to the point of *self-annihilation.* Whenever she'd glance down to check the time, or just to get a feel for how it was doing on her wrist, she saw herself not only as an unselfish, self-effacing, un-self-dramatizing mother, but as an unfulfilled, disappointed human being, as well, one whose needs for drama, excitement, and intellectual stimulation had all been left unmet, sacrificed on the altar of — well, whatever. She couldn't quite finish that train of thought, but you know what I mean.

❧

When the family returned home from America, Mrs. Lazerus got all settled down for the foreseeable future.

Time went by, and she managed. But let's look at the underlying causes behind this incongruity between inner and outer self in order to better understand how such a thing could come to pass. We can start by examining what had prompted her search in the first place.

Certainly not that she needed a new watch. The one she had been wearing when she entered K-Mart was a handsome, stylishly black-faced hand-me-down from her mother, and if she was not thrilled by it, she was fairly content. Wearing such a hand-me-down links one with a larger history, a larger sense of one's place in the world, etc. etc., and also reminds one pleasantly of one's mother. The only thing that was wrong with the watch was that it needed a new battery.

So how did this whole *megillah* start? If truth be told, the story had its genesis one night the previous winter in a parent-teacher meeting. Throughout the evening, Mrs. Lazerus had been trying to keep her eyes, if not her mind, on the principal as he addressed the mothers seated in the high school classroom, when her wandering gaze happened to fall upon the nicely manicured left hand of one of the mothers one seat over to the right, in the row just ahead of her.

She was a blonde, this woman, and Mrs. Lazerus had been confronted with the back of this person's head, and with a slight glimpse of the person's profile, with its perky (surgically corrected?) nose, all evening long. It was aggravating — the glossy fullness of the smooth shoulder-length *sheitel*; the pricey, if clichéd, *savoir-faire* of her tweedy skirt and cashmere sweater; the camel-colored coat, silky lining exposed, that this woman, upon taking a seat, had shrugged off onto the back of her chair.

Above all, though, it was the watch that irked Mrs. Lazerus (not to mention the slender wrist, and the perfect nails with their clear gloss).

First of all, *the band*. Sturdy yet delicate, subtly tapered. Made of soft leather, a light brown color. Not worn-looking, of course, and of course not dirty, but not brassy or right-off-the-shelf, either. It exuded a confident, relaxed, self-possessed, aristocratic sort of air that spoke of New England summer homes populated by extended families whose daughters wear cultured pearls and are good at golf, and go shopping in the village in their tennis whites. Definitely not a life-style to which Mrs. Lazerus aspired.

Secondly, *the face*. A slightly exaggerated largeness not to her taste. Its roundness, also, was not quite to her liking. In addition, it declared the time with phony Roman numerals, which Mrs. Lazerus has always found pretentious and unnecessary. She much prefers straightforward *numbers*. After all, as she sees it, we're not in ancient Rome and let's not pretend we are.

Nor, as I've said, was the gold something she would have worn herself.

But the thing about this watch, aside from the way it suited perfectly the general appearance of its owner, was that on each point, north and south, of the face's generously endowed gold rim, protruded *one tiny golden knob*. These two little protuberances were decorative rather than useful, as far as she could tell (and on that score, as you should have realized by now, not to her taste). But it couldn't be denied, something sumptuous was going on here. Something luxurious and luxuriant. The golden knobs declared in so many unspoken words that in her life this woman dwelled in *a nest of lush comfort*. All her needs were met, and then some. The gold not only matched her blondeness — it was *part of her blondeness*.

As you may have gathered by now, Mrs. Lazerus is not a blonde, not that she wanted to be, and the slight excessiveness of decoration, while not to her taste, and certainly not anything she would have chosen herself, nonetheless conveyed that this woman was accustomed to being well taken care of. And furthermore, she took care of herself without any ironic self-deprecation, guilt, or apology. Her heels (had they been visible) were surely stylish yet sturdy, and were doubtless doing their job knowingly, competently. No fly-by-night, on-the-verge-of-a-nervous-break-down-shoes *here*.

She was a woman protected by self-love.

Mrs. Lazerus wanted that watch.

Not the big round face, or the leather. She definitely did not want some clumsy-looking leather watchband, especially a brown one.

But those two tiny little gold knobs on the solid gold rim, unnecessary and unapologetic — perched there for no good reason in the world at all — she wanted something along those lines.

≈≈

She knew in the back of her mind that one day, after a decent interval, she'd be free to move on. For the present, however, she made it her conscious desire to *mekabel* the K-Mart purchase *b'ahavah*.

Indeed, Mrs. Lazerus did see signs in herself of having risen to a higher *madregah* in regard to this *inyan*, insofar as there were certain things she was coming to appreciate and value about the watch with less judgmentalness, and less insistence upon complete satisfaction.

She worked on appreciating its virtues. First of all, to go over it again, it was silver. She worked on reminding herself that she likes silver, and needs silver, rather than gold, for all her accessories. Secondly, it was neither crass, loud, nor self-dramatizing. No one could say that she was drawing inappropriate attention to herself. Nor was she inadvertently betraying any lack of intelligence, or refinement. Thirdly, each and every time she glanced down for the time, she felt like a good, sensible, un-self-indulgent mother, and an un-wasteful, un-self-glorifying adult.

She knew that the value of all these *middos* was not to be underestimated.

But there was always this: each and every time she checked the time, Mrs. Lazerus also couldn't help but notice what it was that displeased her. The reality had to be faced. *Quite of her own volition — there was no one but herself to blame — she had attached a boring, pedestrian object to her wrist.* And at that precise moment of glancing down, she always had to engage in a subtle little feat of mental acrobatics to adjust to, then disregard, the watch's shortcomings.

Was it worth it? She had to ask herself: Was the spiritual gain — the struggle to come to terms with this self-inflicted violation of her identity, and to believe that the purchase was *gam zu le-tova* — was it worth the little hour by hour, day by day, injury to her sense of self? She didn't aspire to be a flashy person but she did aspire to an expression of her uniqueness, and liked her belongings and appearance to reflect that.

The question persisted. Sometimes, it seemed to her that although the aspect of her inner self that was being negatively affected by this incongruence and dissonance was arguably her *nefesh*, the animal soul, there was also a certain aspect of her *neshamah* that was being denied here. She came increasingly to think that her unease must be arising from her higher self, the so-called *tzurah elyonah*, and that her need for true elegance in her clothing and accessories was not evidence of some gross materialism on her part, but rather, of her exceptionally developed spiritual nature.

One day, out for an errand downtown, Mrs. Lazerus was passing by a window display of watches in a store on Rechov Yaffo and for the first time in the nearly ten months since their American vacation, allowed herself to stop and stare. In all that time, it hadn't occurred to her that she could start looking for another watch. Suddenly, she realized that for the sake of $20, there was really no further need to keep her prior commitment. Buying a watch that she really liked and would feel comfortable with would not now constitute greed, but would, rather, be *a normal event in a normal life.*

Maybe it would be greed, actually, but just normal human greed, from which she was under no obligation to exempt herself. At least she didn't think so. We're not expected to be saints.

Are we?

Well, we are expected to strive to be our best possible selves, but certainly we're not expected to transcend human nature.

It was at this juncture, right there on the spot, that Mrs. Lazerus decided that from now on she'd keep her eyes open.

∞

For several weeks she didn't come across anything she really liked, that really suited her. At least not within her self-imposed price range.

But one afternoon, having ducked into a jewelry store to check out the revolving watch display, and having drifted deeper in, over to a rack of attractive, sparely designed, understated, slinky-feeling black purses — nice rectangular ones with classic sharp corners and little or no excess decoration, Mrs. Lazerus's eyes happened upon a case full of watchbands.

And right off the bat, guess what she found: *a silver watchband that she really liked,* one that she sensed immediately might go nicely with the face, and that fulfilled her various spiritual needs. She asked the man behind the counter if she could take a closer look — and without giving it any further thought, just sort of took the leap.

In no time at all he had removed the K-Mart stretch-band, and, before she knew it, amazingly, had already attached the new one.

The new band was a soft and slinky silver. It was restrained, unpretentious, and possessed *understated elegance.*

Mrs. Lazerus sensed strongly that this was a step forward in personal growth. She had forgiven herself her mistake, put aside regret, and let go of the past. It was so wonderful. She felt this must be a real example of what is meant by learning to nurture oneself, to become one's own good parent. *If I am not for myself,* she thought as she walked out of the store, *then who will be for me?*

Every time Mrs. Lazerus glances down now at her wrist, there is her creation gazing back up at her. If you don't understand why I say "her creation," I just want to make it clear, in case I haven't already, that she *cleverly had a new band attached to her old K-Mart watch-face.* She had found a fresh, ingenious, low-cost answer to self-doubt.

The new band cost more than she expected, actually — maybe the clerk took advantage of her a little, she'll never know for sure — but at fifty-something *shekels* for the band and $19.99 at K-Mart, she figures she still ends up ahead, and she now has a watch that is true to the grain of her personality. (Actually, if truth be told, every once in a while she is struck by the *plainness* of the face, but she is training herself to disregard this and redirect her thoughts.) She congratulates herself from time to time, reminding herself that she has what she always wanted. And she gets a small rush of pleasure each and every time she thinks about it, which she has read is good for her immune system.

She is really very pleased, and proud. She has casually pointed out to her children what she did and could see they were impressed by her unconventional, can-do approach to problem-solving, her fun-loving spirit in such a pleasant mix with the mature, responsible side of her personality. She can tell that her husband is also impressed, and that he appreciates how careful she was not to squander their financial resources. She has caught him looking at it sometimes, and suspects he's thinking how lucky he is to have married such a gem. She has mentioned it off-handedly to a number of her friends, as well.

These days, Mrs. Lazerus is really very happy. It's not a rectangular face, which she knows she would have preferred – that does still bother her a little — but then again, life's not meant to be perfect. *That's olam hazeh for you!* she tells herself cheerfully. The other day, she did happen to catch sight of a very lovely, understated watch — silver — in an expensive jewelry store on Ben Yehudah Street, but hardly even looked it over. *Who is happy? He who is satisfied with his portion.*

The only thing is, Mrs. Lazerus recently read an article in the paper which reported new discoveries indicating that there are many more galaxies in the universe than previously estimated. She quickly forgot the exact figure, and by the time she set about looking for that day's newspaper, realized that she must have already thrown it out. But to her best recollection, it was something like 245 billion.

Such a number did make her wonder.

Should she be taking this much pleasure in a little watch?

No, no, I mustn't diminish my appreciation and pleasure like that! she told herself. *Let us frail mortals be grateful for whatever pleasures we have, for goodness' sake! They say we'll even be asked in the World to Come why we didn't enjoy all that we were permitted to enjoy. The watch is lovely and I'm really quite happy with it, and with myself for the way I handled it, and I see no reason at all I should go around ruining my own happiness with thoughts of two hundred billion galaxies.*

It could have been three hundred. Whatever.

Mr. Lazerus once remarked that one of the reasons Senator Bob Dole lost his bid for the Presidency, back in 1996, was that people made fun of his frequent use of the expression "whatever" during the campaign. But if you think about it, said Mrs. Lazerus, it's really a rather comprehensive expression. It covers a lot of ground.

And besides, she said, I'm not running for President.

That made Mr. Lazerus smile.

25

JUST A SLIGHT ADJUSTMENT OF FOCUS

A friend of mine, someone who has known our children a long time, took me over to the side during a recent visit. "Eli doesn't seem so happy," she said of my 9 1/2-year-old. "Is he O.K.?"

Now that she mentioned it, I realized my little boy had indeed been ornery lately. Maybe there was something going on in his school — something with his *rebbi*, I thought. Reprimands in class, maybe, or not enough joy in the learning. At the earliest opportunity, I asked Eli how school was. "All right," he muttered noncommittally, nothing in his response betraying anything problematic.

Then it occurred to me: in the past few weeks, I myself had been self-absorbed and busy. How long had it been since I'd really paid attention to Eli? His irritability, which I'd kept out there on the fringes of my consciousness, had just seemed like a natural outcome of the normal wear and tear of daily life — his resistance to: *Wake up, it's late — Tuck in your shirt — You can't find your shoes again? So where'd you take them off?!* — And when he came home, it was: *Hurry, you've got a dentist appointment at 5 o'clock. No, I* can't *read a story right now.*

❧ ❧

Fifteen years ago, Rebbetzin Esther Siegel of Jerusalem once demonstrated to me the proper kind of hello befitting a *neshamah* entrusted to my hands. I had confessed that in my tiredness from a new baby's all-night crying, I didn't always give my oldest, then in daycare, an especially big welcome.

The rebbetzin shook her finger at me menacingly. "*Oi va voi la* if you don't give her a big smile when she walks in!" In her tiny Mea Shearim kitchen, Rebbetzin Siegel, then in her late 70's, jumped to her feet and glared at me intently. "I'll show you what to do! You go like this!" She flung open her arms and flashed a wide, radiant smile to an imaginary child standing in her doorway. "'*Shalom, shaina maidele*! I'm so happy you're home! How was school today?'"

The image of the Rebbitzen appeared before me now, and I made a small adjustment in my perspective. I *focused* on Eli.

How is he? I asked myself when he came home from school the next day, giving him a great, big, attentive greeting. Whenever possible that afternoon, I reminded myself to say yes instead of an automatic no. We mothers often feel put upon, and are careful not to give in to our children, for fear of being overwhelmed by their demands. But the result of saying yes more frequently was that his needs got easier to fulfill, rather than harder. In the morning, I woke him up gently, taking care not to jab at him with my voice. When he asked me to look at his stamp collection (and it was no coincidence that it had been some time since it had occurred to him to ask) I recalled one of Rav Noach Orlowek's favorite sayings:

What is love? It's conveying this message: "What's important to you is important to me." If what's important to your child isn't important to you when he's small, then what's important to you won't be important to him when he's big.

It was almost scary — a matter of minutes, not days — how fast Eli started turning into his sweet and happy self again, scary because the transformation demonstrated my amazing power as a mother for good or for ill. But it was wonderful, as well, to see how easy it is to gain access to that power.

All you have to do is recognize that there is nothing in the world more important than the child standing right there before you, and no time more opportune than this moment, right now.

26

MY IMPORTANCE: WRITING AND THE YETZER HARA

There's a story about a revered rabbi on his deathbed, who is asked by his students: "Tell us, what is it like now that you're about to die, when the *yetzer hara* has surely freed you from its clutches?"

And the rabbi says something along these lines: "No, the *yetzer hara* is still bothering me, even now. It's telling me to recite the final *Shema* in such a way that after I'm gone, everyone will say how pure and devout I was during my final moments."

Even though the rabbi is confessing his endless subjugation to his own false pride, his final moments can, from a certain perspective, indeed be considered victorious — not because he had succeeded in vanquishing his *yetzer hara* once and for all, but simply because he was still valiantly engaged in the struggle to keep tabs on it. He was familiar with the *yetzer hara's* unpredictable cleverness at assuming a thousand different identities, and familiar with his own inability to squash it once and for all. But being aware of its machinations was still within his power.

I find the story very comforting. It's a reminder that it isn't conquering the *yetzer hara* that's expected of us, but simply to engage in endless warfare with it, right up until our dying day. Perfect victory isn't possible against an immortal opponent.

We are eminently capable, however, of winning individual battles. The rabbi's confession to his students about what his *yetzer hara* was up to — which smashed whatever false image of his piety they might have otherwise cherished of him at his deathbed — was one such battle won.

Yet no matter how many times we win, new confrontations arise again instantly, time after time. It's ceaseless. It's one definition of being alive. No sooner have we won one battle than another presents itself, providing us with fresh, unwanted evidence that we are not in fact the altruistic beings we wish we were. If we keep our eyes open, it's impossible to feel proud of ourselves for very long. It's impossible to feel holy.

And if we do feel holy, watch out! There's a line that my friend Shifra Atlas told me years ago, that goes like this: "Far is near and near is far." He who takes prides in being close to G-d may very well be far away, by virtue of his pride. And one who feels cast down and far away, may actually be close.

My own *yetzer hara* is, of course, working overtime even at this instant, as I write. What's it doing at this particular moment in time? I'd rather not know. I'd rather you think highly of me. I'd rather think highly of myself. But here goes: Since I am one of those who often feels cast down and far away, I'm taking pride in myself that this must mean I'm actually one of those who are exceptionally close. And having admitted that to you, how can you feel critical of me for my ridiculous vanity? In other words, how can I be found guilty of pride when I'm humble enough to tell you about it? It's like the man who, upon being praised for being humble, says sincerely (or insincerely), "No, I'm really not humble at all."

Wow, we think. That guy is really humble!

Furthermore, by mocking myself as I have just done, by sharing honestly with you the impurity of my intentions, I'm hoping to impress both of us with the purity of my intentions.

The false pride is endless! It's as if there were a tight knot inside that spontaneously keeps on tying and retying itself. If I can just keep untying the string as it reties itself, though, maybe I can become the master of my *yetzer hara*.

How very proud of myself I'd be!

Then my pride would have to be untied.

Or, to look at it another way: It's like gazing into the infinite hallway of mirrors that pops up when you place two mirrors opposite each other and look at your image. You hope to come upon the purity of your own soul, but in the very instant of catching sight of it, it's transformed again into vanity. So you're far away from your goal, once again.

What's the answer to the infinite tunnel of self-deception? It must be this: To stop looking in the mirror for the purity we're seeking. We will always be human, full of pride, full of ego, full of ambition and dissatisfaction and desire for recognition. The desire to find holiness in ourselves is like trying to worship ourselves instead of G-d. Purity is not to be found in me, or you, but in our Creator, and in the rare moments of connection we can find with Him in our prayers.

❧ ❧

Which leads us to —

Writing. My writing, as is the case with a lot of other human occupations, is the monument I build to preserve myself. And again, like most human pursuits, it can be used for good or, G-d forbid, the opposite.

It differs, obviously, from the performance of mitzvos, insofar as we have not been commanded to engage in writing as we have been commanded to visit the sick, or honor our parents, carry out acts of kindness, or do any of the other 613 mitzvos. There's therefore a risk one runs in spending time with pen in hand, or before a computer: We might be deluding ourselves that we are doing something useful when actually we are wasting our precious, irreplaceable time on earth in futility and vanity. That risk is especially great since having one's writing published is such a delicious, filling meal for the ego to feast upon.

The impulse to write, like any other impulse to express oneself to others, to construct one's own particular version of the world, to assert one's presence, arises from, and is cultivated by, all sorts of circumstances and influences that obviously vary from person to person. But it seems to me that people who feel this inexplicable desire to write do all share a similar need to define themselves, to stake a claim — not unlike the mountain-climber who sticks a signpost into the snow and ice upon reaching the peak. "I was here," the mountain-climber is saying. "Look at me, I'm alive!"

For someone like me who as the baby in the family was plagued, growing up, by a sense of unimportance in the world, of powerlessness and smallness, and by jealousy of my big sisters, then getting those words down on the page is like sticking that signpost into the ground, or like setting up a stone monument — (dear me! I almost said "gravestone"!) — to mark the spot where I lived. As the rooster crows and the pony neighs, there's an inescapable instinct to proclaim to myself and others that what I experience has significance, to declare that my life is not nothing, not nothing, not nothing, but something, something, something. Something! Something! Something!

Does that strike you as a worthwhile way to spend a life?

Don't bother answering.

If I harbor any hope at all of being able to look back some day and conclude that my life wasn't wasted, then devoting my days to the goal of *proving I'm not nothing* is not a good bet. This is especially so because in the grand scheme of things, any individual's vain efforts to prove himself do, in fact, amount ultimately to nothing if not nothing.

The highest course to take could well be, therefore, to shift gears and spend my time engaged in something of more immediate, verifiably genuine use to myself, to others, and to G-d.

But before throwing my computer out the window and taking pleasure in the sound of its arrival on the sidewalk, I'd have to consider that our Sages note that if not for the *yetzer hara*, human beings wouldn't do much of anything else, either. No one would learn Torah, or get married, or want children, or build a house. No one would be inclined to lead his country, or to cook dinner and clean up afterwards. If we were capable of ridding ourselves of our egos, it wouldn't be this pitiful little essay alone that would have to go. Our kitchen floors would also get very, very dirty. Our egos are the self-starting engines that goad each of us on to accomplish all the good things that human beings can do.

All of us are ultimately liberated from our false selves as surely as the snake sheds his skin, with nothing left of us but our souls. But for the time being, it is the wondrously amazing phenomenon of the ego that eggs us on from birth to death.

This isn't to say that we aren't also motivated by unselfish motives to do good, to be of help, to spread an awareness of our purpose here in the world. Most of us do share this inborn need to be of real service, to be useful in the eyes of G-d.

It is to say, however, that our purest altruistic impulses are intermixed thoroughly with our desire to be loved, the desire to be recognized: it's an aspect of human personality that cannot be erased; it's woven into the fabric of our being. From the time a baby first looks into his parents' eyes and sees himself mirrored in their smiles, the pattern continues manifesting itself. It has been said that even as the Nobel Prize winner steps up to the podium to collect his check and soak up the accolades, he'll be glancing out into the audience in search of his mother in the second row. *Now she'll think I'm O.K., after all!*

But the desire to be free of this desire is equally universal. Wouldn't we all welcome a liberation from this maddeningly craven craving for appreciation, approval, and respect? Wouldn't it be a relief to attain real humility, whereby one is unduly affected neither by honor nor by insult? Wouldn't it be nice to have as one's central relationship the relationship with one's Creator; to have as one's greatest ambition to be worthy of G-d's approval? Such an individual's self-respect is based less upon pride over his personal achievements than upon an underlying consciousness of himself as an entity created by G-d. He doesn't consider himself superior or inferior; he is blinded neither by self-abomination nor self-inflation nor self-infatuation; he feels no compulsion to diminish others or exaggerate his own importance at their expense; he doesn't crave other people's respect, since he doesn't look to them for his identity. He is more likely than most to perceive the world around him objectively, because he doesn't have a vested interest in distorting it. He trusts implicitly that reality (which includes him) is good, no matter what discomforts and ugliness it may entail, because all that G-d does is good. He's not afraid of what he'll see by forgoing his pride, because in every direction he perceives evidence of Divine kindness, and he would like to serve as an instrument of that kindness.

Yet as we strive toward lofty dreams of transcendence and selflessness such as these, we can rest assured that Hashem knows all the intricate egotistical machinations of our hearts — all the darkness that's in there, and all the light. I can trust, as a humble creation of *HaKadosh Baruch Hu*, that He created me with my particular personality — complete with *yetzer hatov* and *yetzer hara*, not with part of a heart and part of a soul but with all my heart, and all my soul — and with the implanted human drive to fulfill my destined mission in life.

Someone once said to me: If you want to find your mission in life, just look around. You'll see your mission. Is it a pile of dishes? A child needing attention? A neighbor who is alone, a relative in need? Is there something you want to write, or cooking to do? Does the water bill have to be paid this morning?

Perhaps, at this particular moment, it's attending to that hidden problem in your life — the one not many people know about — which constantly requires that you develop all your powers of self-discipline, kindness, patience and *emunah*.

So what's the solution? Perhaps, for me, it's to have the humility (!) not to expect genuine humility from such a one as I.

(Such a one as me?) In other words, not to expect purity from an impure vessel. Purity is G-d's domain.

The only way out of the eternal knot is to humbly accept that I'm driven by egotistical ambitions, no matter how sincerely I try to make my personal goals consistent with G-d's purposes.

❦

Rav Shlomo Wolbe has written that "every person must know he has importance — not illusory importance but very deep and significant importance."

Even as I keep an eye on my unquenchable appetite for false significance, I can try simultaneously to understand that I'm *already* in full possession of the truest possible significance. I can trust that my hungry, childish little ego has an appointed role to play in Hashem's Divine plan, as do we all, as do all living beings He has created in His world.

We don't have to prove ourselves, even though the *yetzer hara*, for better and for worse, may continue prompting us to do so: to accomplish, to contribute to society, to proclaim that we're alive, right up to our last moments on earth. Your importance and mine are not at risk, not in question; not subject to jealous comparison with the value of others.

Just as an infant one second after birth is obviously the most precious thing in the world, so are you, and I. Your importance is beyond any possible calculation, as is mine. My infinite value is guaranteed, as is yours.

During these disastrous times, when our continued existence here in our land has been thrown violently into question and there seems to be no place at all anymore for foolishness, I offer up my own little prayer: May writing constitute an acceptable *avodah*, and the inexplicable desire to spend time absorbed in it not be in conflict with Hashem's larger plans for *Am Yisrael*.

(Given my desire to appear devout in the eyes of others, I should probably distrust my desire now to add: *And may the Holy Temple be rebuilt, speedily in our days.*)

27

WHY IS THIS CHILD DIFFERENT?

Why did my family celebrate the first night of Passover, when all the other holidays were for me, as a child, just strange names? Yom Kippur — I didn't know what that was; the word brought to mind kippered herring. Rosh Hashanah, Chanukah... what were they supposed to signify? And Succos? I'd never heard of it.

But Passover: on Passover we piled into the family car and drove out to Long Island for Aunt Sophie's matzah ball soup and four glasses apiece of sweet wine. Why? I had no idea. I was the youngest of all the cousins. So it was my job to read the Four Questions: *Why on this night do we eat unleavened bread? Why on this night do we eat bitter herbs...*

The questions stirred me inexplicably, but what did they mean? Our grandfather, Pop, took it seriously. His father, Meir, had been the rabbi of their village in Russia. Pop read aloud from a little pamphlet in a guttural, incomprehensible Hebrew, which embarrassed me. It embarrassed all of us children — again, I knew not why. Why was it so uncomfortable to have Pop sitting there with a black yarmulka on his head, reading that old language in a thick, unfamiliar tongue? That's what the Four Questions were really about for me: *Why can't we be like everyone else? Why are we different?* We kids cracked jokes which hard-of-hearing Pop could not make out. He'd look up every once in a while from his recitation, at his giggling, smirking grandchildren sitting there around the elaborately set dinner table, with its white tablecloth and crystal wine glasses, and he, too, must have wondered, "Why?"

Why did our family, like American Jewish families everywhere, recognize Passover as the one thing we would never forget? Aunt Sophie told me years later that she made those Passover Seders in order to forge a bond between all the cousins, and in that she succeeded. But unbeknownst to her, perhaps, and unbeknownst to me, she was also forging bonds between me and my Jewishness, and my people, and G-d.

The Haggadah tells the tale of our bondage at the beginning of our history, and of our liberation. Matzah represents redemption; the bitter herbs life's suffering. We make a sandwich of both of them together at the Seder, enclosing life's bitterness within its kindness. This gesture describes our personal histories as well as our national history. For it's precisely the experience of enslavement that can create inner freedom; the harrowing experience of crossing the desert that makes it possible to earn self-respect; and precisely the experience of wandering that makes finding a home such cause for celebration. Every one of us in the course of our lives passes through an exile of one kind or another, to disconnect us from all our various forms of enslavement. We dream of reacquiring that liberated homeland where everything will be right, and where we'll feel like our own real selves.

In Rabbi Ephraim Oshry's anthology of his halachic responses to the religious queries of fellow Jews in the Kovno ghetto during World War II, he recounts the following incident:

"One morning during prayer at the camp, the man who was leading the congregation in the service reached the blessing, 'Blessed are You Who has not made me a slave.' The man stopped short, and suddenly he shouted bitterly to the Master of all masters, 'How can I recite a blessing of a free man? How can a hungry slave, constantly abused and demeaned, praise his Creator by uttering "Who has not made me a slave"?' Every morning as he led the prayers, he let out the same cry. And many of those who joined him in prayer felt the same way. I was then asked for the Torah ruling on this matter. Response: One of the earliest commentators on the prayers points out that this blessing was not formulated in order to praise G-d for our physical liberty but rather for our spiritual liberty. I therefore ruled that we might not skip or alter this blessing under any circumstances. On the contrary, despite our physical captivity, we were more obligated than ever to recite the blessing, in order to show that as a people we were spiritually free."

During this same era, the mid 1940s, while those Jews in Auschwitz were debating whether or not to recite the blessing, my husband was growing up in Williamsburg, Brooklyn. One of the taunts he used to hear sometimes on his way home, from the parochial-school children, went like this:

Matzahs, matzahs, three by five!

That's what keeps the Jews alive!

My husband would flinch, the Catholic kids laughed, and none of them guessed that those lines were true.

28

WATER, FIRE, AND BABIES

My daughter told me that she learned
there are three things people never get tired of looking at:
Water, fire, and babies.

By water, I presumed,
she was referring to the ocean, and I thought, that's true.
The waves coming in toward us
again and again and
again. We can stand there on the shore for hours, staring.
We can stand on the shore there forever, staring
at waves rearing up out of nothingness,
the Creation happening right there before our eyes
endlessly, something

from nothing endlessly
happening, to a rhythm we know without thinking, a rhythm as
         much our own
as our own breathing.

And Fire. Right,
fire, too.
We can sit for hours at a fireplace, spellbound
by the sparks rising too fast to follow, while outside the
         winter's blowing.
We can stand staring at bonfires on Lag B'Omer, can stand
there for hours and hours and never get bored, gazing at the
flames raging up into the springtime darkness, the shooting
stars flying madly up into the high black night
alight like souls rushing up into the stars.

And babies.

Well,
babies, too,
I suppose.
I guess I could look for
some time at a baby.

Now that I don't have to think about
diapers, and bottles, and all the dangers particular to those days,
I guess I could gaze

at a baby in his mother's arms
for a while
         if I dared.

Why not?

I've got time.

But more than fire, or water.
More than

       babies —

   now it's
you I could look at.
You I could look at
now. *You*

         say the waves of my
heart, say the flames of my
heart repeat
   you.
     You.
   You

I could look at forever

my baby

without getting bored.

     Nineteen years old and
     Eyes alight
     Teaching me something
     That I'd never known.

29

ADAM AND EVE IN THE GARDEN OF JERUSALEM

I t was difficult for my relatives, right from the start.

When did it start?

Not last week, when my daughter got married in Jerusalem. They already knew what to expect: that the men would be on one side, women on the other.

Was it back in the eighties, then, when they first heard we had put her in an all-girl high school? Or before that, in an all-girl kindergarten ? Maybe it dates back to when they first found out about the religious emphasis in the educational curriculum — morning hours, Torah studies; afternoon for secular subjects. *But how will she get into a good college?*

Was it when I myself got married? *This is segregation,* my father had murmured, pained, under his breath. *It makes your mother and sisters into second-class citizens. Can't we enjoy the wedding all together, as a family?*

Didn't it start back in the early seventies, when I stopped wearing pants? When my hemlines got lower, my sleeves longer, when I stopped going to coed college parties? When I wouldn't eat with them at restaurants, when I first koshered one of my mother's pots, one of her pans, a single set of her silverware, when I had to say no to her vegetable soup, that I'd always loved, her homemade herb bread. On Saturdays, when I wouldn't join family outings anymore, when I wouldn't turn off and on lights... The phone would ring and they'd call, "Sarah! It's for you!" I — sitting there on my isolated Shabbat, looking deaf and dumb, befuddled, feeling guilty for all this discomfort I was causing. *Yes, of course it's wonderful you're finding out more about your heritage, but you don't need to go overboard. Can't you discover your Jewish identity without being so extreme about it? You're going back to the Old World.*

⋙ ⋘

Last week they came from America for the wedding. All the relatives — the agnostics and the conservatives, the Orthodox and the atheists and the female rabbi, the Reconstructionist and the Federation activists and the Jews for whom Jewishness seems so irrelevant that they don't bother to define themselves — we kept joining hands to dance. We danced and danced and danced, not for one hour or two or three or four but 'til the wee hours of the morning, men on one side, women on the other, hundreds of us, in what my mother, amazed, called "an explosion of joy that just kept exploding all night."

What was it that lifted us up off the floor like that, almost as one person? For my part, it wasn't only what any mother feels upon seeing her daughter arrive safely on the opposite shore; it was tasting the first fruits. Here was the first generation born into this way of life after the break in continuity which had occurred, in my particular family tree, two and three generations back. Here were a young woman and a young man who have grown up in a society that emphasizes not a person's desires for satisfaction but his or her responsibilities; a society that says everything he or she does in the world has meaning, and importance, in ways that transcend human understanding. And one of this society's more noticeable hallmarks, for those looking on from the side, has always been that daunting separation of men and women — a custom that to uninvolved observers seems so oddly archaic and unnecessary as to be outrageous. Why the all-girl, all-boy schools, why those weddings and bar mitzvahs and synagogues that insist on men on one side, women on the other?

Here was Michoel with his community of beloved friends, holding hands and dancing jubilantly on their side of the *mechitzah.* And in another sphere, hidden from those young men's view: the unrestrained, absolutely celebratory and exultant dancing of Rachel and all the friends with whom she has grown up, young women who were raised to find themselves not in their possessions, or their mirrors, but in their deeds; who have imbibed an understanding from their earliest days that we're each given precisely what we need to get, if we only have eyes to see; that we can rejoice in another person's happiness because it can't infringe on our own. It's a society in which children don't judge each other by their clothes, or their coolness, or their looks, but in which they're taught to perceive the Divine image in every face.

Mine was the joy of seeing with my own eyes what all those years had been for. All those years of mutual embarrassment and mutual apologies for hurting the people we most love, and their subtle sense of having been repudiated by my choice. All was worth it for the two children who have never been wounded by others, so that neither one is afraid of giving whole-heartedly, extravagantly, splendidly.

We were all in an old world together, that's for sure, but not the one they expected — not the stereotyped caricature of Orthodox Jewry to which they were accustomed. We were in the old world that is forever a new world: the world that lives like a hidden oasis within all of us, the Garden of Eden, green and lush and fresh. When all is stripped away, what are we each left with? What matters?

The dream at the center of the world: a young man and a young woman, finding their home in each other and themselves in the Divine.

30

GYM CLASS REVISITED

When I peer into the shadows of the past to find the First Cause behind my becoming an observant Jew, I think I can trace it all the way back to high-school gym class. I hated gym so much, and got into such trouble all the time with Miss McElroy for forgetting to bring back my gym suit after taking it home to be washed, that I had no other choice than to set my sights on more spiritual goals such as writing haiku poetry and wearing dangly earrings. Out on the sunny playing field behind the high-school parking lot, where Donna and Cathy and Cindy and Jane dashed here and there with their blond locks flying, I pretended to take pride, as a Poet, that I couldn't hit the hockey ball. Actually, it was an overwhelming desolation not to look, talk, and jump up and down the way they did.

These experiences led gradually to reading Emily Dickinson and practicing the grapefruit diet, from which it was then just a hop, skip and a jump to fasting on Yom Kippur.

That's why I made it my business to avoid exercising for the next thirty years. Then, one summer, a neighbor asked if I'd like to share a taxi to her aerobics class. At the time, I intuited only that this small step as an athlete would be a giant step for my mental health. I had always sensed that somewhere along the line, certain developmental stages I was supposed to go through hadn't happened. Maybe getting into a pair of sneakers would heal the childhood wounds.

The first time was fun, but frightening. I couldn't keep up. Everyone else in the class, a few of them older than I, many younger, seemed to be following along just fine, whereas I had to keep stopping to catch my breath. "Keep moving," the instructor, Harriet, exhorted me. "The heart rate should be kept at the same level, even if you're just walking in place." Ah, the heart was involved. This wasn't simply a matter of chasing away Miss McElroy's ghost; something real was happening. My internal organs were being affected. My heart was beating.

Months went by. After that first morning's alarming confrontation with my body's weakness, I felt my energy growing perceptibly week by week, lost weight in places I didn't even know I was fat, and developed strength in muscles I didn't even know were there. This was serious stuff. This was a matter of blood pressure, folks. Strengthened immune system. The release of healthy endorphins in the brain.

And talk about healing childhood wounds! And developmental stages! I never asked Harriet how old she was but she had a nice head of undyed gray hair, and the songs she played were the very ones that misguided Donna and Cathy and Cindy and Jane and me through adolescence. I danced to the songs that once broke my young heart, taking untainted pleasure in them now as I couldn't when the isolation of adolescence weighed heavily upon me. In addition, I tasted what it is to be on a women's athletic team, not unlike what it must have been to be on Girls' Basketball, or even Cheerleading Squad.

One morning, we were all down on the mats holding weights. Harriet was taking us through the arm-bend, arm-extend routine and came to the "Heads up!" part. I picked up my head. Since at the time I was facing the wrong way, all at once I was greeted by twenty-five disembodied faces all straining up toward heaven in imperfect unison. Dark skinned and light; religious and non-religious; blondes, brunettes; Rubenesque, toothpicks. Talk about the unity of the Jewish people! This was a spiritually transcendent vision I shall not soon forget.

I know that thousands — make that millions — of people around the world discovered exercise long ago. The streets of the planet are clogged with joggers with their Walkmans, and thousands upon thousands of basements are filling up with exercise bicycles.

But for me, exercise was invented about 1997, and its joys were totally unanticipated.

I remember, in particular, one such joyous moment. Harriet always did this one step I couldn't follow; it took too much energy. You're going heel-toe, knee-up, grapevine, then you straddle the wooden step and jump up onto it with both feet. On that memorable day, before I even knew what was happening, my feet hopped up together onto the step.

It was sublime.

The aerobics industry isn't paying me for this article. I'm much too busy doing dishes and making dinner to hold down a public relations job, and unfortunately, stopped going to Harriet's class nearly three years ago, when my daughter got engaged. But I ran into Harriet at a coffee shop a few weeks ago, and am hoping that writing this article will encourage me to get back to it.

If there's anybody else out there, who — like me — is avoiding exercise, consider the following message a public service announcement: *If I — wife, mother, latent poet — could appear publicly in a leotard and jump up onto a step with both feet, anyone can.*

Try it.

31

THINGS THAT GO BUMP IN THE NIGHT

Behold, the Guardian of Yisrael neither slumbers nor sleeps ... In the Name of Hashem, G-d of Israel, may [the angels] Michael be at my right, Gavriel at my left, Uriel before me, and Raphael behind me; and above my head the Presence of G-d.

(The Bedtime Prayer)

What woke me up at 3 a.m.? That's one of the little mysteries. I lay there for about five minutes, staring vacantly up at the ceiling.

Then I heard something.

I and three of my children had just arrived in Los Angeles the day before, for a summer visit to my mother. I'd gone to sleep in the family room off of the kitchen; they were in the back bedroom. My older daughter had suggested that I take the bedroom, she could sleep on the couch. But I said no, I preferred being out there. *Really, Mommy? I wouldn't mind. No, Mimi, I want to be on the couch.*

That noise ... I'd been hearing things like that at night in my parents' house for the last twenty-five years. A virtually inaudible stirring, as if the walls had the mildest case of indigestion, or a window's eyelid had flickered in a dream. And like all those other times, those ten-thousand other times, the unidentifiable noise — closer to silence than to sound — was inviting me to investigate, even as I'd chide myself for the silliness of it. My mother's dog hadn't even barked this time, as she had on so many other such occasions in the past, when it must have been a squirrel, or the obscure activity of some neighbor dog, that had gotten her going. How stubbornly irrational of me, this ritualistic investigation of the quiet house in the middle of the night. And like all those other times, those ten-thousand other times, as I'd get a drink of water before going back to bed, sometimes I'd wonder: *And what would you do if there* were *someone there?*

But of course, there never had been, and never would be, anyone there. Nothing like that had ever occurred in the two decades my parents lived in L.A., in spite of my nocturnal rounds. It was just this primitive fear I have of sounds in the night.

When, on this particular occasion, I sat up and checked my watch, I realized that I'd fallen asleep with the light on and that I still had on my reading glasses. I took them off, set them on the coffee table, leaned over to pick up John Updike's heavy *Best Short Stories of the Century* from off the floor where it had fallen, set my feet into my slippers, and arose. And there, across the room, was a man. He was coming into the shadows of the kitchen from the shadows of the laundry room.

He stopped short.

Who's that? I wondered.

The man made some gesture of surprise. He wasn't expecting me, apparently. I must say, the feeling was mutual. A broad-shouldered man, Hispanic, black hair cropped short. Muscular, in navy blue T-shirt and jeans.

"Who is that?" I said. It was a low sort of voice, gruffly animalistic but conversational, too. *Overnight guest?* I thought crazily, straining to recall.

"Who is that," I stated, in an odd, flat voice. Surely a legitimate question in the wee hours of the morning. But our guest hadn't the courtesy to reply.

"Who *is* that!" In response to his silence, my question had catapulted to a higher octave and flown over the edge into a scream. The man spun around.

From the far-off tiny corner of my brain where I crouched, curled up like an apostrophe, I could hear the screaming of an unfamiliar madwoman, and through the kitchen's sliding glass door (with the view it gave me of the laundry room's outside wall) I saw the man's head shooting out through the doggie door, and after what seemed to be a two second time-lag (like thunder following lightning) my mind then registered (as an auditory memory to be recovered later) the noisy dull clattering of the thick plastic flaps on Grendel's entryway and then — surprise! — the lock must have burst and the door itself swung wildly open as he dived on through. For what must have been an embarrassing moment, our family friend's big head and abdomen were suspended comically, stuck half in, half out — *that may not be the most convenient way to use the door, but we'll give him ten points for creativity* — before his stout legs materialized in a flash and he was scrambling frantically to his feet. I saw his broad back under the T-shirt as he ran, hunched over slightly, and the back of his large head with its close-cropped haircut receding at the speed of light. (In the mental replay I would retain for future viewing, he would be lumbering off in slow motion, again, again, again.)

Then, like a figment of an overactive imagination, he leaped into the darkness of the bushes and vanished.

Coming back? Partners! Here somewhere! In the house! Where? That weird lady's wordless screaming had gotten a life of its own, high and wild and blood-curdling, rising and falling.

Hiding in the house! The children! Mommy! The children! The children! Still here! The screaming was ascending in a luridly widening spiral, rising and falling and rising and falling.

The children would say later that they thought I was being murdered.

❧ ❧

In response to my emergency 911 call, Officers Ricardo, Hutchinson, and Broadbent arrived a half-hour later, whereupon the dog (now on high alert; she had found her script) barked at the trespassers. *Good dog, Grendel! Better late than never, officers!*

The policemen asked many questions. I filled out a form, they inspected the grounds with flashlights, patted Grendel, reported that the man had gone — *thank you, officers!* — and Officer Broadbent neatly penned a telephone number on a piece of notepaper. "This is the detective assigned to your case."

My mother said not to worry — the man wouldn't want to come back after all that screaming — and went back to bed. Dawn broke. The rest of us tried to lie down and go to sleep but sleep was nowhere in the vicinity. We huddled together like sheep, hung together like magnetic filaments in the living room, were rendered immobile like people after earthquakes who are afraid to go out and afraid to stay in, afraid there will be another one if they close their eyes.

So we kept our eyes open and dreamt while awake.

In the morning, Officer Ricardo came to take fingerprints.

❧ ❧

It's been a week now.

It gets dark and we get watchful; we tense up at small noises.

I pass mirrors and startle at the reflection. My mother enters a room and I jump.

When at night my weary head drops onto the pillow, stumbling over its own thoughts like a drunk falling into dreamland, instantly my inner soldier springs up for guard duty. Atten—*tion*! (My inner child has fled the premises.) No slouching!

How long will this go on, this replaying of the tape? The mind and body keep returning compulsively to relive it: the innocent moment before the discovery of his presence, and then the malevolent discovery, and the stranger's entry into the inviolable sanctuary, my mother's home, where by morning we rise and drink orange juice, where we putter around in our bathrobes and back the Volvo out of the driveway and bring vegetables from the organic supermarket, and in the evening pull up the covers without thinking and say *Shema*.

Yesterday there was a big spread in the Metro Section (that's where The Los Angeles Times publishes the city's daily crime reports; I usually don't read it) that *lo alenu*, an intruder the night before had cut through a screen window in the home of an Hispanic family, shooting some of them.

I tore out that page and ripped it up and stuffed it into the garbage.

My brain feasts on the questions like a dog upon his salty bone. *What if I hadn't woken up in time, and he'd continued on towards the bedro— ? What if I hadn't fallen asleep with the light on? What if I'd decided not to bother getting up this time?* Each question turns my stomach queasily and releases a flood of adrenalin into my million cells: *What if I hadn't fallen asleep on that couch, and he had walked right on back into the bedro— ?*

Maybe he had a gun! Why didn't he use it? What did he want? What did he come here for? What if he'd caught sight of the row of kitchen knives hung behind him on the wall? And, most horrible to contemplate, and I contemplate it again, and shudder as I'm brushed by the sickly flutter of a cold watery wave: *What if I hadn't woken up, and he'd continued on, right past me ... into the bedroo—* My brain compulsively imagines this, and jerks shut, then starts blowing deadly bubbles all over again, forming unanswerable questions and producing the worst possible replies.

It's as if those long kitchen knives are whizzing by overhead and I keep leaping up to catch one as it flies, pulling it down, thrusting it into the softest parts of my heart.

Are you thinking, as I am: *Excuse me, lady, but what's the big deal? With all due respect, people go through a lot worse. After all, nothing happened.*

I start dreaming and the dreams bolt me awake. The eyes of my soul stare obsessively into the tunnel of mirrors where the man is walking through the kitchen, and halting, and there's screaming. My muscles are all busily at work reproducing the questions, and the answers, setting off anew the instant flash flood of adrenalin.

The children sit up in their beds and strain to hear. We keep the lights on. My thirteen-year-old is getting pale. She has circles under her eyes.

Surely time, like a mother, will eventually dismantle the electrified fence in my brain. She'll get the good news across the border that nothing happened. Nothing happened. *Nothing happened.* She'll coax my muscles out of their readiness and tell them again and again to relax, and forget, and ease me away from this fixated gaze, so I can fall asleep in peace.

Can't you see? she'll whisper gently. *Lift up thine eyes.* When nothing happened, something was happening, for the amazing thing, the implausible thing, the humbling thing on which I look back and say, *Thank You,* but haven't found the way to explain to anyone because it sounds so unlikely, is this: before choosing that particular spot by the kitchen, a still, small voice — not with words, but rather, something akin to feelings — had instructed me specifically:

The danger will come from over there.

(Without noticing myself knowing, I knew ... Thought without thinking: something bad, from the laundry room.)

You sleep here tonight, to protect everyone.

32

KEEPING THE BABY

One of the best phone conversations I've ever had is one in which most of the time, I just sat there with my mouth open, listening to a woman I'd never met and whose name I don't recall. A friend had given me her number because at the time I wanted to write about the Jewish mother, and was looking for people who had something to say on the subject. "She'll have something to say," my friend told me.

My friend was right.

"The Jewish mother?" this woman began without hesitation. "Yes, I'll tell you about the Jewish mother. The future of our people is in her hands. The problem with the education being given our people today is that in the *baal teshuvah* women's yeshivahs, they aren't teaching them how to build a Jewish home. The

Jewish home is the foundation of *Yiddishkeit*. Without that there's nothing."

Her second point is generally accepted as a given: any weakness in the Jewish home from one generation to the next will express itself as a weakness in the transmission of Torah itself. What she said about the yeshivahs, though, struck me as wishful thinking. I was about to wonder aloud if any institution could be expected to accomplish academically what should ideally be achieved by a family's living out its *mesorah*. But my voice had already wilted, by virtue of the supreme self-assurance of hers.

"What's the essence of the Jewish home?" she was saying. "Shabbos. Have you ever been at a *baal teshuvah's* house for Friday night dinner?"

I was about to say *yes, as a matter a fact, I* — but stopped short, and with the guilty curiosity of an eavesdropper, girded myself with strength to hear this woman's uncensored opinions.

"Well, I have a neighbor, she's just wonderful, a very sweet person and an excellent neighbor, you couldn't ask for better. But she invited us over for Shabbos dinner a few months ago and didn't even have a white tablecloth on the table. Pink, or light blue, *ich veis*, I forget which. And the menu! Forget about matzah balls. Even chicken soup, forget it. She served vegetable soup, on Friday night! It tasted good, she's an excellent cook, but it sure wasn't Shabbos. This was not a Shabbos dinner. And the chicken, I couldn't believe it when she brought it out. Hawaiian pineapple. On Friday night!"

I noticed in myself a ridiculous, craven desire to mention my chicken soup with matzah balls and my white Shabbos tablecloth. "If there's no problem halachically, don't you think those other ways are legitimate, too?" I interjected tentatively. "People from different cultures celebrate Shabbos in different ways; Yemenites don't make matzah ball soup, and they certainly experience Shabbos."

"Oh, come on, now," she said, "you know what I mean. I'm talking about American *baalei teshuvah*, English *baalei teshu-*

vah. Jews from the Ashkenaz *mesorah*. My mother came from Hungary, and so did my grandmother, and they gave me something so precious, something more valuable than anything material they could have handed down — and believe me, they gave me silver candlesticks from my great-grandmother that are a treasure; they go a long way towards creating the atmosphere of Shabbos all by themselves. But what my mother gave me, what my *Bubby* gave me, was Shabbos itself. No matter what else happens in life, this beauty is like nothing else you'll find in this world. It sustained my mother through Auschwitz, with no external signs, no physical indication of Shabbos there whatsoever, not even a candle flame. It sustains me through whatever I'm given in life to go through, and it sustains — it will sustain — my children, as adults in their own homes. This is what the *baal teshuvah* yeshivahs are not providing. This is what they're not passing on."

I groped for the right way to respond. The right way to think about it. But I was rendered speechless by a sudden, keen sense of loss. It streaked through me like a dark falling star. *Hey, you want me to go back in time and get born in Hungary?* I thought bitterly. *Then would I be authentic?*

"Look," I said, "I'm a *baalas teshuvah*. From the Ashkenaz *mesorah*. And I discovered Shabbos the way Christopher Columbus discovered America. With joy and exultation. And that's never left me. I can't pass on my grandmother's candlesticks — when she came over on the boat from Russia all by herself at the age of fifteen, all she had was a bag of kosher food her mother handed her when they said goodbye. And I can't pass on whatever it is, this intangible consciousness of Shabbos that your mother and grandmother gave you. But I can pass on my joy. I hope." I almost added, plaintively, *Can't I?* "That's a valid legacy, too."

To my relief, the woman didn't now change her tune, to spare the *baalas teshuvah* on the other end. Instead, without condescension, she kept right on sparring with me. We shared some details of each other's personal histories, discussed the transmission of *frum* culture, in general, from one generation to another, then circled around again to the question of the women's yeshivahs. I asked if she was suggesting cooking and sewing classes.

"I wouldn't scoff at that if I were you," she said, and I braced myself. Was this when she'd ask if I serve Hawaiian pineapple chicken on Friday night? "Sewing and cooking classes might not be such a bad idea, if you want to know the truth, but no, that's not what I'm talking about. I'm talking about something more profound. I'll give you an example: The way these women dress. If you're walking down the street and one of them's coming toward you from the other direction, you know from fifty feet away that she's a *baalas teshuvah*. Why *is* that? They can be perfectly neat, it's not about neatness, and well put together, most of them are very well put together. I'm just saying, there's a weakness in their education and you can tell. It's written all over them."

"Oh, so you're talking about *tzenius*."

"No, no. Not *tzenius*. That's not the issue. A lot of them are more *tzenuah* than anyone. They go out of their way about that. It's just that the way they dress, you can tell. Why is that? Why do they dress so strangely?"

Why do they dress so strangely?

Hmmm ... How fascinating!

I usually do well with candor, and this was no exception: I already bore her a certain grudging respect, this straight-talking f.f.b. Nonetheless, I had to admit, for me this had turned into a pretty scary conversation! Maybe she was right that some special sort of curriculum could be developed in the *baal teshuvah* yeshivahs to transmit certain aspects of the Indefinable Essence, but in my heart of hearts I already knew: *There's no solution to this problem.*

Or shall I say, *no cure for our condition.*

We can get our accessories in Meah Shearim and our *shaitels* in Lakewood. Our heels in Williamsburg and our dresses ... we can get the most modest dresses 13th Avenue has to offer. We can button up to the top, pull our *tichels* down to the eyebrows, and throw our vegetarianism and our denim skirts and our pineapple chicken out the window forever and forever and forever. But no chicken soup, or chicken soup with matzah balls — not even a dozen white tablecloths sent special delivery from Hungary — can alter the reality:

Baalei teshuvah grew up in other cultures, *bubbaleh.*

And it was none other than the Almighty Himself Who put us there.

❧

The following thoughts are not meant for the ears of the woman on the telephone. It's to my fellow *baalei-teshuvah* that these words are addressed.

All of us mortals are naturally inclined to perceive those who are different from ourselves as strange, foreign, off the mark; it must be an instinctive reaction that has been instilled within us — like everything else in our human nature — for myriad reasons we can only surmise. When the misconceptions are directed our own way, when the stereotypes are imposed on *us*, well, then, of course we don't like it; we know very well just how cockeyed they are. But when, in the luxurious, comfortable privacy of our own minds, it's we who are looking askance at others ... *they're not quite as O.K. as we are ... they're somehow substandard ... odd ... weird ...* then we scarcely notice what we're doing. Our stereotyped views come so naturally, and the accuracy of our perceptions seems a given. *We've got the goods on those people. We know who they are and what they're lacking and where they're going wrong.* And we're certainly not inclined to question these basic assumptions. *Why should I? I know what I know, and I know I'm right, whether or not I'll say so. And why discuss it except, of course, in my own circles. Those people will know what I mean, because they feel the same way.*

In contrast to those of us who keep our favorite prejudices to ourselves, it will more likely be that woman on the other end of the telephone — who bothers to ask questions, to frankly air her pre-conceptions, to reveal her disdain, and who's interested in hearing what's actually behind "strange" people's behavior — who has a better chance of identifying with those from whom she feels distant, a better chance of entering their realities. It will more likely be she, rather than one who politely conceals her secret biases, who ends up getting insight into all those strange people who *aren't like us.*

As commonly happens to one with a thorn in his side, I started thinking up some good lines only after we hung up. When so many different kinds of Jews from so many different cultures are feeling drawn to Judaism — I wished now I had said — all of us have to start doing what doesn't come naturally, and to appreciate that "strangeness" is relative. If someone seems strange, he is strange *to me.* And my ways may be equally strange to him.

On the other hand, as Rav Avraham Baharan wrote in *The Two-Way Channel,* the more a person believes in himself, the more he believes in G-d and the more he believes in G-d, the more he believes in himself. If my phone companion and I each exhibited limited understanding for those outside our respective circles, she, at least, enjoys an uncompromising self-acceptance that I can only envy. So many of us *baalei teshuvah* fearfully deny who we are and spend years seeking card-carrying membership in the *frum*-from-birth world. If you were to examine this phenomenon from an anthropological point of view, our behavior wouldn't look that different from the social climbing and vying for prestige that occurs in virtually every human society.

This isn't a matter of halachic observance. Each and every sacred tradition is to be adopted in full by the *baal-teshuvah* and by the convert, and complete respect must be demonstrated for the "fences" — including dress standards — of whatever community they join. Nor is there any question whatsoever in regard to his or her respect for the community's *minhagim,* and that he must refrain scrupulously from behavior that would mistakenly arouse suspicion. *Baalei teshuvah* and converts are, in any case, generally known to be stringent with themselves when it comes to these responsibilities and privileges.

The issue, rather, is to what extent, in his quest to fulfill his potential as a Torah-observant Jew, an individual must adopt other people's various cultural habits above and beyond, or outside the domain of, halachic requirements.

There will be as many answers to that question as there are individuals asking it, and the more insightful the *rav* to whom a person goes for guidance, the more perfectly tailored the solution will be, both to his personal history and to his highest aspirations. For some, this involves some simple and straightforward adjustments; for others, an unending, multifaceted growth process.

However, if (given the bafflement that some *frum*-from-birth Jews feel towards the unfamiliar ways of *baalei teshuvah*, and the bafflement and intolerance that some *baalei teshuvah* feel towards themselves) such emulation of the *frum*-from-birth is steeped in an anxious coveting of social approval; if that desire is projected with high-pressured intensity, sometimes with grave negative results, upon one's children; if there's a kind of fearful running away from one's own unexamined self-condemnations; then such modeling-after will be less akin to emulation than it is to mimicry.

One might object that a *baal-teshuvah's* rejection of his own background is appropriate. Since a materialistic culture based largely on the physical can so distort, even shatter, one's life, anyone with a head on his shoulders *would* and *should* be scared of such a culture's impact on himself and his children, and do whatever possible to escape its influence. If you're in a desert and want to cross over as fast as possible to the garden on the other side, it makes sense to leave your baggage behind. One's previous activities and interests — even those with a spiritual component, such as art, science, or "the helping professions" — may have served previously as idolatrous mini-religions, each with its own quaint objects of worship, and altars, and uncompromising dogmas. Much of what a newly observant person once loved *has* to be left behind. It could be too vividly associated with the futile posturing which may have characterized his life. His previous pursuits, no matter how intrinsically valuable, may still arouse in him the mis-channeled striving for social distinction that once distorted his natural desire for significance, recognition, and accomplishment.

Yet if an outward transformation is to be authentic; if it is to bring about a *kiddush Hashem* in the eyes of non-observant relatives; if we are to transform our inner experience as much as we transform our outer selves; then we have to be grounded in trust that the journey which brought us here was meant to be. There is profound meaning to be found in our roots, our beginnings, and in relation to those with whom G-d first set us down in this world — in other words, with our family of origin.

Why do you think it is that Hashem didn't plant us in a *frum* culture? Why did we have to be exposed to whatever we were exposed to? Is there anyone who would claim it was just some oversight on His part?

In the same way that our ancestors had to go through the desert before meriting the Promised Land, so, too, with our individual exiles. To the degree that our nation experienced the emptiness of the *Midbar*, to that degree did we appreciate *Eretz Yisrael*. To whatever extent each of us, at some point in our lives, has experienced alienation from our Creator, to that extent do we long for a relationship with Him.

To trust that every single event in our lives has meaning, purpose, and value, is to believe that no aspect of Creation is accidental.

In the words of Ruth Lewis, a poet whom I met in a religious women's writing workshop in Jerusalem:

So many baal-teshuvas
Throw out the baby
With the bath water.

I did.

I wanted to junk
All my treif past,
To make a thorough job of it.
So I threw out everything,
Including me.

That was scary
  (very)
  not to be there anymore.

Don't make
My mistake.
Throw out all the dirty water, yes.

But keep the baby.

≈≈≈

A Postscript:

Several years have gone by since the phone conversation described in the above essay.

A month ago, I got another phone call, this time from someone who was suggesting a young man for one of our daughters. The woman described his fine *middos*, and his fine character, and his fine ... parents. Such wonderful people, they have no problem at all with their son being in a yeshivah. If I wanted to choose a *bubbe* and *zaide* for my own children, believe me, I would choose them.

I stopped short. *Hey, wait a minute, lady! Hold your horses!* "Excuse me," I said, "you mean his parents aren't *shomer Shabbos*?"

"No, but — "

Well, before you can say *stereotype*, I was calling Rav Noach Orlowek for advice. He knew the young man in question, and knew my husband and me from way back.

"Rabbi Orlowek, I know this will sound a little funny," I said, trying to put this the right way and realizing that there was no right way, "but do you think it's all right for my daughter to go out with a *baal-teshuvah*?"

There was a long silence. I laughed nervously.

More silence, and then: "Mrs. Shapiro, it's O.K."

I had arrived.

33

IN THE SUBURBS

        And all her life
the daisies by the back door
the absent-minded music of her mother humming through
        housework

Feeling her way along the hallways of
childhood without end, and the big rooms
and tall, unopened doors of
childhood without end

Each leaf on each branch
said, "I'm here." Stars were all
whispering weakly: "In this vast emptiness without sound,
we are lights,"

Yet why? The breeze rain birds grass snow stones declared "Yes!"
but *why*
she wanted to know, and naturally didn't say so,
because everybody knew what everything was for.

Station wagons were for: *supermarkets.*
Streets: *for getting there.*
Schools: *for growing up.*
Growing up: *for children.*
Children: *for*
(?)
Children...?
      were for:

??

          A child

               is

                  for asking.

But the question could not be born(e).

34

LIEBERMAN'S CONNECTICUT WASN'T MY CONNECTICUT

My Connecticut was Joseph Lieberman's Connecticut, except in one respect. And that made all the difference.

Hairstyles were the same, the Top Ten were the same, and Stamford was the next exit over on the Merritt Parkway. On Saturdays in the fall, when red and orange elms along Route 7 glowed like fire and the New Canaan Rams played against Stamford High, the cheerleaders jumped up and down as if their lives depended on it, and exhorted the bleachers with all their might: "Two-four-six-eight, who do we appreciate!" On Saturdays in the spring, as the dogwoods bloomed, the junior class crammed for College Entrance Exams. And on Saturdays in summer, the popular kids would cruise down Elm Street as the crickets sang, their existential longing finding its voice in the songs coming over 101 on the dial.

And in what grand event did it culminate, all those long hard years of childhood and adolescence in the adjoining suburbs of Stamford and New Canaan? What awaited at the summit? When did the children finally learn their worth, when did they find out how they'd done, climbing the precariously steep social mountains in his hometown and mine?

At the Senior Prom. That was the ultimate measure of one's popularity and success. Get a good date, have the time of your life at the dance, then all you had left to worry about was who'd they give you for a roommate at college.

≫≪

So Joseph Lieberman's Connecticut was just about like mine, but from what I've read about him in the weeks since he was nominated for Democratic vice-president, it seems his childhood might as well have taken place on a different planet.

For I was a Jewish kid who didn't know what it meant to be Jewish. While I, disquieted by the Jewishness I knew so little about, longed futilely to fit in with the society I scorned, Joseph Lieberman over in Stamford seems to have been securely anchored in his essential identity and enjoying the world around him.

Another way of putting it, more succinctly, is that I'd never heard of Shabbos. What would life have been like if on Friday night, I and my sisters had gotten all dressed up to please not ourselves but G-d, and had joined our parents for dinner, with special linen on the table, and singing, and candlelight? What would it have been like if on Saturday, instead of finishing his weekly magazine article, my father had known he could desist from his incessantly busy schedule and stay home, just to *be?* It's hard to imagine it. To have our much adored and hard-working Daddy and Mommy all to ourselves from Friday night to Saturday night? To not compete for attention with his writing pad and her vegetable garden, his golf clubs or her shopping at Safeway? What would it have been like?

The most immediate benefit would have been the most obvious, psychological one: If parents demonstrate once each week that the family takes precedence over everything else, by erecting a fire wall against interruptions and distractions, their children can't help but get the subliminal message that they themselves are important. In the last decade or so of his life, my father lost no small amount of sleep thinking, in the middle of the night, about how his work had deprived him of his family. If only he'd known that he could have made up for the rest of the week, and all the constant responsibilities his career incurred, with just one day out of seven.

More far-reaching was the benefit that would have come about in regard to our Jewish identity. In those decades, the single most important factor in being Jewish seemed to be the Holocaust, yet what child wants to identify with victims? I knew virtually nothing about Judaism, or religious observance, or Jewish history, and my ignorance was in exact proportion to my sense of shame. My anxiety was such that when a school friend asked in seventh grade if it was true that I was a Jew, I replied, "No, I'm Unitarian," and the cowardice of my lie so bewildered and disgusted me, it took years to get over the self-contempt engendered by the denial. It was this denial, though, and the self-contempt, which started me off in search of my Jewish self. Not until I started becoming observant, as a young woman, did I know what it was to utter the three-letter word without fear.

The most profound benefit would have been in the larger perspective that Shabbos creates in one's mind. The ancient rituals and mundane restrictions of the Jewish Sabbath — the candle-lighting and singing, the father's blessing of the children, the refraining from the telephone, from cooking, from writing, from driving — serve to remind us that there is a reality larger than any particular human being's angle on it. In other words, I the little suburban girl wishing desperately for good friends, good grades, good looks, plagued by an inexplicable sense of being different and out of place, longing for something that felt right, would have discovered that in the immense and frightening void, beyond the traumas and tribulations of life as we knew it, Something was there.

I would have known what Joseph Lieberman as a teenager must have known, when he had to stay home one Friday night in June. He had been crowned King of Stamford High School's Senior Prom — socially speaking, what greater honor was there? — but couldn't attend, because it was Shabbat.

35

A SAFETY NET OF TELEPHONE WIRES

An interview with Rabbi Moshe Speiser in Jerusalem, the director of Kav Baruch, a hotline for religious teens and their parents

On the other end, it's almost always the mothers.

"In most cases," says Rabbi Moshe Speiser, "I never find out who they are. There's one — she called again this morning — who's still anonymous after three months. She identifies herself by her first name only. One time she arranged for her husband to call, and set up a meeting between us. We met anonymously, in the school where he teaches."

An anonymous meeting?

"We arranged a certain spot that's not normally used at that hour, he told me his first name and I gave him identifying signs, that I've got a red beard and wear a tie. In Israel, that's enough."

Rabbi Speiser smiles slightly. There's always a suggestion of that smile playing in his eyes — as if just around the corner, something unexpectedly good's going to happen. "So we met face to face, but I never found out who he was."

Did it help?

"Well, their son's an older *bachur* who's unmotivated. He hasn't gone off the *derech* but she has a hard time getting him up in the morning for *davening*, he doesn't want to start with *shidduchim*. Very little self-confidence. He's afraid to face life. Look, people think you can get involved and right away start changing things. Sometimes, to some extent, that can happen. But most of the time, if it took years to get this way, it'll probably take a long time to get out of it, too. But you can try to give some hope, and some encouragement, especially to the mothers. It's usually the mothers who are trying to fix things, and usually they're the ones who are most broken by the problem. There's often a problem with the fathers, but there's only been one time in my experience that the mother doesn't blame herself, as well. The mother's usually aware that she's part of the problem. In any case, usually one or both of the parents is being too critical, not seeing the good in the child, not being warm enough, enthusiastic enough. But both mothers and fathers, once they arrive at the realization that it's either change themselves or G-d forbid lose their child, then in my experience, most of them are open to the idea. That's not to say they can achieve it so fast, but they're very open to the challenge of changing."

In other words, when it comes to children, that's the one area where our pride doesn't get in the way as much.

"Right. One time I was telling a father that if he was really sincere about wanting to help his son, he would have to change his own attitude entirely, his whole approach, his whole way of thinking about his child. The father sat there taking this in, then he said, 'You mean I have to change my whole personality? Isn't that what you're saying?' I nodded, and the two of us had to laugh. Then I said, 'What we won't do for our children, right?'"

You said that giving hope and encouragement is one of the main goals of the hotline. In your experience, is hope warranted?

"There are no statistics yet because we're in the middle of it, but it's safe to say that a very good percentage of teenagers — after going through what they're going through — realize that there's more to life than the emptiness of what they've run to and they come back. But it's very hard to get that to happen if the parents aren't trying to create a more loving relationship. The goal is to get them to work on changing their own behavior. The parents *have* to be part of the solution. If they don't change, there's far less likelihood of their child changing anything. And if we find that the parents aren't yet able to change their own behavior, in the meantime we try to provide a temporary parent, someone who serves as a big brother or big sister. That's why training people for this is the thing we have to do, because what a child in crisis, or a child wobbling on the borderline, needs more than anything else — it's been said a million times but it's the truth — is simply love, and if you're a loving person, if you tend to be a caring person, you can be trained to really help a child or young adult — or a parent, for that matter — who for whatever reason is on the edge. To know how to do that is a teachable skill.

"I myself learned a lot of what I know in a course given by Dr. Joshua Ritchie, dean of the *MiLev* Professional Training Institute and Director of the *MiLev* Crisis Counseling Hotline for English speakers in Israel. The reason I finally decided to start my own is that after two years of dealing with kids, it became clear that we needed something that *charedim* would feel comfortable with, too.

"Most psychologists here in Israel are not trained for dealing with *charedi* teenagers. In America, people are very psychology-oriented, or they get in touch with a social worker, but here, even if you find a psychologist or social worker who's *frum* or who's adequately familiar with the *frum* community, and who's properly trained, what you usually hear from parents is, 'My child will not go to a psychologist.' There's more a feeling of shame about it. Kids think that if anyone finds out they're going to a psychologist, people will think they're crazy. The courses I give train people what to say to someone in crisis, how to create an atmosphere over the phone line in which people can feel safe, feel they can be open to talk, and if you can do that, then maybe the relationship can develop beyond that, into something face-to-face, in which a person becomes like a surrogate parent or an older, respected sibling. Sometimes that has to be somebody young enough to seem 'cool' in the eyes of the teenager — that can be one of the most powerful role models available."

Who comes to the courses?

"People who'd like to spend a little time helping with something important. It's such a big mitzvah. Sometimes it's parents who see the signs for 'Teenage Crisis Counseling Course' and call up asking if they can take it for their own personal instruction, for their home life, and of course, I say yes, why not. On a number of occasions, I've thought of someone I know who would be good at this and invited them to join the course, someone who by nature is a caring personality. The rest can be learned. The main thing, the crucial factor, is simply learning how to listen."

How do you learn to listen?

"By not talking! Have you ever heard of the difference between a monologue and a dialogue? In a monologue, one person talks and one person listens. In a dialogue, two people talk and no one listens."

What else do they learn in the course?

"How to present basic Jewish values to the at-risk teenager in a manner he or she can accept. It teaches what's going on in the minds of teenagers today and how they're influenced by their parents, schools, community, and society in general. It teaches how to guide teenagers to deal with their situations and to take on the responsibilities of life, and how to guide parents in their role. How to develop patience. How to be nice, not threatening. To not come across as judgmental. To work at not *being* judgmental. To learn the art of looking for the good in people. The way people usually grow is to build on their strengths, so you have to develop a better eye for people's strengths. One of the most important things is building the trust, and learning how not to break it. The caller has to know that if he wants his privacy to be respected, you won't cross that border. That's why the hotline can work sometimes where other approaches can't. People don't have to put themselves on the line. Your identity can remain hidden." Rabbi Speiser pauses thoughtfully. "Sometimes you find yourself in an extreme situation where you must get other people involved. Knowing how to handle that can be tricky. Once, a few years before the hotline was started, I made a mistake in that area and lost my *kesher*."

❧❧

The call came in after midnight.

You were sleeping?

"Yes, but when you get a sense of what's at stake, then being woken up totally loses its power to upset you. So, the phone rang at 1 o'clock and a girl says, 'I'm going to kill myself.'

"I say, look, let's meet and we can talk. She says, 'No.' I say, tell me where you are, I'll take a taxi right now. 'No. I'm killing myself.' She starts talking about her life. Her father's verbally abusive, everything in life is hard. She's in one of the Beis Yaakovs. She doesn't see any point in continuing. I say again, tell me where you are, I'll leave this minute. She says, 'No, I don't want you to see me.' We talk some more and I say, why did you call me? She says, 'This friend of mine, S. — remember her? — she told me about you. She says that one time you talked her out of something. So I thought ... maybe ... why not try him.' I say, why not talk yourself out of it? 'No, it's too hard for me.' What's so hard? 'I have no strength to go on.'

"So then I say one of the things you say in such situations. I say, you know, there's no rush. You can always kill yourself tomorrow. Why don't you get a good night's sleep and call me in the morning?"

❧❧

"I didn't hear from her for a week. I didn't know if she was dead or alive. One night, the phone rang and I knew her voice instantly. I said, where have you been? I've been waiting to hear from you! She said, 'Yeah, I was getting better but now I'm very depressed again. I have a bottle of aspirin and I'm going to do it this time.' During the course of the conversation she dropped a few hints. 'No one in this world is good.' I asked her, nobody? 'Well, one principal was pretty good,' and she mentioned his name. I said, he couldn't help? 'Yeah, he helped me for a while and now I don't trust anybody. I'm going to kill myself.'

"I don't know what put this into my mind, but then I said: Instead of killing yourself, why don't I just kill your *yetzer hara*? She seemed to like that, so I said, but how can I do that if I don't know where you are? No answer. So I say, OK, then, how about this: Why don't you ask your friend a little more about me. Ask her if I ever betrayed her trust. Then you can decide if I'm the kind of person you should talk to.

"She liked that idea so that's what she did, the next day. That night she called back. 'OK, she told me about you but I don't want to go meet you.' Then she hangs up.

"I called the principal she'd mentioned and in half a minute we'd figured out who it was. In forty-five minutes, after some other calls, I'd found out everything about her I needed to know. Before that, I had thought to myself that maybe this kid's playing a big joke on me, maybe she's just having fun, but after speaking to the people involved, no, it seemed she was capable of hurting herself. So the next time she called I decided to take a little tougher stance. I said, look, I know who you are. I know this and I know that. She was caught totally off guard.

"So you know who I am.' She sounded shocked. 'We'd better stop having conversations.' Then she hung up."

Then what?

"That's the last time I spoke to her. She never called again."

Can't you speak to the family?

"No. Because it turned out that the reason she'd lost trust in people, the thing that had precipitated that last crisis, was that the principal had let slip something to the parents that the girl had said in confidence. So I'm in touch with the principal, and a few of the teachers, and some other people. They're watching after her. Under the circumstances, that's as much as I can do. And every day, there are around twenty-five boys and girls I *daven* for — she's one of them."

≈≈

Can you tell some other stories?

"All right. One Friday afternoon, not long after the first ads for the hotline had appeared, the phone rings and when I pick up, there's nobody there. Hello? No answer. I say, is anybody there? Nothing. Then I hear somebody breathing.

"We're taught not to give up. Sometimes it's hard for a person to talk. So I say, 'Look, if it's hard for you to talk, take your time. I'll be ready when you are.' Now, not many men call up, but this time it's a man. He says: 'I think my son is on drugs.' I say, can you tell me what makes you think so? So he lists the various signs. I say, 'Look, I'm not an expert on drugs, but it doesn't sound like drugs to me. If you'll hold, I'll call a drug expert on the other line and ask him what he thinks.' So I call a friend of mine who knows all about these things and he agrees it doesn't sound like drugs, but says, that boy will probably end up on drugs if you don't do something fast. So from that point on, the father and I started working on it.

"Another time, a fifteen-year-old girl, clearly very nervous to be calling, started off by saying, 'I don't know if you deal with this kind of thing, I don't know if I should talk to you about it, it's not really a serious problem. It's only about friends.' I told her it took a lot of courage to call, please go ahead. It turns out her family had made *aliyah* a few years earlier and she's had trouble finding friends she can confide in. Her best friend, one of the only English-speaking girls, is always on-again, off-again about their friendship, dropping her and taking her back, so she never knows when she can count on their friendship and when she's going to be ignored. She said it was making her very depressed.

"After talking awhile, it became apparent that there were also family problems. The girl had no one to talk to, she didn't get along well with her mother, felt she couldn't confide in her. She felt she had nobody.

"While we were talking, I got an idea — a woman who I thought would be just the right big sister for this particular girl. She's a mother of a large family, she's warm, caring, smart. Good at finding the good in people. So I approached her about it and asked if she would give it a try.

"The woman had never done anything like this before. She was a little scared to take on something like this. It's a responsibility, somebody's life. But she went ahead and got in touch, and they spoke, and they've been meeting. I'll just have to watch that it doesn't get to be too demanding a situation. You have to be careful on behalf of your volunteers, to guard against their getting burned out. You have to take care not to give them more than they have time and energy for."

⋙ ⋘

"One time, a teenager said he'd seen the ad and was calling because his twelve-year-old brother was driving him crazy. 'He starts up with me all the time, especially Shabbos, and it makes me furious.' I said that he was probably doing it to get his big brother's attention, so maybe if you ignore him, he'll stop bugging you. I asked him if he wanted to come to my house for Shabbos and he said no, he didn't, but a few days later he called back and said he'd tried not reacting to his little brother over Shabbos and it had worked. He obviously felt very good about it. I told him he was a *gibor*, and said, 'Look how much you gained by being able to control yourself.'

"A child can come to view self-discipline as being something for his or her own benefit.

"Parents are often not aware of how negatively they come across when it comes to their children. They convey a pessimistic attitude. Like with that unmotivated *bachur* afraid to go out on *shidduchim*, the mother used to say things such as, 'How are you ever going to get married?' I told her, wake him up in the morning with a kiss instead of a push. When he comes home, give him a hug hello. We have to give enough loving attention that it will be able to counteract the outside influences. We have to fully grasp what's going on in the minds of teenagers today. Outside influences are pulling at them. The Internet, television, magazines, billboards, the way people walk on the street, the availability of drugs. If I tell parents to be more loving in such and such a way, sometimes they say — and they're right — *my* parents didn't do that and *I'm* O.K. But this is a different generation. It's not that today's parents don't feel love — in the grand majority of cases, they do — but that they have to communicate the love so that it's felt.

"There are all kinds of calls. Sometimes problems arise when a child has been put into a school that's inappropriate for his personality or his goals. Sometimes, it's because of undiagnosed or misdiagnosed medical conditions, or learning disabilities.

"Around a year ago, I got a call from the parents of a boy who was failing in school and had consciously decided to rebel. Failure in school is a high-risk factor, because of what it can do to self-image, and sure enough, he'd become less and less religious. They'd put him step by step into more and more modern schools, but it hadn't worked. He dropped out completely and got involved in drugs. Some of his friends tried with some success to persuade him to stop taking drugs but nonetheless he almost died of an overdose.

"I was in touch with the parents throughout this period, pleading with them not to throw him out. To be more firm on some things and less firm on some other things, but not to give up.

"They didn't give up on him. They went through it with him and today their son is doing much, much better and going to a school he's succeeding in. Just this week I got a letter from the mother,"

— Rabbi Speiser takes out a paper from his pocket —"She says her son has started keeping Shabbos again, that he's taking high school courses and wants to start attending a Gemara class. 'We are so thankful for what has happened with E. I can't express to you our gratitude. I hope we can pass on the *chessed* to others in return.'

"A woman once called up very upset because her teenage daughter was wearing inappropriate clothing. But in talking to her, it became evident that this was a problem not only of a parent not knowing how to give it over to her child in a good way, without trying to shame her, but also that the mother herself didn't have a good grasp of the philosophy behind *tznius*. We have to approach these things from the standpoint of what they stand to lose and what they stand to gain."

To appeal to the child's self-interest?

"Yes, but something that goes beyond self-interest, too. Today one of the major problems is that observance of Judaism in general has become shallow. There's more learning than ever before but the heart behind it is lacking. No kid ever ends up on the street because of philosophical issues — in my limited experience, it always has something to do with the family life — but *hashkafah* issues are real and we have to know how to address them. The truth of Torah especially, along with *tznius*, these are the two issues that counselors need to be well prepared for on a profound level. The children are picking up that there's nothing intrinsically uplifting about what we're saying. We're not making them feel good in such a way they will want to do what they're being told to do.

"For example, a father takes his son to shul. He sits down, expects the kid to *daven*, but doesn't lovingly tell his son that Hashem is listening, that Hashem loves him and wants to hear from him. Why should that child want to continue *davening*? If we would find a little more meaning in our *Yiddishkeit*, I think our children would follow along.

"We have to love our children unconditionally, no matter what they do. If a child feels he's loved when he does something good, and not loved when he doesn't, then that's a strong source of rebellion. He feels, 'If you knew the real me, you wouldn't love me.'

"There was a problem between a father and his son, and the boy had become rebellious. I told the father, you must give your son personal attention. Why don't you take him out by himself to eat? He did, and a third party reported to me later that the young man had said to a friend, 'What took him so long? It took me becoming a *chiloni* to get my father to start listening to me.'"

At the start of our conversation, you mentioned that a mother called you this morning, the one who had arranged an anonymous meeting between you and the father.

"Yes, she called the hotline this morning crying, saying, 'My husband thinks he knows everything.' but I was on the other line so I asked if she could call back."

Did she call back?

"Not yet, but she will."

By the way, what happened at that anonymous meeting?

Rabbi Speiser goes silent for a few seconds before speaking. "The father told me something he said he'd never told anyone. He said, 'Of all our kids, this was the one child I never loved.'"

36

M.R.I.

A sudden loss of hearing in the left ear ... The doctor scheduled me for an M.R.I. He said the hospital waiting list could take a month or more.

The next morning, someone from the hospital called. "You have an appointment tomorrow night at 11."

"Tomorrow? But at E.N.T. they said it would take at least a mo —"

"Tomorrow, Thursday, 11 P.M."

"At *night*?

"Be here at quarter of."

I knew what they were all thinking. "Do they think it's a tu —"

She'd already said goodbye. *Dum-de-dum-dum,* the rolling of drums in the background.

～～

In the middle of the night
Why give me such a fright?

≋≋

Down, down, down the stairs, and down yet another flight, deeper into the dank, dim bowels of the bright, enormous hospital. Peeking here and there, but as yet no sign of where I was going. Fewer and fewer lights as I descended. Old mops and extra chairs, a half-open door, a glimpse into a low-ceilinged Bluebeard-type chamber, whose entire length and width was a grey tangle of overlapping various-sized pipes snaking all around the room. One of the pipes, near the door, was leaking, and the little drops were plopping quaintly into a plastic bucket.

Such modest intestines for the shining institution!

How odd, to be feeling my way along like this in the dim hallways. It must be the wrong way. *Had I heard the nurse's instructions wrong? Am I losing my hearing?* But then there it was, a little sign. Just three little letters, and a small tidy arrow pointing the way.

≋≋

"Are you carrying any weapons?" asked the nurse behind the partition. "Do you have any pins in your body from an operation? Is there shrapnel lodged anywhere in your body?"

"Shrapnel?"

"Such as from a terrorist attack. Do you have a pacemaker? Are you expecting? Remove all hairpins. Remove all jewelry."

I felt through my hair for hairpins, then took off my necklace, my bracelets, my watch, my earrings. More than the tunnel itself, for some reason, it had been the prospect of taking off my jewelry that had aroused some flutter of dread. Another nurse ushered me somewhere for the insertion of an intravenous tube and I looked the other way. Then she ushered me into another room, where there it loomed: a huge, blunt, dense, off-white whale, taking up perhaps a third of the space, and it had a round gray mouth — for me.

She told me to get up on the table, told me to lie down, and then to lift up my head so she could put on earphones. She asked what music I would like.

I thought this over carefully. "Baroque."

"Baroque?"

"Like Bach, or Vivaldi. Do you have any?"

"I'll check."

"Don't move when you're in there," she said.

"What if I fall asleep? And move when I'm asleep?"

No answer. I was on my back; she slid me backwards, head-first into the ovens. She shut the round tunnel door and all at once I was seized by terror. Maybe I hadn't found all the bobby pins! If I'd missed any, would they turn into flying magnets that would whizz like arrows through my skull? I should scream for her to stop the presses!

I remained mute.

People had told me about this: enclosed in a tunnel, the ceiling a few inches overhead like a sarcophagus. Maybe this was what it's like to have died. I closed my eyes and all at once — no warming up period necessary? — the noises began that people had told me about: Odd thunder, rumbling and vaguely spreading as if before an earthquake, then a gun shot. A second gun shot, some fuzzy baritone knocks, and then — I jumped — machine gun fire! My paratrooper son in Lebanon!

I opened my eyes for a second — it was better to keep them shut. But then — a distant horizon came somewhat into view. My eyes blinked back open and right there over me, the gray, sterile ceiling was two or three inches over my forehead, and the inner walls of the tunnel curved snugly all around. My friend Renée's mother — She and Renee's father had hidden in a bunker dug out underneath a pigpen. The Polish Catholic farmer's son slept over the spot to guard them every night for three years, until the war ended.

Suddenly there was a radio coming through the headphones, an Israeli radio station, a man talking loudly and a woman talking loudly back. Back and forth, back and forth — surely the nurse would turn the channel now to the classical music station.

But no, then rock music came on! Not soft rock, either, but horrible 90s teenage music! And then machine gun fire again. I jumped. Turn the channel! A single gunshot, and then another. Music like this at a time like this? Of all things to be assaulting my brain with at such a time! Stop it! Turn off the music! If I call out, will she hear? Where is that woman? Am I allowed to move my mouth? Renée's mother. This must be the definition of hell! Change the channel! "There were twenty-four people altogether," Renée told me. "For a while, some of the other people in there were thinking of killing my mother."

"Why? She got hysterical?"

Renée nodded.

"Turn off the music!"

A few more seconds, then the rock music stopped. She had heard me.

And then — Bach did arrive. Weaving between the gun-shots, circling in and around the thunder, coming forward and bowing joyously to me, noble symmetry behind the machine guns, a peacock fanning out. Danny in Lebanon, hiding behind a rock. I wanted very much to move. I must not. The Bach curv-ing around and around like seashells, colors harmonizing in an unfolding prism.

I had been dreaming of a window in the side of the tunnel. I must have fallen asleep, even with the gunfire. My legs, my arms. My head at a slight angle. I wanted, I *had* to move my head. Shall I scream?

I was going to scream!

She was sliding me out.

"Is it forty minutes already?" I asked.

She nodded.

∽∾

On my way out of the whale room, I passed the next person in line, an Arab girl about ten years old, frail and thin, blue-black hair in a ponytail. Her lips were parted with uncertainty. She glanced back at her father in the reception area, who had a black mustache. He was standing like a military signpost alongside the mother, in a long grey *chador*. He nodded to his daughter to continue on in, and she turned. The door shut behind her.

Finding my way out of there, I noticed that in a glassed-off room to the left, my nurse was sitting before three computer monitors. Could those be pictures of me, maybe, that she was looking at?

I stopped and took a step inside. "Can I see?" I asked. She nodded. I stood looking over her shoulder. She was at the keyboard, entering into the computer memory a series of brightly backlit images. I said, "Is that my brain?"

She answered crisply. "Yes, it is." She pointed to two thin little white threads, a half-inch apiece, tilting upwards on either side. "This is an auditory nerve. See? And here's the other one."

I said that there didn't seem to be any suspicious globs or masses of anything extra in there.

"Well, the doctor will have to look at it."

My brain — *my brain* — laid upon a luminous white screen. I'd never seen it before.

My brain!

It was rather disappointing. That was it? Hard to believe. It looked — like a lily pond. But not a very lovely one. Just a swampy kind of thing. Very organic, just a vulnerable looking thing, like a smudge of moss upon a rock. So surprisingly low-tech! All the people I'd ever known were in there? My elementary school friends, and everything I'd ever learned? Ancient history, the constellations: Big Dipper, Little Dipper. The kings of England, the capital of Pennsylvania.

It looked like a dingy sort of cloud formation. Irregular and — not at all like the new iBook laptop from Apple Computers, with glossy orange or blueberry exterior and fast shining innards.

Poor strained brain. The floods it must endure regularly of my anger, my desires. It could be washed out, overwhelmed; it could overflow its poor little wavering shoreline. My whole life is in there?

She said, "You can call for the answer in ten days."

In the taxi on the way home, I rolled down the car window and tilted my head back against the seat. The warm black velvet night breeze rippled on my face. The stones of the high wall alongside the hospital parking lot, that loomed up outside the window for a few seconds as we pulled out, were textured like the moon's surface, all kinds of variegated grayish bumps and hills, and then: way up high on the ceiling of the sky — the moon itself at 1 a.m., the perfect shining sphere, sailing through the endless black emptiness among a handful of tiny scattered diamond stars.

Just then, along came some darkly gray wispy floating clouds, like an old pond drifting across the sky, drifting right over the moon's brilliant shining white radiance, like — a translucent — veil. My brain, in the sky. My brain was everywhere.

37

ON ANGER

You and I know what it's like, because we're both human: the certainty that we've been wronged, and our sense of innocence. The rising indignation; the festering of our wound in silence; the self-righteousness that builds up within. The keen desire to craft some put-down that will diminish the other as we've been diminished, to put him back down and ourselves back up; to restore our dignity as it must be restored. The bottling-up of our cutting retort, or, alternatively, just really letting this person have what's coming to him — after all, he deserves it.

How good it feels to be so strong! It's such a relief until — our conscience speaks up. Then we must defend ourselves. There's guilt, or embarrassment, or shame over the way we've spoken, and then all the external consequences that are already out of our hands: all the reactions and responses of those upon whom we've vented our spleen. If we love them, it's hard to bear the distance that has opened up like a chasm between us.

Then there's the loss of self-respect, which always, without fail, results from any loss of self-control.

It's that ancient infant within us, our anger, in all its many manifestations as they vary from individual to individual. And as on so many other occasions, it has gotten the better of us once again. Anyone who has ever had parents, or children, or friends and relatives and neighbors, or co-workers, bosses, employees — in other words, as anyone who has ever been a human being knows, life constantly provides good reasons to feel angry, and the reason for this is obvious: *the world has a way of not coinciding with our wishes.* Therefore, when crossing paths with anyone or anything on the planet, including ourselves, there's a good chance we'll experience some frustration of our will.

How should this reality of life be dealt with? Sometimes, it seems the only answer is to make people and things do what you want. One's children often fall into this category. Most of us, however, eventually discover that in spite of its strong appeal, this solution leaves something to be desired — mainly, that it doesn't work.

I will never forget my own moment of realization in this regard. One day early on in my motherhood, sinking down onto the couch after an afternoon spent yelling at my innocent little kids, something dawned upon me: it's hard and exhausting work, getting angry. And in the next few moments, two brand new ideas crossed my mind.

Submitting to force runs against the grain of human nature, even if the person in question is only 2½.

If I'm trying to control any other human being, including my own child, that's a sign that I've lost control of myself.

These realizations touched me so deeply that my anger vanished into thin air and I remained imperturbable for the rest of the day. But when, by the following afternoon, I was once again tired and bored, I had to start all over again from scratch. Like all abrupt awakenings, this one may have had a significant impact upon my general level of understanding, but its effect on my behavior was transient.

We may be appalled by the destructiveness of our anger on ourselves and the people we most care about. We can understand very well that old saying, *anger is like acid, it destroys the vessel that contains it.* We can even have tasted the bitter truth in the double meaning of that word *mad.* Losing one's temper is akin to losing one's mind. But the *middah* of anger can only be changed by conscious long-term effort, until self-restraint becomes habitual. To achieve that goal, what is required above all is a modification of our basic beliefs about life itself.

⋙⋘

Rosh Hashanah is dedicated to the principle that G-d is King of the universe. The holiday's chief goal is that by the end of the day, we will not only have tasted a number of apples dipped in honey but will also have arrived at the recognition, on some level, of the fact that Hashem is truly — that means actually — the source of all events. G-d is here, as I type. G-d is with you as you read, as your eyes take in these words. The sounds you hear out the window, the memory in your mind of what happened this morning, the fragment of memory that appears instantaneously in your miraculous computer of a mind when you see the phrases: *the house I grew up in,* or *1975,* or *white curtains.* Your breath, the one you've just taken, and the one you're about to take. The child in Botswana crying for his mother and the Israeli government that's about to collapse, the birth at this moment of a star seventy million light years away… An underlying recognition of the totality of the Creator's presence is the necessary foundation for whatever truthful self-examination we engage in during the Ten Days of Repentance.

Why is that recognition necessary to accurate self-confrontation? Because if we carry within us an awareness that Hashem is the Source of all phenomena, those that loom large and those that appear trivial, those that are earth-shaking and those that seem meaningless, then everything's cast in a different light.

If such an understanding prevailed, we would be less inclined to get mad at the children for fighting during dinner, or to retaliate at so-and-so for her snide remark, or to get upset when stuck in a traffic jam.

Although anger can quite literally destroy us, it isn't an enemy that can be crushed and banished. It's an intrinsic facet of our personalities, and is purposefully designed into our being, and needn't, cannot be denied. It can provide us with superb insight into our own usually hidden selves. What is it that irritates, annoys, infuriates us? The more developed our capacity to identify what's really bothering us, and to recognize that the true object of our anger always lies within, not in the external phenomenon, then the better our chances of becoming our own masters. Anger, which can work so powerfully against happiness, is the very tool we've been given to get a handle on our invisible, elusive inner selves. *What aggravates me? Why does it inflame me?* The more truthful our answers, the more light that's shed on what makes us tick. It's precisely in the struggle to get control over that which seems uncontrollable, that we have a chance of becoming the people we aspire to be. Rav Moshe Feinstein was once asked how he could possibly stay as calm as he did in the face of intense provocation. "Do you think I was always like this?" Rav Feinstein replied. "By nature, I have a fierce temper, but I have worked to overcome it."

It's uncontrolled anger that brings murder and war to mankind, anger that dissolves marriages and makes for unhappy childhoods; anger, in general, that drains life of its joy and shatters a person's self-respect. If someone were to wave a magic wand and offer to free us of this internal scourge once and for all, who among us wouldn't jump at the chance? But by the same token, who among us finds anger easy to let go? As attractive a proposition as it may seem on paper, letting go of it feels like a sacrifice. It does not come naturally to relinquish the belief that *we know what's happening and why, and that if I'm suffering, then something or someone is responsible for it.*

The world is larger than I think, and the causes behind all things infinitely more mysterious than my mind can grasp. May we learn to look without fear into the mirror, and open our hearts to a world we can't control.

38

THE FLOWERS
ARE GROWING

I'm in a bad mood and I sit on the couch.
My children run in and out,
avoiding my eyes. The grouch
of the house, the mother.

They're laughing, and report to me occasionally:
"Mommy, I opened the water outside."
"Mommy, the boy on the slide hit me."
"Mommy, I want to drink!"

They are like grass. I depend
on their goodness,
on the way they all spring instantly back up

in the wake of my heavy step.
They are there, green, sweet.

Outside there's silence, then a burst of laughter.
I get myself up and go to the door.

They have taken the flowers I threw in the garbage
this morning and have stuck them into the dirt
and are watering them with my coffee cups.
Yellow wilting roses
bending under the weight
of their own dying.

"We're making a garden, Mommy!"
The roses nod in the flood.
"Look! The flowers are growing!"

39

SPEAK, UNIVERSE

We couldn't have found a more fitting symbol for the end of the twentieth century than the failure, in November 1999, of NASA's mission to the Red Planet. Nor could we hope for a more eloquent message to celebrate the birth of the new millennium than the meek Mars Lander's continued silence.

"Mars Lander's Apparent Loss Dashes Spirits and Raises Fears," read the headline in The New York Times, when the expensive little robot designed to send us data from Mars vanished in space without a trace, as it approached the destination. "Little hope remains that flight controllers will establish contact."

In those two lines can be detected the eternal desire to connect with the unknown; the impossibility of conquering it once and for all; and mankind's never-extinguished hope even in the midst of failure. "Hope is the thing with feathers," wrote Emily Dickinson, a hundred fifty years ago,

That perches in the soul
And sings the tune without the words
And never stops at all…

I've heard it in the chillest land
And on the strangest sea,
Yet never in extremity
It asked a crumb of me.

Here we were once again, thrusting ourselves towards some unseen horizon. Once again were we being driven by some inexplicably passionate curiosity to explore an undiscovered frontier, and once again were we thwarted by uncontrollable natural forces, left with an unarticulated sense that somebody or something was rebuking us — not only for our hubris but for our innocence. We human beings toss our questions out into the universe as if they were prayers, but our love for answers seems unrequited by a Sphinx-like void which would rather not respond. The hopes and fears of all the years — Are they not met in thee tonight, little robot (already forgotten by us on Earth) that never saw fit to send back any message to us from beyond?

Is there anyone who cannot identify with those who worked on this project? Who among us has not known such failure? "We are all crestfallen," said Wayne F. Zimmerman, head electronics engineer on the team that developed the 6.5-foot mechanical arm. "Man, it's tough when you put in that much work for years into designing, building and testing, it's hard to lose it all. Not to have an opportunity to do that science is pretty depressing."

For Mr. Zimmerman, hope's devastation consisted of a lost opportunity for scientific achievement. But the failures life has to offer come in all shapes and sizes: The book that wasn't published or the dream house not built. The waiter who doesn't bring what you ordered. The health that's been lost, the friend who died before you got there. The child who talks back, or that you never had, or didn't do right by … The dirty dishes in the sink.

Education errs, the author Kurt Vonnegut has written, in trying to teach us how to succeed; what it should do is teach us how to fail, because that's usually what happens.

Three decades ago, the Times reported, the Mars Lander project's chief planetary geologist, Dr. Bruce Murray, predicted that volumes of water were probably frozen in the Martian polar regions. "This was his first [and last] chance, at the age of sixty-eight, to learn more... [and] there is no follow-up mission."

A scientist such as Dr. Murray — looking for signs that the conditions on earth which make life possible are not unique, and that the human species came about by a natural chain of fortuitous physical reactions — may not call his quest a religious one. But its undercurrents are intrinsically akin to those of any spiritual search, and its conclusions equally immune to definitive proof. For no matter what we discover and how much more we learn, we interpret it according to our predilections. What's out there? People have always wondered. How did it begin? Is life the product of coincidence, and — by virtue of the mathematical inevitability inherent to an infinite cosmos — bound to be duplicated elsewhere? Or are we the only ones around in an otherwise neutral, unhearing cosmos? Are we here for some reason yet to be discerned, or that will never be spelled out? Is there anything out there that can give us a glimpse of our own future, our own origin, our true nature? That we have failed to get a call-back from our man on Mars, our diminutive alter ego with his long robotic arm, is par for the course. That basic desire to get some response from "out there," the desire to speak and be spoken to, is not unrelated to the modest joy we experience when our e-mail program says "You've got mail," and the little flash of disappointment when it says, "No new messages." But there is a message in the robot's silence: to co-exist with unyielding mysteries. G-d hides His face, neither more nor less today than thousands of years ago, when the Creator asked Job:

Where were you when I laid the foundations of the earth? ... when the morning stars sang together, and ... shouted for joy?

Or who shut up the sea with doors... as if it had issued out of the womb? When I made the cloud the garment thereof ... Declare, if you have understanding." And Job finally replied, "Truly, I have uttered things that I understood not; things too wonderful for me ..."

Our own conversations with G-d seem to be monologues, not dialogues, yet Judaism teaches that G-d speaks with us through the events in our lives — totally loving messages which each of us is ultimately compelled to decipher all by ourselves. As the year 2000 began, at thousands of celebrations around the world, what millions of people wanted was to not be alone at that moment, to assure themselves for the record that their lives are successful, that they'd found someone to love and be loved by — We look for mirrors to tell us who we are. We want the universe to talk back.

But aloneness is a basic premise of our existence, and each of us must rediscover what we're here for. It's a lonely mission, and like that tiny robot lost somewhere out there in space, we're stuck with it, as individuals and as a species. "People must understand how difficult these things are," said Mr. Zimmerman. "Your playing field is the whole solar system and it's full of hazards and unknowns."

We need those hazards and unknowns. The soul by definition thrives on the intangible, the invisible, the inscrutable, and it's our good fortune that the world has been designed in such a way that we're in no apparent danger of comprehending very much at all. There will always be an infinite supply of emptiness into which to project our inquiries and dreams. There will always be our failures, large and small, to compel us to connect to something greater and more perfect than ourselves. And when it comes right down to it, there will always be your aloneness and mine, which prompts us to speak to an unseen G-d.

Ever since man walked on the moon, we might well imagine, when gazing up at that white shining entity, that we've been there, done that. But the moon and its reasons for being are still as foreign to us as Mars, and as unknowable as our own minds.

The whole thing — earth, universe, our own consciousness — is one wall-to-wall carpet of miracles.

Our humanity is not to be discovered in our success at getting answers, but rather in the persistence of our quest in the face of overwhelming disappointments. We can't refrain, just because we fail to pick up any reply, from turning our hearts once again up to the starry night, and asking again, and asking again, and asking again.

40

Two Sisters At War

Peace in the Middle East may be hard to find, but on Thanksgiving Day two Jewish sisters in Los Angeles found their way to a cease-fire, courtesy of Peggy Post. Peggy Post is the granddaughter of Emily Post, who, as we all know, served for several generations as the world's greatest authority on manners.

Now, etiquette is not a traditional "Jewish" subject, and this is especially so in present-day Israel, where people are too busy thinking about survival to remember how to fold their table napkins. But on the day of which we speak, Peggy Post rescued the above-mentioned sisters, one of whom lives in Jerusalem and the other in Oakland (and both of whom were visiting their mother, who was due to undergo major surgery a few days after the American holiday) from an outbreak of hostilities which could have hindered both the executive and the legislative branches of family government for weeks, if not months, on end. At the very least, their enjoyment of the kosher turkey would have been much diminished were it not for Ms. Post's timely intervention.

The war began with CNN, when dinner was still a few hours off and the family took up positions on the couch to see how Florida was coming along. But instead of the ongoing recount of Gore ballots in Palm Beach, they were presented with a news bulletin.

An Israeli bus had been bombed in Hadera, near Haifa. The family saw the nose of the bus plunged headfirst into a store, the awning of the store imprinted with the Elite Chocolate company logo, which to the sister from Jerusalem was jarringly and profoundly familiar, as was the sight of the rear window of the Egged bus. They saw the street, a dark vision of blood and shattered glass, and people running and screaming.

The sister from Jerusalem went into a kind of panic. One of her children's in school near Haifa.

❧❧

You see that? she exclaims bitterly. *Arab civilians attack Jewish civilians, but Jewish civilians don't attack Arabs.*

Israeli soldiers attack Palestinian civilians, says the sister from Oakland. *Israeli soldiers are shooting at unarmed children.*

Unarmed children, says the sister from Jerusalem. *That's ridiculous. That's how CNN presents it.*

NPR, says the sister from Oakland.

I couldn't believe it yesterday when I heard someone on National Public Radio say that Israel is "aggressing" against the Palestinians, says the sister from Jerusalem. *That's absurd. The Palestinians are shooting at us.*

Israel prevents the Palestinians from having their own army, says the sister from Oakland.

That's because each of the five wars in Israel's history since 1948 began when the armies of our Arab neighbors invaded.

That's why Israel occupied the West Bank — or Judea and Samaria, that's their ancient Jewish names — in the first place. I know we should be more cooperative and help the Palestinians establish an army and fulfill their national aspirations, says the sister from Jerusalem, *especially since the Palestinian Covenant declares that its people's national goal is destruction of the Zionist entity. But there's something,* je ne sais quoi, *that rubs me the wrong way about generously promoting our own destruction.*

Israel is occupying Gaza, says the sister from Oakland, *as well as the rest of the Palestinian homeland. Even in the midst of the Oslo negotiations, Israel was permitting new settlements to be established in the contested territories of the West Bank. No wonder the Palestinian people are furious.*

They're furious because Arab pride is wounded by our existence on sacred Muslim soil, says the sister from Jerusalem. *They're wonded by our existence, period! Violence against Jewish infidels is sanctioned by Islam. Saying it's because of settlements is their lie to make it more palatable to the world! Arabs have a unique capacity for brutality. It's a cultural characteristic. They have a particular capacity for committing uninhibited violence and cruelty.*

That's a stereotype, says the sister from Oakland.

It may be a stereotype. It's also a fact of life. The sister from Jerusalem thinks: I am not going to lose my temper. *I'm sorry, but you just don't know what you're talking about. You don't live there.*

There are plenty of people who do live there who agree with me. How as a Jew can you ignore the Palestinians' suffering? The Palestinians were forced off of their land when Israel was created.

Excuse me, Jerusalem was founded by King David. The land of Israel has been occupied by Jews for 3,000 years. And you have no idea what's going on there now between left and right. Even Leah Rabin said her husband Yitzhak would be spinning in his grave. Rabin told us not to be afraid, the Palestinian Police would never dream of shooting at Israelis with the guns he agreed to give them at Oslo. They'd only use them in our joint fight against terrorism. But surprise! Jerusalem hears her own voice rising up sharply to a higher octave. *They're using the guns against Israelis. All around the country. Look, there are thousands of Arabs who would prefer to co-exist with us, at least for pragmatic reasons, but countless more who would consider it an act of heroism to kill anyone in our family.*

How can you condone the suffering that goes on in Palestinian refugee camps?

I don't, but it's the Arabs who are keeping them there. Look, now that I see the news media here, I understand why it's impossible for you to comprehend what's going on! All you see about this is what you get from all the American newspapers! And American television! Jerusalem thinks: I have to keep my voice down! *What would you say if for fifty years Israel hadn't gotten Jewish refugees out of refugee camps? Arabs don't want to absorb their own brethren.*

Israel has the right of return but denies it to the Palestinians.

Their right of return would mean the end of the Jewish State! Can't you see this? The Palestinians are right next door to several immensely huge Arab countries! The only place on the planet that belongs to the Jews is this incredibly tiny spot! Three Israeli children lost limbs a few days ago when Arabs attacked their school bus in Gaza. Get it? Jerusalem lights up like a rocket. *A school bus? What do you think has to be on a man's mind to attack a school bus?*

I'm very, very sad about the children on the school bus. Oakland's eyes fill suddenly with tears. Jerusalem loves this sister as much as she loves her own life. *I'm also very sad about the Palestinian children. And don't say Arab,* says Oakland, *say Palestinian.*

The land of Israel is your birthright, too! Jerusalem is yelling. *It's not only my children's, it's your child's! Look, either you think Israel has the right to exist or you don't, that's what it comes down to, and I really don't care anymore if people agree or disagree, because we'd rather live. To be or not to be, baby. What do you want? You want us to commit suicide for our enemy's sake? Here we are in the worst situation we've ever been and you manifest that marvelous Jewish tendency to see the other side more than our own!*

I am not taking the other side. All I'm saying is: both sides are guilty. Both are responsible.

G-d forbid, screams Jerusalem, *let's just see how even-handed you'd be if they killed —* Here the sister from Jerusalem says words that go too far, and both sisters become abruptly conscious of their mother, seated between them on the couch, head lowered as if she's been struck.

⁓

The sisters were never ever going to speak to each other again in their lives. Wolf Blitzer was reporting from Tallahassee that the Supreme Court would hear arguments on Friday about the counting of the ballots.

Jerusalem stormed out of the room. Oakland drove off to Ralph's Supermarket, to get a basting brush and a bunch of celery for the stuffing. In the car — she would tell her sister later that afternoon — she heard Peggy Post being interviewed by Linda Wertheimer on National Public Radio. *When families get together on Thanksgiving Day,* said Linda, *sometimes old tensions have a way of surfacing. Do you have any advice for our listeners in this regard?*

Certainly, said Peggy. *If there are old family issues that have been a source of disagreement in the past, these are usually best avoided for the duration of the holiday festivities. We might want to save those things for later on. And if there are family members at the gathering who don't see eye to eye on political issues, it might be best to just sort of steer clear of whatever might touch on somebody's sore spots.*

Would that include the election? You know, the whole recount issue? asks Linda. Peggy laughs politely. *Oh, yes! That could certainly spoil the family get-together!*

The sister from Oakland stopped off at a florist to pick up a bunch of pink tulips for her sister from Jerusalem. The sister from Jerusalem went out and got *Best American Essays of the Year* for her sister from Oakland. They exchanged the gifts (as their forefather Yaakov learned to appease his brother Esav, when he feared the latter might kill him), resolved to refrain in future from discussing G-d, Israel, Jews, Judaism, Arabs, Jewish identity, and Jewish history ancient and modern, at least until they were out of earshot, and agreed to talk only politics — American politics — since they and their mother are all Democrats.

So tell me: if even sisters can lay down their arms, can lions and lambs be far behind?

41

MER NISHT KEIN KINDT — IN THE LOST AND FOUND

To stand outside a room in the intensive care unit, where my mother is hooked up after her operation...

I'm standing outside the glass-walled room. *Is this happening?* She is recognizable, but not here. Her face and body are unanimated by *Mommy*, the person who is the ground of my being.

Is that the way to put it? These words I'm scribbling seem like such cheap and vulgar artifice for the sake of writing about it! Am I trying to keep my distance by writing at such a moment? Am I trying to *use* this experience? Ugly girl! Selfish!

After they buzzed me on through the electronically controlled double-doors into I.C.U., I followed all the way around the horse-shoe-shaped department until I got to Room 12. The Filipino nurse outside the door, busy with medical charts, saw my hesitation, and apparently thought I needed encouragement. "You can go on in."

I stood there not liking her encouragement, detesting her white tennis shoes and pink lipstick and pretty black pageboy. Now I see that all of that was because I didn't want to go in. But I didn't know how to think about that, that I didn't feel like going in there! I could see through the window.

I went in, of course. Who in the world would go to visit her precious mother in an intensive care unit and not go in? What kind of selfish daughter would do such a thing!

Having entered, I stood a few inches away from the bed. A number of minutes went by.

Oh, it was a no-man's-land, a gray void. *I should be doing — something else! Should be feeling something else. I am wrong. Faithless!* An awful place, this hospital room with its camera eyes and pale blank window high up over her head, too high to look out of, and this nice wallpaper trying to convince us fools this is some kind of Holiday Inn with maddeningly rising and falling graphs and beeping monitors. I'm suspended in some limbo of unexplainable self-contempt. The indignity for her, the unfairness and disrespectfulness of looking at Mommy when she can't look back. The person who has given me not only life, but all of the unconditional love and selflessness a daughter could dream of in a mother. She is a helpless, inert physical object, trapped in her body, but I am still privileged to be body and mind properly aligned.

This room's a horrendous hellish limbo between nothing and nothing.

I let a magnet draw me out of that void, into the corridor.

Now I'm back out here, standing next to Room 12's open door again, hating myself as I scribble in this notebook, looking back in at her through the glass. If not for the discernable rise and fall of the white hospital sheet over the shallow mound that is my mother upon the hospital bed, I would be plunging head-first this minute through a crevice into a black hole.

Next door, in room 13, there's an elderly Oriental woman, frail as a… as a… what can be said! Stupid words! This woman is so weak that she's already a dried-up rejected leaf, ignored by her family, wherever they are, her life crumpled up and being blown away, by itself, off into some unknown place. What can I say! Head fallen onto her own frail left shoulder, thinnest of faces collapsed in upon its own features.

I just looked up from my scribbling and my mother has... opened her eyes!

Mommy!

She's looking up at the ceiling!

<hr />

*To have your mother open her eyes...*The universe shifts, the stars shift into their proper spots. My heart starts beating.

Now my tongue belongs to me. I say, "Mommy?"

Her head moves slightly on the pillow. She looks at...*me!* Who? Am I the grandmother I am?

"Mommy?"

She smiles!

At me!

Az men farlirt de elteren, goes the Yiddish saying, *iz men mer nisht kein kindt.* "When you lose your parents, you are no longer a child." And as long as I have my Mommy's love, I myself am a little girl.

42

IN A TAXI

O n an October afternoon in the Old City of Jerusalem, waiting for a bus near the Western Wall and in a big hurry to get home, I approached a taxi for the five to ten-minute ride. "Are you available?" I asked, but after one glance at the driver's face, I abruptly walked off. The current wave of terrorism, which we would soon dub the second *intifada*, by far worse than the first one, in the 1980s, had just begun, on Rosh Hashanah. A few days before, an American Jewish student had been taken by a Palestinian taxi driver to an Arab neighborhood, where he'd been dragged from the car by a group of men and beaten.

But some hunch prompted me to turn around for another look, and sure enough, the car sported a bumper sticker, in Hebrew, *Shalom*. I hurried back, regretting the affront. "I'm so sorry," I said through his half-open window. "I thought you were an Arab."

I never used to talk like that.

The driver's profile, averted as I greeted him, lifted up towards me slightly — dark eyes running into mine then instantly flickering away. A man in his forties with an angular face, a thin line of black mustache, and the high-cheekbones and olive skin of a Yemenite Jew. *"Ani ken Aravi,"* he said with just a shadow of a strained half-smile. *I am an Arab.*

Silence fell. I stood there, and for a fraction of a second my narrowed eyes searched his, and his eyes deflected my gaze. That fleeting smile — though faint, uncomfortable, evasive — had somehow not aroused my fear. The bizarre question on the tip of my tongue, *Are you going to kill me?* didn't need articulation. He knew what I was thinking. "Can I travel with you?" I said, for some reason expecting him to answer honestly. "It would be all right?" which meant, *is it safe?*

He lowered his eyes and gave a quick nod.

"B'emet?" Really? Even as I chided myself for being ridiculous, my eyes were requesting the simple truth from this stranger, as if he were momentarily on my side, as if he'd say what was in my best interests, as if he wouldn't rather have me dead, as if, in fact, he'd care that a Jewish mother had to get home on time for her little girl's arrival from school.

He nodded fast several times, with some more tense smiling. He seemed strained by the humiliating nature of this conversation, but tolerant of it, too, for the sake of his fare. His eyes were replying, *I understand your fear, geveret. I understand why you insult me in this manner. But I pose no danger.*

I got in.

～～

At the junction by Dung Gate, a few hundred meters away, he did not turn left, which could have taken us toward the nearest Arab village, but right, along the curvy, uphill route that would take us in four or five minutes to downtown Jerusalem. The familiar, ancient hills that surround the capital came into view as we climbed, and the gray skies, that in this city always seem hung closer to earth, hinted at the rainfall for which we Jews, and probably Arabs, too, were praying.

In the back seat, I relaxed. We stopped at a red light. "Sir?" I ventured. He glanced back at me over his shoulder. "Do you mind if I ask you something?" He shrugged. "What do you think of everything that's happening?" I didn't need to explain.

"Everything that's happening?" he repeated in Hebrew. "Not good. Not good."

"You think we're going to have a war?"

"War? Oh, no. No, no. It will be all right."

"It will?" Optimism from an Arab was nice to hear. Maybe he knew something I didn't know. But of course I wasn't stupid enough to put stock in it. That week, two Israeli reserve soldiers, one a newlywed and the other a father of three, had been lynched after taking a wrong turn, and that was, for me, a turning point. For the first time in my life, war struck me as the mandatory response, simply the only appropriate reaction. I imagined, too, that I was ready for it now, whatever war involved, though I knew very well I couldn't fathom the suffering signified by the word. In any case, it was an interesting novelty for me, this anger that was so overwhelming it had turned to fearlessness. It produced a pleasurable illusion of strength. "What," I said, "you think we can live together?"

"Yes, certainly."

"But Arabs hate us."

"No, no. No, no."

"You don't? I sure find that hard to believe."

"No, no."

"Well, a lot of you do. Millions of you do."

"*Geveret*," he said in a low voice, his face turning momentarily to the back seat, as the walls that surround the Old City rose up on our right. "I do not hate Jews."

"That's nice. I'm glad. But I wonder how many other Arabs feel that way."

"It depends on what the parents teach their children. I have taught mine from their earliest years that when the other children come and say to them, 'Come, let's throw stones at the Jews,' they are not allowed to participate."

"Hmm. Does your wife feel the same way?"

"Yes, the same. You should speak to her."

"You want to live your life in peace with us?"

"Yes, *geveret*. I teach my children that Jews are people, too, just like us. That some Jews are good people. We have the same root. Our father Avraham. Our blood is red. Their blood is red. I wish you could hear me when I talk with my children. I tell them many Jews are good people, who just want to live their lives in peace and quiet."

"How many Arabs do you think there are who think the way you do?"

"Twenty years ago, thirty years ago, there were very few, but the number is growing. It is slow but the number is growing."

"How many of the Israeli Arabs do you think want to make peace with Israel?"

"Sixteen percent."

This brought a smile to my lips. "Sixteen percent? How do you know?"

"This is what I have read. I want peace with the Jews. They give us *parnasah*. If Arafat takes over, what *parnasah* will he give us? Our problem, *geveret*, is our leaders. Arafat gets money from all over the world. The Arab governments give him millions of dollars. And he gives none to us. He doesn't care if we suffer. It is all about meals. I cannot put meals on the table without tourists. With this violence, the tourists don't come. I don't understand what he wants. We have no choice. We share this land. We have to live together."

"What do you think of what happened in Ramallah?"

"This was not right. Not right at all. It was very, very wrong. Not the way to do things. They think that if you kill a Jew, you get *Gan Eden*."

It surprised me to hear the Hebrew word for Paradise on his lips. "You don't think that?"

"No. I tell them, if you want paradise, go right ahead, but I want a good life here in this world. I have to support my family."

"Oh, so you're not religious?"

He shook his head.

"Is that why you don't hate Jews?"

"No, that is not why. I studied the Koran and know it very well. The Koran does not say what they claim that it says. They want the Koran to say things it doesn't. You know what the Koran says? It says it is forbidden to kill a child, a woman, or an old person."

I wondered if the Koran held that it was meritorious to kill Jews as long as they were adult males, but thought better of it. What made me imagine he'd tell me the truth, anyway, and if he did, would I believe him? I just felt like keeping the conversation pleasant. "We go left here, at the stop light."

We turned into the narrow lane leading into the parking lot next to our apartment building. A garbage truck was blocking our way. As we sat there waiting, he said, "May I tell you the truth, *geveret*?" I nodded. He turned off the meter. "When I come in here, a Jewish neighborhood, and I see them collecting the garbage, and I see flowers planted, I think, why not our neighborhood? I live five minutes from here." He gestured toward East Jerusalem. "When I drive along our street, my car goes bump, bump, bump. All the potholes in the pavement that the municipality has never come to fix, no matter how many times we have requested it. Why? Because we are Arabs. And why do they only come once a week to collect our garbage? The smell is difficult to live with. Why? Because we are Arabs. I ask myself, Why? I pay taxes, I pay *arnonah*, thousands of *shekels*. My neighbor has many children and wanted to build another room and the municipality said no. So he built it anyway, because he hadn't enough room for his children. And they came with a bulldozer and destroyed his house. He is now without a house."

I sank into the back seat like a stone. I remembered a comment made about twenty-five years ago, by a friend of my father's, a Jewish lawyer in Connecticut: "If they don't improve the municipal services for Israeli Arabs, it will turn into a time bomb."

He went on. "I learned in Alexandria for four years to become an architect of ports. After the four years I went to Haifa and looked for work and they told me they could not take me because I am an Arab. Every time I walk into my house, I see the diploma staring at me from the wall. I got good marks. And I feel angry, what did I work so hard for? I feel I am in a corner."

"The people in the port probably couldn't hire you for security reasons. Because of the terrorism."

He nodded, then gestured to the roof and grinned sadly. "I know, I know. G-d made me an Arab. What can I do?"

"You wouldn't want to move to an Arab country? Where you'd be able to work in your field?"

He shrugged. "My father is here, my mother is here. My brothers and sisters. I was born here. This is my home." He paused. "And we cannot go to the Arab countries anyway."

"Oh. You mean they don't want you."

He didn't answer.

The garbage truck was starting to back out of our way. Then he said, "Can I tell you what I really think? I think Jews want to do to the Arabs what the Germans did to them."

I couldn't believe my ears. "What did you say?" He repeated himself. At first I thought he was just saying that for the sake of argument. Then I saw that he really believed it. For all I knew, maybe he had met Jews who gave him good reason to believe it.

"That's preposterous," I said. "Jews do *not* feel that way, there's no comparison whatsoever."

"Don't you see what's happening? Jews treat Arabs as if they're not human beings."

"That's only because of the fear. The terrorism has made normal relations between us impossible." I thought: all these roots are too entangled, too deep, to ever be straightened out, and was about to say, "Only G-d can solve this problem," but felt too dispirited.

"Don't you see how Arabs are treated here?" he went on. "All people want *parnasah,* but most of all we want to be treated like human beings. I don't ask for more than my portion. Just my portion as a human being and not more."

"I understand, but *adoni,* when you're afraid someone's going to pull out a knife, you're not looking at him normally. If not for terrorism, Jews would want peace with you, and you know it. We'd co-exist in a second. Look at this: you know what happens to us in Arab neighborhoods, but here you are in a Jewish neighborhood and you're not scared at all, because you know that Jews are not going to attack you. It's not our nature. Right?"

He nodded. "This is correct."

"Why is it that when a Jew does something wrong to an Arab, Jews all over the world protest, but when Arabs do something wrong, we don't hear anything. If you felt strongly enough against what your own people are doing, you'd protest. Even if there were a risk involved."

"*Geveret,* you do not know what I feel. I write for a newspaper every week and after the events in Ramallah I wrote in my column that it was wrong, that this was not according to the Koran. If you want, my wife and I will speak with you. I will give you my telephone number."

He asked for a pen and paper. "Can you also write down that line from the Koran for me?" He said yes, and after a minute returned my pen and spiral notebook.

The garbage truck lumbered off and he pulled up next to our entrance.

"This is from G-d that we have talked," he said. "You can come and visit us. You can talk to my wife."

"Thank you," I smiled. *And one of your neighbors could lynch me.* I looked at the meter, took out my wallet to pay, and we bid each other *shalom*.

Today, while cleaning out my purse a month later, I came across a page torn from my notebook and was startled by four lines of Arabic written in my own black ink, along with his Hebrew translation, his name, his wife's name, and their phone number.

I hesitated, not knowing at first what to do with it.

43

ONCE UPON A CAPPUCINO

The moment I'm going to tell you about, when I looked down at the cracked linoleum in the coffee shop and experienced peace, happened the same Tuesday that we realized our refrigerator was on the blink; the food was melting and dying faster than we could eat it.

In addition, the refrigerator breakdown occurred, oddly enough, the same week that my fax machine failed. I had received two faxes and nothing was on them.

So you can be forgiven for thinking I'm making it up when I tell you that just a few days before that, my laptop had started acting strangely. At first, it just wouldn't delete anymore, but I was able to fix this problem by pressing different keys until I undid whatever it was that I had done wrong. Then, however, it did something more ominous. It malfunctioned in conjunction with the printer: I'd press F7, as usual, at which point it's supposed to start printing. But instead, it would fall silent and do nothing whatsoever.

I sat at my desk and pressed F7 several hundred times. Each time, the printer's "online" light flickered hopefully, then went dark.

There was nothing to do but absorb the reality that this approach would probably never work. I pressed F7 a few more times, then called the computer people. Someone named Moshe told me I could bring the laptop and the printer to their Petach Tikvah branch and they'd take a look at them.

"Oh no!" I exclaimed. "All the way to Petach Tikvah? Don't you have a delivery service?"

At the delivery service place, I watched as they put my printer and my laptop into two boxes and set them on a counter under a handwritten sign saying "Tel Aviv." In my own mind, I prepared myself for losing them. Perhaps this would be the last time I'd ever see my laptop (I didn't care as much about the printer) because one thing I'm learning as I get older is that unexpected things happen, and that this is to be expected. Someone could tell me later that one of my machines had gotten lost in transit. Someone could claim that I'd never sent them. Someone could drop one of the boxes by mistake, like a baby from the arms of a negligent babysitter.

A few days later someone named Shmulik called to say the printer was ready.

"What about the laptop?" I asked.

"Yes, yes. Also the laptop."

I rushed out. When I arrived, Shmulik said that they hadn't found anything wrong with either the printer or the laptop.

Strained by the effort of being civil, as if I were a mature, spiritual person who doesn't fall apart when her machines do, I said, "There was something wrong with them!"

Shmulik connected the laptop and the printer and turned them on. When he pressed F7, nothing happened.

"Well," he said, "there doesn't seem to be anything wrong with the cable, but for some reason the computer's not communicating with your printer." I already knew that, but it felt good to have him say so. "You can bring it in to Moshe at the Talpiot branch and he'll take a look."

"The computer or the printer?"

"*Ken, ken.* Both."

Lucky I asked. I rushed over there with both of them, which made for an exciting story in its own right but one which I'd rather forget. Moshe plugged in the laptop and the bubble-jet and set up everything so we could enter a file, then pressed F7. My printer did not fall silent and go dark, as I had just said it would. Instead, it instantly and confidently started printing a document in what appeared to be a Cyrillic alphabet. My printer had never done that before. Moshe said it must be a problem with the board, and I'd be better off buying a new one.

"A new board?"

"A new printer."

"Oh, no!" My heart sank deeply. I packed up both machines and left.

Out on the sidewalk of Rechov Hillel, it had gotten hot, and the inarticulate buildings looked big and dense. Now what?

It was noontime. I lugged my two burdens over to a public telephone. A tall blonde Russian woman in a sunhat was speaking, to my satisfaction, in a Hebrew not as good as my own. At last it was my turn.

"There's no use hurrying home," said my husband, as I gazed up the hill at an El Al sign over Promised Land Tours. "You wouldn't be able to do anything in the kitchen anyway. I emptied out the whole refrigerator and there's water all over the floor."

"What do you think is wrong with it?"

"It needs defrosting. Ice got into the wiring, I think. So you can go do something in town, if you want. I'll be here when the kids come home. Have fun." I said goodbye and wondered who I was. It was vacation. I was losing my identity.

I called Mr. Stein to ask if my fax was ready.

"Yes, yes, you can come take it."

"What was the problem?"

"Oh … well, it was just a few things." He knows from experience that I ask such questions but never understand his answers. "It's working all right now, *baruch Hashem*."

"How much do I owe you?"

"Oh … no problem. No charge for this." Mr. Stein, whom I've heard is a brilliant *talmid chacham* at Mir Yeshiva, makes his parnasah fixing electrical equipment to perfection, but he often declines to accept payment if he considers the job to have been too easy.

"That's what you said last time."

"No, it was nothing, really. You can come get it."

I hung up and glanced at the sky for an answer. I wouldn't be able to go get the fax without first going home to drop off the laptop and bubble-jet, and I didn't want to go home, where there was water all over the kitchen floor. And I couldn't go shopping for anything while carrying the laptop and printer. These two machines were certainly weighing me down.

That's when the happy thought came to me that I would go have a cappuccino. This was followed by the unhappy thought that it would be a waste of time. Then came the happy thought of my dear sister Andrea. I could practically see her, right there next to me. How I wished she were here now, instead of so far away over the gray Atlantic! I'd suggest going out for coffee, she'd bring along a Sunday Times Book Review. Oh, how I wished! Wasting time in her company would make it all right. It wouldn't be a lost moment in the day, a blank gap; it would be something precious in itself.

As it was, I had only myself, with whom I would not be able to converse fondly across a table.

A few minutes later at my favorite little corner table in my favorite coffee shop, waiting for the waitress to come get my order, I was telling myself that theoretically, there was no reason I couldn't be as happy by myself as I would have been if Andrea were there.

Two young waitresses were absorbed in conversation at another table, taking deep drags on their Time cigarettes, and for some reason I didn't feel indignant about the second-hand smoke drifting over into the non-smoking section. My gaze went out the window. One flight down, out on the plaza, a man and a woman and a small child were eating at a round white plastic table, partly concealed under an umbrella imprinted with the insignia of the falafel place next door. I spied upon them from my bird's-eye view.

Was this a happy family or an unhappy family? Whenever the husband's gaze was drawn off abstractedly towards passersby, I figured they were unhappy. Then the woman would say something and smile and he'd smile back and they were happy, after all. They loved each other. How nice. The baby dropped her pita and the mother, in the middle of saying something to her husband, didn't get mad as she leaned down to get it. A good mother. I love good mothers. Then, a minute or two later, the father again got a bored, discontented, empty look, and I pitied them the futility of their lives. They don't realize that the obligations incurred by Judaism would connect their daily lives with the things that are eternal, I thought, that's their problem. They both looked very weary and drained, and seemed to be trying mightily to resist the body's natural tendency to disintegrate.

There was neither a writing notebook nor a pen in my purse, no way to jot down something about The Endless Frustrations of Daily Life, or: Here We See Various Members of the Human Race Having Falafel and Cappucino, Feeling Alienated From Their Creator. Would that be about me or them? Both, I decided. Maybe that topic would go well with the title, "Once Upon a Cappuccino," which had occurred to me years ago but for which a suitable subject had never come to mind.

In any case, I was so used to my laptop that writing with a pen was out of the question.

The waitresses were just starting to get on my nerves, sitting there talking and smoking like that instead of coming to take my order, when I noticed an International Herald Tribune two tables over, which someone had left behind amidst empty iced coffee glasses. How lovely! I got up and grabbed it, and was just descending into the robotic state provided by newspaper-reading when the waitress appeared abruptly at my little table and declared that she was sorry to have kept me waiting.

"That's all right," I said.

"I'm sorry," she repeated, with such frank, sincere regret that it took me aback. Since when does a waitress care about her responsibilities like that, and expose her vulnerability by admitting it so sweetly? I ordered cappuccino, making sure to specify extra whipped cream, then turned with relish to the as yet unseen inside pages. *Voters Not Buying Dole's Economic Message.* Good. *Disputed Tunnel to Be Opened in Jerusalem.* Hmmm. What's that? *Suspect in Penn State Killing Had Tried to Kill Herself.* Sad! *Swiss Banks Holding Gold Deposited by Nazis after WW II.* Ha! *Sensitive Papers on Tobacco Research Secretly Destroyed by Philip Morris.* Ha! Pay attention, girls! *Iraq Said to Have Evaded International Inspection of Chemical, Biological Weapons.*

I didn't want to think about that.

Fourth Chernobyl Reactor Exhibiting Evidence of Chain Reaction: Sarcophagus Developing Radioactive Leaks.

Chernobyl's a few hundred miles from Israel. Whether nuclear radioactivity is released underground, underwater, or into the atmosphere, it is indestructible and indiscriminate, and eventually travels everywhere, with no regard whatsoever for boundaries, concrete or otherwise: it enters the soil, water, and air, the cells of our bodies, and the ground beneath my sister's feet, and into her water, and air. Once released, there's no controlling or evading it. Ultimately, the ludicrous concrete sarcophagus built after the Chernobyl accident will no more contain the lethal radiation than would a coffin made of aluminum foil.

I didn't want to think about that.

Down on the plaza, my happy or unhappy family had vanished, and two women tourists in their seventies were now in the mother's and father's chairs. My waitress arrived, setting down before me a tower of whipped cream, along with a long silver spoon, poised upon the saucer. The spiraled dome was rising up in all its tempting smoothness — all mine, all white — and just then, from the speaker overhead, a Bach harpsichord came on! My favorite music! I lifted the silver spoon to my lips; said the *berachah* with intense kavannah; the spoonful of calm whipped cream entered the dark pool of my mind like a little stone sending out silvery glittering ripples on black water. What an inexplicable phenomenon, sound waves in the eardrums that produce an emotional response! My glance then happened to fall upon my right shoe, spotlighted inside an oblong rectangle of sunlight that had alighted there weightlessly and laid itself down upon the cracked linoleum, and the shoe was in the middle of the light proclaiming its splendid brown ordinariness on the unpolished gray-spotted floor, when suddenly, out of the blue, an unexpected stream of happiness rose up out of nowhere.

It was a current electrically nourished by caffeine and sunlight, and it was ribboning upwards and spreading out into a pool of shining tranquility.

It was growing still larger. It seemed to be enclosing within its swelling diameter all my life's small stupidities and dissatisfactions. It was tenderly encircling my greatest fears, and the apparent emptiness of so many quotidian things, and the apparent absence of meaning. *The point is not what happens to us in our lives* — Rebbetzin Heller once said something along these lines in a shiur — *but who we become in the process.*

But even as I sat there enclosed by melody, filling to the brim with harpsichord, I was getting worried about losing this splendid and rare consciousness; I knew all too well that any second now, this ephemeral flow of perfection — in which all aspects of life bore the Name of the Creator — would slip away. How long could it last, this sublime, peaceful acceptance of the absence of peace, especially since I was already worrying about losing it? How I wished it were possible to quickly draw everything in the world into the scope of its rare illumination.

I looked outside to the plaza down below, and lo and behold, who of all people should be passing by just then, but Yehuda Wachsman. His teenage son, Nachshon, of blessed memory, had been kidnapped and executed by Arab terrorists a few years before. It was Mr. Wachsman who had comforted the thousands of people who had come to the Kotel to pray for his son's rescue with the line that became famous: "Sometimes a Father says no to His children."

Mr. Wachsman was walking along with one of his other children, around 12 years old. He was talking to her as if everything were all right, though as everyone knows, he had suffered one of the most painful and tragic losses possible in this world.

That did it. My mind couldn't expand adequately to contain the reminder of that event. Bach went right on going but the current had already been cut, and the afternoon restored to its broken, obscure self.

The ribbon of light, the radiant pool ... gone.

A few weeks later the Hasmonean Tunnel would be opened, eliciting Palestinian protests and global condemnation; the world does not welcome archaeological evidence of the Jews' historical presence in the land we are accused of stealing from the Palestinians.

Soon thereafter, the rifles which were given by Rabin's government to the Palestinian Police Force, as an act of trust during the Oslo Peace Process, were for the first time used not, as promised, against Hamas but against Jews — catapulting us into what would quickly become our new, unpredictable, exponentially more dangerous, turbulent era. A sharply increasing number of Israelis would now start undergoing the most painful losses possible, in wave upon wave upon wave of attacks. Over a morning cup of coffee in my living room, I would read an article in The International Herald Tribune about "Palestinian Rage and Despair" and would be shot through with rage and despair. If only I could recognize that the rage and despair and the radiant pool, the water on the kitchen floor and the waitress's regret, the escaping radiation, the whipped cream, the global condemnation and the cracked linoleum ... all of them emanate from one Source.

By the time you read this, that oddly behaving laptop will have crashed and been replaced long ago, and the Tuesday described here will have already slipped into oblivion, as will all these words spent in a futile attempt to capture and redeem it.

The printer was beyond repair, but the fax and refrigerator are working.

Unexpected things happen.

There's sunlight under our feet.

44

ON FINGER POINTING

One spring morning in Jerusalem, a few weeks after the end of the Gulf War, I found myself in line at the local supermarket behind the mother of Esther, one of my neighbors. Passover was fast approaching and this woman's shopping cart, like mine, was full of such things as Scotch Brite and silver polish, bottles of bleach and rug shampoo, but neither of us seemed overwhelmed, as we might have been in other years, by the prospect of household slavery. We were much too full of joy for that.

With gusto, we'd torn down the plastic sheeting that our husbands had installed scrupulously over the windows; had tossed our ghoulish gas masks back into their boxes and stored them on the highest shelves. Ever since Iraq's invasion of Kuwait the previous summer, the prospect of some horrible death had been looming over us. We had faced an unthinkable unknown for seven months, ever since Saddam Hussein first threatened to retaliate against United States intervention by using chemical and/or biological weapons against Israel. Now we were free. Hussein's abrupt surrender had taken us all by surprise. And its wonderful timing — the news had been announced on Kol Israel just as Megillah scrolls were being opened throughout Israel — had instilled into the event an implausible dimension of the miraculous.

The rescue was as inexplicable as the strange Gulf War itself had been and we were not only grateful but proud. For we had stayed. We had weathered the storm, and our ample reward for not fleeing had been to witness with our own eyes the bizarre unfolding of events.

But amidst all this rejoicing there was something about the whole experience that I, and Esther's mother, and many other American immigrants, were not thinking about anymore, in the wake of our liberation.

It was our own secret and solitary inner wars, about the children, that we were already forgetting. *To stay or to go?* It had been a daily torment. *To leave is to lose faith, but to stay is to expose the children to...* We didn't know what. *To leave is to reveal ourselves as cowards, to give the children a role model of cowardice. But to leave is to protect them. Are we risking their lives for the sake of our pride? Perhaps it's sheer madness. To stay is naïve idiocy. But to leave is to teach them to run. They'll always remember our lack of faith. To leave is responsible. To leave is irresponsible. To stay is responsible. To stay is irresponsible.*

Casting its vast shadow over all this was the Holocaust. It was never far from our thoughts. *Maybe we're doing what they did in Europe, not getting out while it's still possible. But then again, nobody ever claimed Europe was the Promised Land. Hashem never said, Lech lecha, get thyself to Poland.*

Now, standing there on the checkout line, I inadvertently stepped onto this minefield. *Where's Esther?* I said. *I haven't seen her around.*

The woman's face underwent a faint change. *Esther's in Borough Park.*

Oh, that's nice.

No. It's not. She wants to come back.

So... why doesn't she? I thought, I shouldn't have said that. There's an illness in the family.

Because she left right before the war, so she's ashamed now to show her face in Jerusalem. She'd even made an appointment with a professional security man from the municipality. He came over and told them that as far as gas was concerned, it wasn't ideal they were on the ground floor, but he thought it would be O.K. He advised them how to prepare the house, which room was best for their sealed room, etc., etc. They bought bottled water, the canned goods. They had the gas masks all set. Everything. But she started to get almost ill, from fear, of something happening to the children.

≈≈

These issues have surfaced again during the present *intifada.* Should Jews in the diaspora lend us their moral support by permitting their children to come here? Should they publicly demonstrate that Arab terrorism will not succeed in scaring them away?

Ascertaining statistical risk is an ambiguous business. Is the current *intifida* such that children are in more danger here than they are from earthquakes in Los Angeles, highways in Long Island, or drug dealers in the suburbs? We who see the daily situation firsthand obviously think not. Otherwise, the Torah commandment of *pikuach nefesh,* to guard our lives, would have obligated us to leave long ago. One of the perks of getting older (no matter when in history you happen to come along, and no matter where on earth you've settled) is that time, of itself, does gradually reveal the reality that danger is intrinsic to human life on the planet. If we design our existence around the futile effort to evade it, we expose our children to the greatest danger of all: the life devoid of trust in God.

Yet we as parents are wired for cowardice. Another name for that is protectiveness, and another name for protectiveness is love. Like Esther, most of us are subject to the self-doubts, fears and harrowing decision-making which any responsible parent knows only too well. It is a unique brand of agony.

I'm forever thankful we stayed here during the Gulf War. The act of faith did strengthen us in unforeseen ways. Most of our children — one of them is a mother now herself — are adults making their own decisions. They're voting with their feet. Their roots are here, and I'm glad beyond words, and there's nowhere else I want to be, or want them to be. But back in 1990, if my husband had just given the nod, I would have forgotten my pride, and my faith, and anything else that seemed to threaten their safety. I would have scooped up the kids — as *my* parents were begging us to do — and gotten out on the first available flight.

The Jewish way, it seems to me, would not be to demand, or even to encourage, parents to bravely send their children into situations they perceive as dangerous for the sake of a political goal. In my opinion, those of us who live here should take responsibility for our choices and not impose them on others.

Who can judge others when it comes to the lives of children? It is a realm of behavior off-limits to dispute. A worried parent — even an unduly worried parent — might well expect his brethren to empathize, not criticize; to identify rather than to judge.

45

"HAKADOSH BARUCH HU ... IS NOT GOING TO LEAVE YOU"

AN INTERVIEW WITH MRS. MIRIAM BROVENDER

The beating itself isn't what she seems most interested in discussing. Yet the reason I've come here, to her home, for an interview, is to find out what actually happened. The few, brief newspaper accounts hadn't provided details. That her husband had taken a wrong turn and had ended up in a Palestinian village, I have already read in The Jerusalem Post. That he had been speaking to her on his cellular phone when the connection was lost; that when someone finally got through, a man speaking Arabic had answered, "He's dead," and then hung up — these uncorroborated reports I had heard through the grapevine.

Miriam Brovender nods when I say that there had been little about it in the papers. "Why didn't the secular press call me? An Israeli reporter from Maariv came to the hospital when my husband arrived that first night, and asked permission to take pictures of him, but publishing a photograph of Rabbi Brovender in that condition did not seem right. For what purpose? I felt the reporter was looking for a certain sensationalism. It's a shame. If they had publicized the story, maybe we could have avoided the lynching. The story of the lynching was almost exactly parallel."

The incident to which she is referring took place a week after the one which involved her husband, Rabbi Chaim Brovender. Two Israelis on reserve duty, one a father of three and the other a newlywed, took a wrong turn, ended up in Ramallah, and were taken to the Palestinian police station, where they were beaten by a crowd and dragged through the streets. The two Israelis died. Their bodies were mutilated.

So as we in Israel are pressured, from within and without, to bring to completion the destruction of our country called the Oslo Peace Process, it's my intention to accurately record Rabbi Brovender's personal encounter with the particular brand of uninhibited violence which characterizes Arab culture. But Mrs. Brovender doesn't seem to be responding exactly as I expected to the gist of my inquiries. "My husband has his story," she says, "and I have mine," whereupon she begins, not with the evening of October 5th — when Rabbi Brovender was ordered out of his car by two Palestinian policemen — but at another point in time. It becomes apparent that for her, the main story isn't the cruelty. As she sees it, to convey the meaning of the event which has changed her life, first she has to take a few steps back, to a different era altogether.

❧ ❧

"My Zeide, Eliezer Krulovetsky, came to America in 1901 and brought over the family from Baranovitch at the turn of the century. He saved up money and brought over my great-grandparents, my great-aunts and uncles, my cousins, and got them all set up in New York. The relatives lived with them in their house when they

arrived, then he would find them housing and jobs. My grandmother's two younger sisters, Malka and Osna, were among those
whom he brought over.

"Osna got married at the age of 30, which was very uncommon in those days in an Orthodox family. She only wanted to
marry a man who had *yiras Shamayim*, who wouldn't work on
Shabbos, and at last she found what she was seeking when she
married Meshulem Yoel Zuckerman. Osna had three children.
Those three children have over 150 great-grandchildren, and at
the time of her death, Osna was *zochah, b'li ayin hara*, to have
just had her ninth great-great grandchild.

"October 5th, that Thursday, turned out to be a very unusual day. That morning, we went to Osna's *levayah.* She died
at the age of 102. I know Osna as well as I know myself. We
were very, very close. I can't begin to tell you about who this
pure woman was. Her *emunah temimah*, her love for *Klal
Yisrael.* Everyone felt special with her. Her warmth was overwhelming. She always blessed whoever was in her presence that
Hashem should always give us everything good. She would always say, 'Don't worry, Hashem has to help. He *will* help.' When
the beating was going on, just hours after her *petirah*, I really
think she was crying up in *Shamayim*, 'You can't let this happen.
You must do something.'

"At 6:40 that evening, I was talking to my husband on his
cellular phone. He was on his way back from Efrat early, to be
menachem avel Osna's son, and was calling to say that he would
be a little late because the tunnel in the Gush had been closed.
Two Palestinians who had thrown fire bombs had been shot by
Israeli soldiers. I asked him where he was going and he said he
was going to follow the car in front of him that had an Israeli
license plate. It was already dark and I got nervous. I said,
'Where are you going? How do you know where you're going?'
All of a sudden I heard a sound — an unfamiliar sound — and
the mobile phone turned off. I dialed him back. There was no
answer. I kept dialing and dialing and all of a sudden somebody
answered and I could hear it was an Arab. I shouted, *'Mi zeh?*

Mi zeh?' I wanted my husband to hear me, I wanted him to know I was calling, that I knew something was happening. The Arab said, 'Mistake, mistake,' and hung up."

≈≈

"It was *aseres y'mei teshuvah.* My girls were out doing shopping for Succos. So I was alone in the house. And I was overwhelmed with a fear that I've never had before in my life. I've experienced all kinds of situations in connection with war here in Israel. There have been many times I was very afraid. But this — it was fear of the unknown — it took over every bone in my body. It must be what's meant by the fear on the Day of Judgment. I think it's what *HaKadosh Baruch Hu* wants us to feel on the Day of Judgment.

"I decided there would be no purpose in telling the children yet what was going on, that I should try to deal with it by myself, so I called a friend in Efrat and said, 'I'm scared. I'm terrified.' I told her what happened. She said, 'Let me call the *Moked* [central command] in Efrat.' In a minute Danny, in charge of the *Moked,* called me and said, 'Give me the number of his mobile. Don't worry. It will be all right.' Danny dialed my husband's number, there was no answer, and finally after many tries, someone picked up. Danny said, 'Where is the owner of the car?' And a man said in Arabic, 'He's dead. We just killed him.'

"Now, Danny had the good sense not to call me back with this news. He called Rabbi Shlomo Riskin of Efrat and said, 'Sit down. I have information to tell you and I don't know if it's accurate.' Rabbi Riskin ran out to the yeshivah in Efrat and told the boys to start saying *tehillim* for the *matzav* [general situation]. He didn't want to say yet what he had heard from Danny.

"By this time, an hour later, my daughters had returned from shopping and I was getting phone calls from the army and the police, so of course they felt something and I had to tell them. They started screaming and crying, crying out to *HaKadosh Baruch*

Hu." Miriam smiles to herself with a look of deep satisfaction. "They did some great *davening.*

"How come I answered the phone at 6:40? Usually I would have been in my office working then." Miriam Brovender does marital and adult counseling. "How come the Arab answered my husband's phone when I called, and then when Danny called? Upstairs, *HaKadosh Baruch Hu* was ringing the bell: 'Now is the time to *daven.* I will do My part, you do yours.' And the yeshivah *bochurim* were *davening* out there in the yeshivah. *Avinu Malkenu,* rip up the bad decree. *Avinu Malkenu,* tear up the bad decree. Even after Succos, that line kept coming back to me.

"And while all this was going on, and my daughters were crying out and saying *tehillim,* something else was going on with me.

"I have a study session three times a week with Shifra Slater on *Nesivos Shalom,* the *sefer* of the Slonimer Rebbe. We've been doing it for a year and a half and it has had a tremendous impact on my life. That evening, throughout the hours that I was waiting, I had the *sefer* open and I just kept reading a few paragraphs again and again, I kept hearing him say over and over again, 'We are the children of *HaKadosh Baruch Hu. HaKadosh Baruch Hu* is not going to leave you.' I was listening to the Slonimer Rebbe, and it was as if he were speaking to me. I was engrossed in the words I heard him whispering in my ears: "We are the children of *HaKadosh Boruch Hu. HaKadosh Boruch Hu* is not going to leave you,' and I heard myself saying to the girls, reassuring them, everything will be O.K., *HaKadosh Baruch Hu* will help. And this is because of the *emunah temimah* of my grandmother, and of my great-aunt Osna. I grew up in my grandmother's house and I always used to hear her say a Yiddish expression, '*HaKadosh Baruch Hu* is just and His decree is just.'

"How is it that my husband didn't die from the beating? It's as if Hashem wrapped him up with pillows. His body and face were bleeding from being kicked and beaten and dragged, two ribs were broken, one of his lungs was perforated. The Arab who answered the phone thought they had killed him. When we got to the hospital and saw him in the emergency room, it was too painful to look. We greeted him, then had to walk away to cry. Only then did I realize what could have been. Hashem had *rachamim.*

"They X-rayed him in the hospital for an hour and a half. He had turned grey from not breathing properly so right there in the emergency room they performed an emergency procedure on the membrane of his lungs — they couldn't delay it. He was released Sunday morning, *erev* Yom Kippur, but then had to be brought back on Monday, Chol HaMoed Succos, because of a life-threatening *shoshanah* [cellulitis] infection in the muscles, from being dragged along the ground. It looked the way it does when a child falls and bruises himself but they were long bruises, long red scratches, very raw, all over his body. The infection was spreading to the rest of his body. He received a tremendous amount of intravenous antibiotics. He's still on antibiotics. When the dentist arrived early the next morning and looked at his face, he thought he'd have to do extensive work, but found that there was no damage, *b'li ayin hara*, to his teeth. There were bruises and cuts right next to his eyes, but not in his eyes. All around his ears, but not the ears themselves. Then he had another operation to draw out and drain the pus from inside his leg.

"*HaKadosh Baruch Hu* prepares the cure before the affliction. The Slonimer Rebbe had such a love for every Jew, and after Shifra introduced me to his writings and I started to learn his Torah — which she suggested that we study together on the phone from 8:15 to 8:30 — I started taking the *sefer* wherever I go.

"I am *frum* from birth, and was nursed on *tefillah*. The adults in my childhood ingrained in me that we are never alone. Never alone. They ingrained the idea that when faced with a difficult situation — no matter how overwhelming — all we have to do is cry out, and He is there. So because of how I was brought up, it came naturally. I grabbed his *sefer* and just kept reading this paragraph over and over and over: 'Even in times of darkness you have to know that *HaKadosh Baruch Hu* loves us and takes care of us.' It's the truth, even though we don't know it.

"That moment when I heard the voice of an Arab, a stranger, it brought to mind Nachshon Wachsman, of blessed memory — how it was when he was out there somewhere in the hands of enemies, darkness covering all. I had to tell myself, *Stop! Focus! I'm not alone. I need You desperately now, this very moment. You are still with me, it's hidden but I can allow myself to feel the concern, Your love. I've been preparing all my life for this moment. I sense in every part of my being Your protection and warmth and love. I'm safe. My husband is safe. I have You.* For the three hours of that terrible fear, during which I didn't know what was going on and the fear of danger all around was overwhelming, all-encompassing, I read those lines again and again and again, right up until the moment I heard my husband's voice again. *Ahavah rabbah...* I read again and again the lines that *HaKadosh Baruch Hu* loves us. Count how many times in the paragraph before the *Shema* those words appear, *ahavah rabbah*. You have to know that and to start to believe it. Those words — now they jump out at me."

〰〰

"Let's go back to the story.

"The taxi my husband had followed was that of an Israeli Arab, and suddenly he found himself in Beit Jala. Two Palestinian policemen stopped him, and waved on the other cars as they signaled to him to get out of his car. He locked his doors and gestured that he just wanted to turn around, but the road was too narrow, a single lane, and there were cars before him and behind him. Then they took their rifles and started banging on his windshield, so he got out and started explaining to them that he had made a mistake. They didn't want to listen. They grabbed him and threw him against a wall — this was happening very quickly — on a dark, narrow street. He saw them calling someone on their mobile phones and all of a sudden there was a band of about thirty Arabs. Adults, not children, who threw him on the ground and started to stomp him with their army boots, jumping on him, beating and kicking him all over his body. They had no knives and thank G-d, my husband doesn't believe in carrying a gun, because they could have used it on him. The thing I can't understand, aside from his survival, is that he didn't pass out. He stayed conscious the whole time. The beating lasted between five and seven minutes. He says now that the pain was a *chessed*, because while it was going on, he got so involved in the pain that he wasn't able to think. He says that had he been able to think, he might have gone crazy. It seemed to him like a scene from the Holocaust. The Palestinian policemen stood by watching as it was going on.

"Then a jeep arrived — it seemed to him to come out of nowhere — and all of the men ran away. Two policemen got out who were apparently a higher rank than the first two, and they pushed him into their jeep. This is when he realized they were not going to kill him. Only later did I find out how it was that the second jeep arrived. After Danny spoke to the Arab who had my husband's phone, he called up high authorities in the Army, who called higher authorities, who got in touch with the Palestinian Police and said, 'We know you have him.'

"The second pair of Palestinian policemen drove for about five minutes. My husband didn't know where they were taking him. Then they told my husband to get out of the jeep, and he found himself being directed towards what turned out to be the Palestinian Police building in Bethlehem. This very police headquarters was blown up a week or so later, when a bomb that was being prepared, for use against Israelis, prematurely exploded and blew up the building.

"In the compound at the entrance to that building, the two policemen stood and watched as another group of Arabs came and beat him up for another three, four minutes, then they told the men to stop. The policemen helped him up and took him inside, where he was met by two men who said they were doctors, though there were no visible signs of their being doctors, and that he was now in the infirmary, though it was an empty room.

They took some cotton and alcohol and wiped off his face and hands, and lifted up his clothes and wiped off some of the blood. With hindsight, we understood that they wanted to clean him up a little before handing him over to the Israelis.

"One of the 'doctors' at this point made a little speech, in which he was saying how wonderful Arabs are. He said, 'You're a very lucky man, because if you had been an Arab and we were Israelis, you would have been long gone.' Now, my husband is not the type to keep quiet at such a moment. He is a person who by nature will say what he thinks. This is one of the many things about the story that amaze me: Hashem closed his mouth.

"They put him into a detention cell, where they gave him a drink of water. He wasn't able to breathe and he asked for an inhalator but they didn't have one. He became aware that in the other room, a Palestinian official was negotiating with an Israeli officer. At that point, he asked the Israeli if he could use his cellular phone and that's when he called me."

Miriam Brovender pauses here and her eyes, cast down, are averted. I can see that she is crying, and that she is focused on regaining control of herself. "When he said my name, I said, 'Chaim, how are you?' And he said, 'I'm alive. In Bethlehem.'"

After some moments, she continues. "His voice sounded horrible. Then he hung up. Later, he explained to me why he hung up. He was unable to focus. His head was not so grounded, and he wasn't sure that that official was really an Israeli. He thought it might put me in danger that he was calling me.

"The Israeli army then called me to tell us that he was safe but wounded, and they were transferring him by armored army ambulance to Gilo, and from there by civilian ambulance to Hadassah Ein Kerem." Gilo is now being shot at daily from Beit Jala, so at the idea of Gilo as a safe haven, Miriam and I exchange ironic glances. "I know. I know," she says. "Gilo. It's a joke. Before being transferred, though, first he was taken to the office of the governor of Bethlehem. He produced Chaim's briefcase and told him to open the briefcase and check that everything was there. My husband knew where he had put everything and it seemed that everything was still there, even including the $300 in cash that he had had, but then he checked his wallet and there were 4,000 *shekels* missing. He said so, and the official pretended not to hear.

"This is part of the miracle.

"We believe that *teshuvah, tefillah,* and *tzedakah* remove the evil decree, and know that *tzedakah* saves a person from death." Miriam smiles her smile again. "Where were the 4,000 *shekels?*"

❧ ❧

"Before the Holocaust, my mother-in-law had been told by the Rebbe in Rokitna, in the Ukraine, to leave, and so she did. Later on, her whole family was killed in the Holocaust. With one exception, she found information about how each family member had perished. But for the next twenty-five years, she didn't know what had happened to her brother, Chaim Zandweiss.

"After the Holocaust, Chaim Zandweiss ended up in Siberia. After fifteen years, somehow he got out, via Poland, and from there went to Israel. He had lost his wife and his child in the Holocaust and he never remarried. My mother-in-law finally located him here, and my husband put up a *tzedakah* fund in his name, *Keren Chaim v' Chesed.* The 4,000 *shekels* was money my husband had collected for that fund and had planned to distribute on *erev Shabbos Shuvah.*

I feel that this uncle was crying out, 'This *tzedakah* is in my memory. You have to do something. You have to let my name live on. You have to save him. He's carrying on my memory.'

"On October 6th, Friday, the morning after the incident, I started getting phone calls from all over the world. People had seen the paragraph that had appeared on the front page of The Jerusalem Post, and were asking me what they could do to help. I said that they should please give thirty-six *shekels* to any *tzedakah* of their choice, and that this money would be for *ho-dayah*, thankfulness to *HaKadosh Baruch Hu*, and for a *refuah sheleimah* for Chaim ben Sara Rachel. I didn't want to mention that fund in particular, but when people in both Israel and America started hearing about what had happened to the stolen 4,000 *shekels* earmarked for *tzedakah*, they started sending in money to it, and in the end, there was more money in the fund than before the incident.

"My husband's former *talmidim* from all over the world, some dating back thirty years, started setting up *tefillah* and *tehillim* groups for his *refuah sheleimah*. And a thousand people came out on the streets of Riverdale saying *tehillim* for his recovery. So, all these people were crying out, 'You have to let him live. You have to let him work.'"

～～

"If I had been granted a wish when my husband came back to the emergency ward on Chol HaMoed, it would have been for a father to be there in the hospital to guide and advise me, someone knowledgeable about medicine and surgery who would have known how to direct the doctors and tell them what to do. If I had written a letter to *HaKadosh Baruch Hu*, a little selfish part of me would have said, 'Please, don't leave me alone here to make decisions. I can't do it.'

"On Thursday morning in the hospital, one of my daughters came to me and said, 'There's somebody here to see you.' It was a 21-year-old boy and his parents. This young man had once been one of my husband's *talmidim*, and he had come back to spend this Elul in the yeshivah. He had lost his father when he was five years old and his mother had brought him up on her own. My husband had been like a father to him. I said, 'Binyamin, how are you?' and his eyes filled with tears. He said, 'I only want to see the Rabbi for two minutes, I'm not going to disturb him. I just have to see him.'

"It is written, 'May you always be blessed to be givers and never have to take.' My husband has always tried to follow that, and it's very difficult for him to take. But lo and behold, the boy's mother, Chavy Neiman Hirschman, had in later years married Dr. Sholom Hirschman, who for twenty-eight years had been the head of the Department of Infectious Diseases at Mt. Sinai Hospital in New York. He was the doctor for the Satmar Rebbe, the Klausenberger Rebbe, the Lubavitcher Rebbe. And now, the Hirschmans had come to Israel to spend Succos with Binyamin.

"This is where my wish came true. This man walked us through the experience we were about to undergo. The doctors knew who he was and showed him tremendous respect. He was in Israel until just after Succos, directing my husband's treatment, and when he left, he said, 'We're leaving the country, but we are just a phone call away. Call me at any hour, day or night.'"

≈≈

"We've learned so much about what *chessed* is. When you're a recipient, you learn about it in a whole new way. For instance, in Hadassah Hospital on Simchas Torah, my husband wanted to go to the shul downstairs but he couldn't get off the bed. A *chassid* was there on the ward for his father, and he said, 'Wait here, I'll be back in five minutes.' He came back with a wheelchair and said, 'Come, we're going down for *Minchah*.' My husband was so overwhelmed.

"*Chessed* is about doing. It's about getting the job done. Making it happen. That's what we saw, over and over again.

"Why is it so difficult? Why do we procrastinate, avoid it, turn away from those moments that *HaKadosh Baruch Hu* presents to us? It's so simple, yet so hard. A phone call, a smile, an encouraging word. Noticing what the other person is in need of. We are all so busy, so preoccupied — with valid reasons, of course. If we open up, just a tiny bit, that's all it takes to begin our journey. The rewards are so great and fulfilling, may Hashem guide our first steps, and from there, on and on.

"I thought I understood a lot about people and interpersonal relationships. But I just think that what happened has sensitized both of us in such a profound way.

"This is the love that *HaKadosh Baruch Hu* has for us. For each of us. *HaKadosh Baruch Hu* gives each person his or her own special talents for how to do *chessed*, and each individual's talents are unique. No two people have the same talents. We have an obligation to develop these talents, to keep developing them, to sanctify *HaKadosh Baruch Hu's* Name in the world.

"I don't think either of us will ever be the same."

"The morning before the day of my husband's discharge, he woke up and remembered that it was the day of a *chasunah* at which he had been asked to be *mesader kiddushin*. I thought he had forgotten about it. He said to me, 'Make arrangements for leaving the hospital at 3:00 so that we can get to the *chasunah* on time.' He dressed in his Shabbos clothes and it was like the beginning of a closure. The experience started with the story of a great woman who built her *bayis ne'eman*, and now he had the *zechus* to help a young couple at the beginning of their building a *bayis ne'eman*.

"Last week, we had the *zechus* of the *bris* of the first grandson to bear the Brovender last name, and whose father, our son Eliezer Menashe, is named after Zeide Eliezer.

"I hear the Rebbe's words over and over again. *HaKadosh Baruch Hu* loves us, we are His children, and here I am witnessing once again the miracle of birth. And somehow the continuity of *HaKadosh Baruch Hu's* kindness... I can't put it into words. They say that a child born brings a *refuah* to a family. I feel very much Hashem having mercy upon His

Creation. Now I'm crying for happiness, with *hakaras hatov*. When I say the morning *davening* now — things I've said a million times, all of my life — all of a sudden the words jump out at me. They have a personal meaning for me now. I cry out as I have at the appointed times during the year but now it's different. All the *davening* has become a personal *tefillah*, and as I *daven*, I feel that now I own this *tefillah*. I join all the generations who have cried out at times of sorrow, and my small little voice becomes greater by tenfold, because all these generations are crying out with me.

"What my husband went through is part of our history, like what Jews have gone through over the centuries, and what many other Jews are going through now during these days. The blows are coming. But the *tefillos* are overcoming the blows. The moment of connection has come.

"At the *levayah* of Osna in America, on the day before the incident, her son Aharon said in his *hesped*, 'It is a time of trouble for Yaakov, and from it he shall be saved.'

46

WHO IS RICH?

When the doctor delivered the news, we were abashed and afraid. How much time did we have? When she started to walk haltingly, we were abashed and afraid. She'd never moved around slowly like that before in her life!

When the lab test came back, we were so relieved. It looked like she was going to make it! When she got some of her energy back, we were so happy!

When she started to sit down a lot, we were abashed and afraid.

When she stopped reading everything except the morning paper, we were abashed and afraid. She had always been such a big reader.

When she stopped driving, we were abashed and afraid. She had always driven everywhere!

Now she sat in the passenger's seat.

When she stopped reading the morning paper and we'd read to her, we longed to see her with The New York Times in hand.

It took her forever just to make herself breakfast.

When she started lying down right after breakfast, we got worried. We wished she would spend her mornings sitting up.

When she'd drop off to sleep while being read to, we wished she'd listen all the way through.

When she could no longer stand there to make breakfast, we were abashed and afraid. She was the one who always fed everybody! She had always made herself breakfast! We couldn't believe what was happening. We made her breakfast.

When she could only eat half, we longed to see her finishing everything on her plate, the way her father had taught her; all her life she'd obeyed him.

We longed to see her in the passenger's seat.

When she didn't have the energy to listen, we looked back wistfully at the way we used to read to her, and wished we had read to her more. We could have read her various things. Why hadn't we taken her places? Maybe she would have enjoyed the museum.

We longed to see her in her chair.

When she couldn't get out of bed, we thought: Just yesterday she got out of bed! It seemed so long ago. She'd walk across the living room to the kitchen.

When she couldn't feed herself anymore, we fed her, shyly.

When she could only finish about a third, we yearned for the time when she'd eat half.

When we realized she couldn't swallow, we thought to ourselves: Just yesterday she was able to eat.

When she stopped speaking, we looked back on our little conversations as if they were diamonds.

We sit and watch. She doesn't seem to be seeing us.

But she is breathing!

We rejoice. She is breathing!

47

TO BE OR NOT TO BE

I t has always struck me as bizarre, mysterious and absurd that Israel's essential right to exist is ever a question in the eyes of the world. That which for other nations is a given, is for us something we must try to prove, in each successive generation. No matter that the one spot we claim as our own takes up less space then New Jersey. No matter that our presence here goes back three millennia. For Israel, it always becomes, again and again — as it has for Jews throughout history — a matter of "to be or not to be." We find ourselves repeatedly in the position of justifying our existence.

Yet everything in Jewish history which seems senseless, meaningless or unfair is eventually revealed to us as meaningful, and purposeful. Absurdities are not absurdities. Bizarre and mysterious, yes, but not accidental, or random. It's no accident that we should be repeatedly compelled to explain our presence, to have to figure out what we're doing here. It might not be such a bad thing, to know we're in constant peril of losing what we love. It might not be to our detriment that our right to live is ever in doubt, that we're thrown back constantly onto the basic fact of our being present, and Jewish. Being a Jew is an *issue*, whether or not you want it to be. Our simple existence does pose a question.

Small events in our own small lives are as significant in the grand scheme of things as that which occurs on a larger scale. So, in a universe created according to a single blueprint, surely our personal histories are similarly designed — that the less we can take our existence for granted, the more we come alive. The more we lose of ourselves as years go by, the more we're compelled to find our real identities. My friend Esther told me that after her mother got two knee transplants, she said, "Look at this. I don't have my own knees anymore. My heart's run by a pacemaker. My hearing's gone — I hear with my hearing aids. My sight's going. My teeth are false. Who am I, anyway?"

From the Gulf War in 1990 to the collapse of Oslo in 2001, Israel was catapulted from one crisis to another. The "peace process" staggered forth through seven years like a bloodied beast leaving grief in its wake. Yet amidst the deep and widespread suffering of individuals, threats to our survival as a nation were repeatedly diverted. We witnessed with our own eyes how we were repeatedly and unexpectedly plucked from the precipice. To the extent that each catastrophe had seemed impossible to escape, to that extent was each unforeseen rescue beyond anyone's ability to predict.

≫≪

It is written that truth comes out of the ground. One morning back in the mid-nineties (when the Peace Process was going nicely and the Israeli government was promoting our future in "The New Middle East") I was leafing through The Jerusalem Post in a dentist's waiting room, looking forward to a root canal, when I came across the following news item: A speech given by Yasser Arafat in Arabic, before a closed gathering of Arab ambassadors in Stockholm, had been secretly recorded and published by the Norwegian daily Dagen. According to The Jerusalem Post, which delayed publication of his remarks until the report could be verified, Arafat told his audience that Israel would "collapse in the foreseeable future. We Palestinians will take over everything, including all of Jerusalem. Within five years we will have six to seven million Arabs living in the West Bank and Jerusalem... If the Jews can import all kinds of Ethiopians, Russians, Uzbekians, and Ukranians as Jews, we can import all kinds of Arabs... We plan to eliminate the State of Israel and establish a Palestinian State. We will make life unbearable for Jews by psychological warfare and population explosion. Jews will not want to live among Arabs." Then he added: "I have no use for Jews. They are and will remain Jews."

Arafat, as usual, later denied that those were his comments. The Israeli government, as usual, said his remarks were "just words." And I, as usual, went out of my mind, imploding in a kind of crazed inner frenzy. If not for the dentist whose excellent work kept me quiet for the next few hours, who knows what words I myself would have come out with? What in the world was happening to us? What dangerous insanity! The Arab leader was speaking truly of his true intentions, and it was precisely on such occasions that Israel's leaders sincerely doubted his sincerity.

Ultimately, an event took place which in its abruptness and implausibility was reminiscent of the sudden end of the Gulf War on Purim Day. An outgoing Prime Minister, eager for the Peace Process to finally yield fruit during his tenure, hurriedly offered the Palestinian Authority 97% of the territories it had always demanded. The Palestinian State along our border was about to be born, embracing the area Arafat had sought most urgently to possess, the Temple Mount, which includes the Western Wall.

The unthinkable — we were going to lose the Kosel — had somehow become the inevitable, and it suddenly became excruciatingly obvious that all these years we'd been taking free access to the Wall for granted.

My daughter's in-laws in the Old City told us wryly that the proposed borderline ran through their living room. To get from their kitchen to the front door, they would have to get visas.

A Jewish Quarter *posek* said that the proposed transfer to Palestinian control would constitute danger to life, and that under such circumstances, Jews might be obligated to abandon their homes.

One rainy winter morning, I was seated on our living room couch having my first cup of coffee, reading on page two of the paper about the latest shooting incidents. A Jewish woman in Jerusalem's Gilo neighborhood had been shot while walking along a sidewalk, by a sniper in the adjacent Arab village of Beit Jala.

I looked up from the page. My gaze drifted through our newly dry-cleaned white curtains, drifted out the window, through the bare outstretched branches of the trees, wandered across the street, over to the familiar rooftops of the adjacent Arab neighborhood of East Jerusalem.

And something occurred to me.

When the upcoming transfer of military control took effect — my eyes roamed here and there among the houses — then somebody standing at any one of those windows, if he so chose, could, with impunity — shoot right into this living room.

A few days went by.

Then what happened? Get up and dance, get up and shout for joy! Illogically, wonderfully, *absurdly,* Arafat said Israel's offer was insufficient. Instead of taking his wife out for dinner that night and lining up the Palestinian Police Force for a victory celebration, he gave the nod to another *intifada,* thereby publicly lifting the veil on his true intentions. And that was the end — at least for now — of the Oslo Peace Process.

❧ ❧

It is an irony of the computer age that the same technology which has brought about much loneliness and dehumanization has also given us the phenomenon of e-mail. Letter-writing — which thanks to the telephone had been largely abandoned — is now a resurrected art.

At a particularly violent juncture in the current *intifada*, when the fear was overwhelming and there seemed no realistic possibility of escape at all, I received an e-mail from my friend Bayla Sheva Jacobs, in Flatbush.

She was forwarding something she had received from someone else online — it could have circled the globe three times before getting to me — a quote from one of the masters of Kabbalah during the Middle Ages, the author of *Tomer Devorah*, Rabbi Moshe Cordovero.

His words — *just words,* spoke to me across the centuries that separated us.

> *At that time, in the future, the descendants of Yishmael (the Arab nations) will awaken together with all the inhabitants of the world to come to Jerusalem and start talking peace amongst themselves. This talk of peace will have one underlying goal, though: to destroy Israel. And their rationale shall be: because they [the Jews] established for themselves their own government. And though the Jews will be in tremendous danger at that time, nevertheless they will not be destroyed. In fact, from that very situation they will be saved.*

As of this writing, our future is as veiled in ambiguity as ever, and the present is equally concealed. Lynchings of Jews, drive-by shootings, car bombs, suicide bombings — these things have become commonplace. The morning news reminds me sometimes of Holocaust diaries from the Lodz ghetto (*this one has been killed, that one has been killed, this one has disappeared.*) A 6-month-old baby died tonight from a stoning.

It is widely assumed that in the not-too-distant future we will be at war.

One evening a few weeks ago, a Jerusalem wedding hall collapsed and approximately 600 people, including the bride, fell three stories. Many were injured, many were buried alive. In its apparent randomness, that incomprehensible event overwhelms the mind, like a flooded river overflowing its banks.

We who were spared stand at the border, and gaze over at those who have crossed to the other side.

≈≈

It is written that at the border where understanding fails, *emunah* begins. How many losses, accidents, and disasters — and how much kindness — will we experience, individually and collectively, before I learn how to believe that each incomprehensible event is bringing us closer to our real identity and purpose in the world?

Until such time as we serve as a light unto the nations, every one, including us, will be asking what we're here for. And somebody will always come along to say, "They are, and will remain, Jews."

To be alive is to be in conflict. No matter where on earth one is, there is no such thing as safety, only the illusion of safety. *I thank you*, we say each morning as soon as we open our eyes, *O King Who is always alive, for returning my soul to me in compassion.*

Maybe it's not such a bad thing to be reminded, hour by hour, that the next hour is an unknown. To be a participant at this point in our history is to realize that there's no escape. There's nowhere to go but where we are. To be alive today is to be brought back, again and again, to the miraculous phenomenon of our being, here, in this wondrous present moment.

48

CIRCLES IN THE SAND: A QUESTION OF QUESTIONING

O nce upon a time many years ago, I read about the coming-of-age ritual of a certain African tribe.

Upon reaching a designated birthday (though my memory's vague, the number seven comes to mind) each member of this tribe would be escorted hand-in-hand by his or her parents to a particular site. As the rest of the tribe stood in a circle around the three of them, looking on, and with the child himself standing alone in the center, the mother and father would then, together, draw a circle around him in the sand.

And at that moment, the child would experience a physical inability to step outside the circle.

When I first came across that account in a psychology book, I was eighteen years old, and was myself standing, frightened, at the circle's edge. My non-Jewish hometown environment was comfort-

able, attractive, orderly, predictable, and to my mind opaque: I couldn't see through it. Nothing, it seemed, could shake its apparent self-confidence as the center of the universe. I was haunted by the feeling that truth (with a capital T) lay just out of sight, on the other side of the visible world, but to me it was inaccessible. No matter what route I used to reach it, truth remained elusive. My instincts drew me to nature, to literature, to art. The beauties to be found in the forest that surrounded our house spoke in a language I could understand; the messages I got from Edna St. Vincent Millay's sonnets or Van Gogh's sunflowers seemed to me more in tune with that invisible other dimension than anything I was being taught in school.

But I hadn't found answers, and knew it. I hadn't even found the questions.

My father — whose own childhood had been largely a matter of stepping out beyond a Judaism which had been drawn like a mental prison around him, a religion he had never been allowed to question — had instilled in me the idea that I could think for myself, that there was nothing I was obliged to accept on faith.

Armed with that certainty that truth would prevail, I took a step out into the void. And after what felt to me like an eternity of wandering, but was actually just a few brief years, I came, much to my own surprise, upon ... nothing other than Judaism.

It was the Judaism of my father, that's for sure, but a Judaism that didn't appear to be small, or confining. I couldn't even see the circle's edge, the Torah was so vast, and I was glad. There was room for awe. All the questions that I hadn't ever even articulated to myself, much less to others, because I was so sure they were stupid, began to emerge, and all at once, being inside a circle made sense. God was with me at the center, and present everywhere, beyond my sight.

I'd ask: "What are human beings for?" and somebody would answer. Then I'd ask again, and hear another answer. I learned that the Torah has seventy faces.

Thirty-something years went by. One day I got a call from the secretary of one of my children's schools.

"Your daughter," she said, *"is asking things in class that we would rather she not ask. I don't know why, but we don't see why the other girls should be exposed to these questions if they themselves don't have them."*

So ... it's a question of questioning.

∾∾

"Everything that happens here, it's all a miracle." said 8-year-old Haya Schijveschuurder from her hospital bed, during an interview on Israel Radio's morning news. "Nothing happens for no reason."

She paused occasionally between words; a listener could tell she was articulating her thoughts carefully and hesitantly as she went along, the mix in her voice of shyness and self-confidence revealing a child unaccustomed to expressing herself to strangers, but accustomed to getting attention at home. It sounded somehow as if she were being prompted gently to go on by some smiling, nodding parent, though neither parent was present; I felt as if I could hear the internalized parental voice telling her that in this new situation it would be a mitzvah to speak openly to the interviewer. A few days earlier, she had lost her mother, father and three siblings in the August 2001 suicide bombing at Sbarro's Restaurant in Jerusalem. "Hashem knows what He's doing," she declared with total certainty in her soft little voice. "He wants to tell us that we need to behave a little bit better and that soon *Moschiach* will come and that then all the dead will rise again."

Standing by the radio, hurriedly scrambling some eggs in the hope that my little girl would have something to eat before leaving for school, I imagined how Haya's mother and father would have felt, hearing their child talk like that. Their deaths had deprived them suddenly of any further role in her life, any further say in her education, but apparently they had managed to leave in her possession the only lasting inheritance that any observant Jewish parent has in his power to bequeath: belief.

This child's core perspective, I thought to myself, is that she knows Hashem is present, that He's kind, that all events have Him as their source. These truths had been established in their proper time, in her earliest years, so whether or not questions arise later — what happened to her family is likely to arouse a lifelong quest — the parents had already succeeded in setting her down on firm ground.

Chances are she'll be all right.

Whatever that girl is destined now to undergo — I wished that her mother and father could have heard the interview — there's reason to hope that eventually all life's joys will be within her reach.

〜〜

It's three days after the terrorist attack upon New York City. I'm sitting in a coffee shop in Golders Green, the plane I was traveling in on September 11th to Kennedy Airport having been diverted midair to London.

I'm stuck here. There will be no flights out, they say, for at least several more days; for the time being I can neither return to Israel nor continue on to America. The phone lines are down. Like everyone else this week, I've been swept up like a mote of dust in a furious wind and set down in a new, changed world. I'm overwhelmed by a sense of helplessness and isolation.

But a visual metaphor for the kind of belief that Haya expressed that morning appeared suddenly just now in my mind's eye. The image probably doesn't correspond to any sort of architectural reality; nonetheless, the mental snapshot was of the World Trade Center's deeply laid foundation — powerful steel pillars twisted and damaged but soaring up amidst the ruins.

So it is with belief. If an unshakable trust in Hashem's goodness and love is established early on in a child's mind then these massive underlying buttresses and girders will endure, no matter what else is lost or destroyed.

Here I am at this little marble-topped table, with an unfinished slice of seven-layer chocolate cream cake and a too-bitter cup of coffee — I suppose that's how the English take it — and what comes to mind is story about Auschwitz. It's an incident I heard about a few years ago during a stopover in Manhattan, when my non-observant hosts set me up for a kosher meal with their Orthodox neighbors.

If resolute agnosticism and resolute belief can be imagined as opposite ends of one long continuum, then an unanswerable question lies at one extreme and an unquestioned answer on the other. In the space of one evening I took a whirlwind tour of the shortcut from doubt to certainty. Doubt's endless limbo was up on sixth, total *emunah* one flight down.

⧼⧽

My non-observant friends — the two of them were intellectuals, writers, college graduates, ethical, honest, kind — had been telling me that one of the main things stopping them from believing was the Holocaust. If God is kind, just, and omnipotent, as Judaism claims, then how could He have allowed it to happen?

One needn't go so far as to bring up the Holocaust, I said. If you were to follow that proposition to its logical conclusion, the suffering of just one or two basically decent individuals would be more than enough to prove your point. Take just one young mother who dies in a car accident, for example, or a child who gets cancer, or another who (for no constructive reason that we can see) falls down and skins his knee. By your definition of an omnipotent Deity, any of those events is adequate evidence of either His non-existence or His cruelty. In fact, thousands upon thousands of apparently unjust accidents and calamities are surely taking place at this very moment, even as we speak, all around the globe. That's without even taking into account, say, the ordeal endured by babies as they emerge from the womb: what better example is there of undeserved pain, brought about by the very phenomenon — human birth — which for many, ironically enough, evokes belief in God? And if we could compute into this reckoning the intensity of human misfortune in general (forget about the suffering brought about throughout history by war, famine, and bad weather; the suffering that occurs on any single sunny day in May would suffice for our purposes) then according to your premise — that a kind, omnipotent Deity would not have allowed evil and undeserved suffering to exist in the world — then yes: He would certainly have designed Creation in such a way that reasonably well-meaning people would always be happy and contented.

So, I said, it's true: an omnipotent, kind Deity could certainly have prevented the Holocaust.

But there's another possibility. Given the abundant scientific evidence of an inexplicably orderly universe, perhaps our human capacity for doing evil is part of the design, as is our capacity for pain when we are evil's victims. Maybe human existence is meant to include suffering, calibrated perfectly to the unique developmental requirements of each soul that Hashem has created. Perhaps there's an underlying purpose to every individual's suffering, whether or not we believe it; whether or not to us it will ever become apparent.

They'd heard this argument before.

My friends were not impressed.

I then went down to dinner at the home of Rabbi and Mrs. G. The story that emerged in conversation was as follows:

One particularly freezing, blustery winter morning in 1944, Rabbi G., then 19 years old, was atop one of the watchtowers perched high above the camp, engaged in the task of repairing the tower's broken light. Down on the ground some distance away was some kind of large pit, in which something was burning. An acrid smell reached him faintly on the wind.

The SS guard who had ordered him to do the job was standing on the platform behind him, rifle over the shoulder, looking on, attired in winter overcoat and boots.

As he crouched there with the Nazi at his back, working with stiff and uncontrollably trembling fingers, something caught his attention, a strange sound. At first he wasn't sure he was hearing anything at all. The blasts of wind were blowing the sounds away. But more than the cold, something about what he was hearing froze his blood.

He knew better than to turn around to look; for that he could be shot. So he just moved his eyes to the side, and in a moment or two, recognized that what he was hearing was screams.

A dump truck sped by through his line of vision. For a few seconds — for now the wind was carrying the sounds toward him — his ears were filled with screaming, crying and wailing, and he caught sight, in the back of the truck, packed in together, of about a hundred naked children.

He kept working, eyes downcast, glancing off for a second here, a second there. He saw the truck coming to a stop, back up into position alongside that pit, jerk momentarily into reverse. The screaming rose louder. Then, as with any dump-truck emptying its load, the back lifted up and its contents slid down, into the flames.

He learned later on that at that point the Germans had been running out of time and money. To conserve resources they had devised a way to dispose of children more quickly and inexpensively.

For the rest of his life, he said, he had not been able to entirely remove that dump-truck from his line of vision. (Did he ever dare to imagine, when he was 19, that there would be a "rest of his life"? That he would one day be very happily married, that he and his wife would live in America, in New York City, in an Orthodox community, and have children, and grandchildren?)

When he finished telling the story, I asked, "When you were in the camp, did you ever doubt God's existence?"

His eyes regarded me with sharp surprise. "No," he said, "I wouldn't permit such a thought to enter my mind."

The meaning of a symbol is in the eye of the beholder. The circle in the sand can be used to illustrate any number of different, even opposing, themes, depending on what point you're trying to make at any given time. One could use it to argue that circles in the sand *should* be drawn around children, or *shouldn't* be drawn, that circles do work or that they don't. But one thing does ring true: for better or worse, in all societies such circles are in fact drawn.

Today, it seems to me self-evident that the human mind requires circles which surround one's consciousness and set limits on awareness; they serve as organizing principles on which it becomes possible to "hang" one's perceptions, to interpret the world and to function in it coherently. By the same token, human societies need those circles to be drawn; it is circles which create order, community and a shared social perspective. Furthermore, from my present perspective as an Orthodox parent, that circle in the sand symbolizes early Torah education, during which it is the parents' and teachers' responsibility to indoctrinate children while very young with Torah and the reality of Hashem's existence.

But as a teenager in a white Anglo-Saxon Protestant American suburb, engaged in the struggle (as is natural to adolescents anywhere who find themselves out of sync with their surroundings) to define myself rather than be defined, the circle in the sand resonated for me as a symbol of social hypnotism wrongly perpetrated on children to control their thought and behavior.

The particular Connecticut town in which my conscientious parents had settled down had been chosen by them for its highly reputed public education. There were many things they might have said they'd been looking for in that quest for a good education for their children: a school system that would imbue us with American democracy's highest ideals; bestow an appreciation for literature, the arts, and western civilization's humanitarian values; put at our disposal the 20th century's grand sweep of scientific inquiry and discovery, impart to us its spirit of unhindered inquiry. But above all, if what they were looking for had been put into a nutshell, it would have been for us to emerge from our education with that most precious of mental faculties: *an open mind.*

Another way of putting that is that they wanted us to be free of organized religion.

Judaism, particularly in my father's boyhood experience during the 1920s, had been imposed on him and his peers with scant regard for whether or not a child understood what he was memorizing, and certainly with little concern for whether or not he was being "inspired" by any of it. Even belief was given short shrift; it was simply taken for granted, as was obedience. Like many other Jews of his generation, my father endured countless baffling afternoons in Hebrew School (while the other boys were out playing baseball) cramming for his bar mitzvah, and — in an effort to avoid being run out of school — ignoring the many theological questions that gnawed at him.

The questions were many. But the hallmark of his Hebrew School education was that questions weren't uttered, and if they were, seemed to displease people. Maybe the rabbis just didn't have answers.

In any case, the result was that a few decades later, his daughters found themselves in a society free of religion, and from tribal Jewish loyalties. Unbeknownst to my parents, however (and unbeknownst to me, who couldn't have articulated that this is what was going on) the mental freedom was scary. One could say that in a certain sense, there was no circle around me at all. While my parents had inherited a traditional Jewish orientation toward the world, which for them still endured as a given, my own childish mind (freed from Judaism's structuring of the universe) was in a state of perpetually silent free-fall, in which I was constantly trying to figure out from scratch what the universe was all about.

On the other hand, one could point out how I was surrounded not by one circle but by many. Multiple circles —

multiple assumptions about life which were so accepted that they were viewed not as perceptions but as underlying realities. In this land of open minds, as I labored away at social studies and arithmetic, I knew better than to speak up in school about the things that were really bothering me — otherworldly, futile questions such as: *Why am I here? Is there a God?* I knew better than to ask weird questions, lest I be considered strange, or silly, or dumb, or superstitious. The half-visible guidelines which encircled me were not circles that lent structure to the universe, or referred to things eternal or spiritual, but circles that pertained specifically to that culture: the rituals and rules and regulations applied to sports (which I did not do well in) and the conjugation of French verbs and the National Honor Society, and college applications — none of which bore any relation to my inner world. The surrounding culture felt inconsistent with my inborn Jewish nature. I didn't understand why I had such a nature. I didn't want it.

But one thing I did acquire for sure: an open mind. A painfully open mind.

And ironically enough, what was the outcome of that open mind, that ability to think for myself which my deeply loving and kind parents had nurtured? I ended up stepping out of those circles, one after the other, until at last I had stepped out of the very circle they themselves had drawn. The truth-seeking they themselves had encouraged led me ultimately to Judaism, from which they had liberated me.

≈≈

"Personally, I don't know why she needs to ask such things," the secretary of my daughter's Bais Yaacov high school was saying, "but if she feels she must, the principal has said that she can meet and ask him privately."

Before the woman on the other end had even finished talking, and before I had time to formulate a civil reply, I had already filled to the brim with a highly unpleasant cocktail of toxic emotions. There was a certain tone in her voice which equated questioning with an unfortunate lack of *emunah.* Had we placed our daughter into a school system that was going to suppress her wonderful inquisitive mind, the lifelong philosophical bent she had exhibited as early as kindergarten? *My dear woman,* I had to restrain myself from boasting, *that girl's got more emunah in her little finger than you do in your whole hand!* The last thing on earth I wanted was to tell my own daughter not to ask questions! Such a thing was unthinkable! It was anathema to me!

When my daughter got home from school I told her what the secretary had said and told her that maybe she shouldn't ask questions in class anymore, for the sake of the other girls.

She knows me well, my daughter, and saw I was upset. "Mommy, don't worry, I understand why they don't want me to ask in class. It's really no problem."

I know *her* well, too, and saw that as far as she was concerned, it really *wasn't* a problem. Had her schooling made her too resigned to ignoring her own thoughts? Was her intellectual growth being nipped in the bud? Or was this a case of my having been sensitized by my background to something that for her was not really an issue?

Either way, I found the idea of a private free-ranging session between her and the principal very appealing. "So would you like to meet with the principal?"

"No, I'd feel funny. It's not like I go around with questions all the time. They just come to my mind when we're in class."

≈∞≈

A young woman I know has told me that when she was about nine, she asked her older brother, "What does Hashem look like?"

Her brother, a few years her senior, responded angrily: "Don't ever say that again!"

She didn't.

Some years ago, a *baal-teshuvah* couple in Jerusalem's Old City hosted two *frum*-from-birth girls from Brooklyn for Shabbos lunch. The discussion at that table was wide-ranging, and in the course of conversation, one of the girls, who was attending seminary that year in Israel, asked, "How old is God?"

The hostess was taken aback. How had her guest gotten through an entire childhood of Torah education with a question such as that still on her mind? The young woman replied that this particular puzzle had bothered her sometimes when she was little, and she might have mentioned it to her mother (her mother usually didn't have answers), but she just knew somehow not to ask it in school. She knew that whatever is written in the Torah has to be accepted, so whenever questions arose and she wondered about something, she just let it pass.

Another young woman, from South Africa, has told me that several years ago while she was attending a Jerusalem seminary, she had been called in for a talk with the principal. He said that some of her fellow students had complained to him about the questions she was asking. "I never knew what to make of that, that it was the other girls in the seminary who didn't like it. They resented it, I think. It made them uncomfortable."

I asked what kind of questions.

"Oh, things I really wanted to know the answer to, like, 'How do we really know that the Torah is from God? How do we know it's true?' The other girls must have thought I had some kind of agenda or something, but really, I didn't. I was 18. I was just asking whatever occurred to me. I don't think people that age know necessarily what questions they have until they start talking about them. All they know is they're in a world that is confusing, coming at them from all directions. Especially in Israel. You go there for a year of seminary and there's all this secular-religious conflict, and bombs going off. Even if you don't know what you want to ask exactly before you ask it, you have to know you're not going to be thought badly of if you think out loud. You can't really learn if you're always cut off at the starting point. I mean, that's what real education is, isn't it? That you're in a place, and you're with someone, a teacher, where the bottom line is honesty?"

I asked how things had turned out.

"Well, one night I came back after the 11:00 curfew, and they told me I would have to leave the sem. It was only 11:15, and I'd just been at some relatives — I'd never done anything against the rules, like going to town or something — so I was pretty sure that wasn't the real reason. I felt they just didn't like having me there. I felt very bad about it. You know, I was very young. But the whole thing was *gam zu letova.* I moved to another seminary, where they didn't have any problem about my asking things. I asked whatever I wanted and it was wonderful."

Someone else has told me that the daughter of a friend of hers attends a Bais Yaacov in Jerusalem, and that the principal makes a habit of doing the following: Every once in a while he'll come into a classroom and exclaim, "All right, girls, here's your chance! Questions! Questions! Any questions you want to ask!"

The girls love him.

⋙⋘

It is written that a few moments after receiving the Torah, when *HaKadosh Baruch Hu's* voice was no longer being heard but while they were still standing there on Har Sinai, the Jewish people had their first stirrings of doubt.

It is a paradox that *emunah* can be built on a foundation of questions, that questions can arise out of faith. But Judaism has never been a religion incapable of absorbing self-contradictions. I've read that in the physical world, as we get closer to the core of anything, positive and negative charges become neutralized. Similarly, it has been said that what looks like a contradiction is often a matter of our not yet seeing the whole picture, of looking from only one perspective; that much of the time, reality is such that apparently irreconcilable opposites eventually join up together. It brings to mind some kind of Möbius Strip, wherein opposites are revealed as different points on the same continuum.

"To think" is a synonym of "to question." One could even speculate (especially in light of the deeds perpetrated on September 11th, by people whose belief is unquestioning) that our particular capacity as Jews for questioning is intrinsic to the enduring sturdiness of our belief. Maimonides once raised the question of the apparent contradiction between God's foreknowledge and man's free will, gave a partial solution to this problem, and was criticized by the Raavad for raising a question that he could not satisfactorily answer. Commenting upon this, Rav Yaakov Kaminetsky explained that Maimonides wished to teach us that there are questions in life which we cannot satisfactorily answer, but they need not deter us from moving on.

We need to make room in our faith for what we cannot know, for that which is beyond our understanding, just as the architect of a skyscraper has to take into consideration the likelihood of earthquakes (and bombs, and from now on, I suppose, jet planes) if the building is to last. He has to design into the blueprint not only a profound foundation but a capacity for moving when the earth moves, and for leaning into the wind.

It has often been said that if Hashem had meant for belief to be an easy thing to come by, He would have made human beings into robots, or angels. The inclination to ask questions is one of the defining characteristics of being human, and a salient characteristic, in particular, of our people; it's intrinsic to our nature. Belief and questioning are not incompatible.

To be a child is to wonder. Even in the absence of external conflict, the mind of a child is a growing, changing organism — more so than the physical body. We needn't be afraid of a child's questions, even if we ourselves don't know how to reply, for every question, if pursued truly, leads to truth.

49

LIVING WHERE GROUND ZERO IS EVERYWHERE

It's a mysterious thing, this impulse to live here. Like other things that are so much a part of me that I take them as givens — such as my maternal instinct, or the desire for a roof over my head, or coffee first thing in the morning — this inner prompting to be in Jerusalem has proven itself to be as inexplicable, as unchanging, as the natural inclination of a compass to point north.

If I stand aside and try to observe this phenomenon objectively, it arouses an awe in me for my own inscrutable self. What was it that drew me as a young woman, and held me here though I was alone, separated from family and home in America? Where did it come from, my certainty that the person I married would have to be someone who wanted to stay in this turbulent Middle Eastern land where Ground Zero is everywhere; where bombs have been going off since my arrival twenty-five years ago; where for as long as I've been a mother, I've bid the children a secret unsaid good-bye whenever they leave the house? Where prices are high and salaries low, where people joke that in this country, you can't count on making a fortune but you can surely count on losing it?

This inner compass is a mystery, but something else strikes me as stranger, still: that so many other Jews feel the same way. People from societies as different from mine as the one in Georgia (in the United States) or Georgia (in Russia), or Ethiopia, or South Africa, experience the identical impulse, as if we'd all been made in the same factory. This country may be accused of racism, but the fact is that the Jewish State is a veritable Benetton ad for racial and national diversity, as has been the case down through the centuries, ever since the first Jew, Abraham, heard a Divine call to *"lech lecha." Go, to the land that I will show you.*

≋ ≋

It has been said that the best way to love something is to realize it can be lost, and this was self-evident when I was in Manhattan the week after September 11th. Love was in the air.

Here in Israel, that kind of love has had three thousand years to grow.

On Saturday night, we heard the explosions, watched the ambulances from our kitchen window, heard the sirens in our sleep. The next morning in an act of defiance, a refusal to be intimidated, I took a number 18, the line I've been too afraid to travel on since the double suicide bombing of two number 18's a few years ago. The long, so-called "accordion" double-length bus was packed. There were about a hundred-fifty people on board, almost all of whom were traveling in silence, bearing a remarkably similar facial expression, which I then realized was on my own face, too: stillness.

I was a standee. When a news report came on loudly over the bus radio that there had been a suicide bombing of a bus in Haifa in which at least ten were killed, the elderly man in the seat before me asked, "What? Did he say in Haifa?" I nodded. He threw back his face, raised his arms palms up and yelled, *"Elokim! Elokim!"* [G-d! G-d!]

Last night I attended the funeral of a 15-year-old boy, who was killed in one of this week's four suicide bombings. His mother, who kept collapsing as she was escorted to the cemetery, was crying, "I can't bury my son! I can't bury my son! I'll die!"

This morning I went downtown and got a cappuccino in the Rimon Café, where a number of customers had been seriously injured, then walked over to the spot where candles of remembrance had been set up. Two Newsweek photographers, a man and a woman, were trying to pass through the police barriers, and I chastised them. "Look, lady," the woman snapped, "we're just trying to record this so people will know what's going on here! The Palestinians pull out the dead children for us to take pictures. I don't understand what these Israelis are thinking! Isn't there anyone around here who wants some PR?"

Groups of store owners and workers were busy up and down the block installing enormous new windows for the store-fronts that had been shattered. Glass crackled under my feet. I looked up and saw that rows of second- and third-story windows were also blown out. Red-brown blood was spattered over the nearest brick wall.

I thought for the umpteenth time of Yasser Arafat's statement some years ago that Israel would collapse in the foreseeable future. "We Palestinians will take over everything," he declared, "including all of Jerusalem ... We plan to eliminate the State of Israel and establish a Palestinian State. We will make life unbearable for Jews by psychological warfare and population explosion. Jews will not want to live among Arabs. I have no use for Jews. They are and will remain Jews."

As I turned to go, I caught sight, in a blown-out storefront of a silver goods shop, on a charred, otherwise empty display shelf, of an eight-branched Chanukah menorah. Someone had apparently stuck it out there though there was no glass anymore in the window to keep it from being stolen.

A sudden joy flickered through me like fire. In a few more days, in windows throughout Israel, the lights will be burning.

50

ORPHANS AT ANY AGE

*I wish I had words of wisdom or advice, but I know — and
you know — that we each proceed through this type of experience in an individual, unique way. One of the things that
helped me — particularly in the early days — was the realization that friends of mine had experienced such a loss, yet
they had survived.*

*The loss of a second parent is pretty devastating, espe-
cially when it's your Mommy. Becoming an orphan, at any
age, is a terrible thing to confront.*

Paula Van Gelder, October 30, 2001

One morning last summer, not long before the world
was altered forever, an article appeared in The Los
Angeles Times about the pilot of a small plane that had
gone down while crossing the Atlantic. I wish I'd had the presence
of mind to save it; like so many other things in life, it's only with

hindsight that I realize the value that story would have had for me later on. But I was in America on a visit to my mother during her final illness. My mind was scattered and unsettled.

I don't recall if the pilot said it was a case of engine trouble, or if they'd run out of fuel, or into bad weather. He sounded like a friendly, sporty, All-American type from the Midwest — unpretentious, good-humored, easy-going, not a man ordinarily given to sharing his introspective or philosophical musings. The plane had suddenly fallen into a steep dive and plunged down through dense fog. When it broke through the mist, he saw the water about a hundred feet below, and had one split second to steer for a landing.

It happened at night. There were three or four passengers from Japan on board.

Surprisingly, the plane didn't break up and sink upon hitting the surface. He and his passengers donned their life preservers, inflated the plane's vinyl lifeboat, and climbed out. They were instantly and completely drenched.

There was a full moon. The black waves roaring up were huge.

Through the night the pilot bailed out the icy seawater that ceaselessly filled up their tiny vessel. "It gave me something to do," he said. "If I hadn't had to keep bailing out, I would have thought about what was happening to me and gone out of my mind."

Being out on the ocean at night, he said, alone, with land nowhere in sight, clinging to their lightweight, slippery little raft as it rode atop the huge waves, evoked a terror he'd never before experienced.

The dark ocean, vast and turbulent under the white moonlight, was the most terrifying, the most beautiful thing he'd ever seen in his life.

<hr>

I finished my coffee, left the newspaper behind for the next customer, and drove back home to my mother's house. It was late

October. The Twin Towers had fallen. The caretaker whom we had hired was changing the sheets.

It was an elaborate procedure: the rolling first to one side, one hand holding my mother firmly, the other hand snatching the sheet and pulling it out from under; the rolling to the other side, and the deft, quick insertion underneath of clean linen; the gentle, sure turning, and turning back; the lifting under the arms and pulling her backwards up along the bed; the careful setting down of her head upon the pillow, and readjustment of the neck and shoulders. The folding down, tucking-in, and smoothing. And then, the patting of my mother's hands, inert upon the blanket.

"That's much *better* now, isn't it, Mrs. Cousins?"

I stood back a few feet from the bed, useless.

I'd been gone for more than an hour.

"All clean and fresh for you now, right, Mrs. Cousins?" The nurse, kind and competent, cajoled in her musical South American singsong, as if to a small child. My mother, having already been confined to bed for about a week, in what had suddenly turned into a fast plunge through the final stages of cancer, had had a stroke a few days before. She who had always personified giving, doing, working — there'd never been anyone so much the embodiment of the word "giver," never anyone so much the antithesis of laziness, as she — was now the prisoner of her body: the beloved, sturdy physical vessel which had given us life and taken care of us all since time began. I couldn't bear to imagine the mental torture she must be experiencing.

"There we go now, Mrs. Cousins, *all* finished!"

A plume of hot anger, scattering sparks, shot mutely through me in an arc. I couldn't stand this violation of my mother's dignity; the nurse had no idea whom she was talking to. Surely Mommy should chafe mightily at this silly condescension. Leaning over to look her straight in the face and exchange a private wink of indignation, I was relieved, then frightened, to find in her eyes no answering glimmer of annoyance.

No irritation.

Would I have preferred some sign of torment, rather than the benevolent flicker of greeting I did detect in the pale green corneas, placidly returning my gaze?

"Mommy?"

A loosely slurred grumble. Was I mistaken, or was that recognition? Wasn't she focusing on me?

"Mommy?"

No answer.

They say that aging is the way of the world, that death is part of life. My father was fond of saying, "No one gets out of this world alive." But just as ten years before, when one day without warning, in apparently excellent health, he had been there one day and was gone the next; had suddenly, in an instant, vanished totally off the face of the earth, so was it now with her, whose strength had been fading unevenly for four years and who had just recently dropped out of orbit into a vertical free-fall; a free fall which had quickly gained such momentum that she was flying under the radar; we couldn't keep track anymore of all that was being discarded along the way. All the essential, hitherto unremarked, crucial aspects of her which had made her herself had been vanishing day by day, and then, hour by hour.

And now: this random drifting not far from shore, aimless, to and fro, in shallow waters of consciousness.

Both phenomena, his and hers, seemed bizarre, abrupt reversals of the universe's regular designated course, as if a sweet blue sky had all at once turned inside out and revealed its unnatural, malevolent inner lining. The two of them, my father and mother, had been the great bright sky, the background for everything. It was impossible that one day his voice, resonant with kindness and understanding, had been on the other end of the telephone and was supposedly, the next day, never to be heard by us again. Impossible, now, that I should be standing here by my mother's bed struck grotesquely, stupidly dumb while she who was at the warm center of my life, of all life, who had kept him with us after his death, was turning before my eyes into a faceless gray infant slipping maddeningly out of my grasp and I into an impotent mother in a nightmare, holding nothing in my arms. Impossible, this repeated slipping of my mother from my hands; impossible that I should be standing here, helpless, as right before my eyes some vast malignant undertow beneath the surface was drawing her away. Sinister waves. I'd never sensed the existence of these subterranean currents before in my life. The undertow would tug at her, then relent slightly. Draw her farther out, and relent, like contractions during delivery. Was I being left alone on shore? Was I being sucked out along with her, riding the waves, farther and farther out? My mother was my life raft, as she'd always been, of course, and I was trying to hold on. Then she'd be nowhere in sight. Then she'd reappear. She was unrecognizable. Neither she nor I was anyone I knew. I'd never been way out here by myself before. Only the white moonlight was familiar.

For a horrible moment, I was my daughter, standing there helpless, looking on, and I my mother, in the bed. Drifting away.

Someday. Perhaps not too far off, if we and the world lasted that long.

No matter that my mother was eighty-seven, and I more than halfway through my journey. If I was expected to construe all this as reality, if I was to understand and accept, like an adult, that this was simply the way of the world, and that along with birth, nothing could be more natural or commonplace; that we had supposedly reached this time, this season, *"shehechiyanu, vekiyemanu, vehigiyanu la'zeman hazeh,"* then as far as I was concerned, reality wasn't realistic.

Reality was nowhere in sight. Towers we'd never dreamed could crumble were turning to clouds of white dust, and falling, magically, in a dream.

≈≈

Shortly after it became apparent that what had happened was that she had died, the phone rang. My sister answered.

"It's for you," she whispered. "It's Mimi."

I took the phone. "Hi, darling."

"Mommy, how are you?"

"O.K."

"You are, Mommy? Really? It must be so hard. How's Mom?"

"Mimi, Mom just died."

"*What?*"

"Yes."

"*What are you saying?*"

Words didn't appear.

"*Mommy!*"

Words... Nowhere around.

"*How do you know?*"

I saw again... began to see it again, then closed my mind's eye. "I know."

"Where is she?"

"Right here."

"What do you *mean?*"

"Here. She's in her bed." Yes, dear daughter, surprise! Death's big and famous otherworldly kingdom is just the other side of... The other side of a... thin translucent membrane. It takes just a second, nay, less than a second... to go all that way. All the way from here to there. A fragment of an instant... to sail a trillion miles.

"Mommy —" She was crying.

"Yes, darling."

"When did it happen?"

"Just now."

"*Just now? What do you mean?*"

"A few minutes ago."

"No! You were with her?"

I nodded.

"Mommy?"

"Yes."

"You were with her?"

"I can't — talk. I'm sorry."

"Oh, Mommy, of course! But just tell me, are you O.K.? Was Candis with you?"

"Yes."

"Oh, I'm so glad."

"And Dovie's here."

"Dovie's there? He's with you now?"

"Yes."

"Oh, I'm so glad! That's so good that Dovie's with you! Was he there when it happened?"

"No, he walked in about a minute afterwards."

"Oh! Poor Dovie! What did you all do?"

"We cried."

"Oh!"

"Yes."

She was crying.

"Mommy. *Baruch Dayan HaEmes.*"

"*Baruch Dayan HaEmes.*"

"Mommy, you sound — you're not like it was with Saba. You sound different."

"Yeah, I'm O.K."

"Yes, Mommy? That's so good. Is Dovie O.K.?"

"Yes, sweetheart."

"And Candis?"

"Yes, she's OK. We're all O.K."

"Really?"

"Yes. darling. Well, so I think–"

"Mommy, does Daddy know?"

"Not yet."

"Should I call him?"

"No. I want to."

"What about the kids?"

"No. Oh, but — I guess you can, if you want to. Oh, but you know what, no. I want to. Later."

"Mommy, I love you."

"I love you, sweetheart."

"Are you really O.K.?"

"Yes, Mimi. Are you?"

"Yes. I'm O.K.."

"Goodbye, then, darling."

"Good bye!"

"Good bye."

"Good bye!"

～∾∾

My sister had left the bedroom. I asked my son if he could stay with Mom while I called Rabbi Eidelitz. He nodded.

I walked into the hallway.

The bookcase was on my right. I walked alongside.

This is it.

I permitted myself a side-glance to the left, into their living room. There, incredibly, presided the two off-white couches, as blithely serene as if they hadn't just lost the one person in the world who'd taken care of them for twenty years. The ingratitude of inanimate objects! The large, low glass coffee table, and the magnificent stained-glass Tiffany lamp from my Uncle Bobby, that he'd made by hand for his sister and brother-in-law, and the floor-to-ceiling windows, with my mother's and father's view of their ever-changing sky. And the antique teacup on the fireplace that hadn't broken in the earthquake.

It has happened.

The thing I've always feared.

What I had dreaded above all things, through the years — I'd always known, of course, that one day this moment would arrive: the unimaginable, horrible time that I'd be standing in this house when my mother was no longer here.

It's happening now.

I looked around.

Things were — the same.

I walked toward the phone, thinking to myself, "Am I all right?" I seemed to be, surprisingly so. I wasn't falling apart. What was wrong with me?

Was it good or bad?

It felt bad. I was relieved. With Daddy, I had collapsed, imploded, crashed into myself.

All was calm. A large, spreading stillness. I sat down on her black leather chair and leaned forward, as she always did — I felt as if she were in me, leaning forward — to look through her rolodex. My fingers flicking through the cards. The skin on the back of my hand. All things were moving slowly. Everything had come to a quiet place. A still, expanding place. The opaque gray afternoon sunlight descending from the skylight. Next to her black chair, as usual, stood the Danish lamp from the Connecticut house, and in a row along the wall, my father's photographs, that she had gotten framed.

Could it be?

This was happening.

What was happening? No sooner was she out of sight than I was already betraying her? It was insulting. Something I would have wanted to hide from her, that things could — that I — could just go on. If I died, wouldn't it hurt me to see everyone simply carrying on like this after a few minutes? Or would I be glad? I guess I'd be glad. Yeah, probably I'd be glad.

Could it be that I'm just tired?

I was sitting there waiting for Candis to finish talking on the phone. I gathered that she was talking to our sister in Massachusetts. The next thing I knew, Candis was across the room, walking hurriedly back towards the bedroom. Now it was my turn.

As I leaned forward to pick up the phone, I noticed, next to my mother's magnifying glass, and partly covered by a To Do list in Candis's handwriting — "Dr. Nalick, ask about CA-125, physical therapy/Thursday O.K.? almond butter, eggs" — the little blue box from Robinson's/May which had held a pair of earrings. It looked as if it might be right where Mommy had left it, months ago. I reached for it and took off the lid.

There they were. Two small tear-shaped pendants, pale green. To match my mother's eyes. "They're really quite lovely," she had said. "Thank you."

Too late.

There was no answer at their house. I dialed his cellular phone. To my surprise, he answered. Everything was surprising.

"Rabbi Eidelitz, I'm so glad to get you."

"Yes, hello. I was just going to call to find out how things are going."

"Rabbi Eidelitz, my mother just died."

"*Baruch Dayan HaEmes.*" He spoke of my mother. An unusually giving and unselfish person, an extraordinarily positive outlook. Incapable of stating an untruth. Totally unpretentious and down-to-earth. Her wonderful spirit; throughout her illness she was devoid of self-pity. He and Debby were just remarking on how they'd never heard her complain once; she'd always been so upbeat, always said she was doing just fine, that she had the most wonderful doctors. And that's the way she perceived her situation. That's the way she experienced her life, with humility, modesty and gratitude. An *emes'dik* human being. During her visits over the last few years, they had noticed her interest in Torah. They'd had a number of very interesting conversations. May your mitzvos be a *zechus* for the *aliyah* of her *neshamah*.

I pushed away those words. They were true.

My mind was a shut fist.

"Rabbi Eidelitz, what am I supposed to do now?"

He told me to open a window in the room in which the *petirah* had occurred, to symbolize the arrival of an angel to guide her and the departure of her soul. He said that from now until the time of burial, she was not to be left alone.

"Do I have to cover all the mirrors or just some?"

All of them.

"My sister says she thinks we're supposed to cover her face. That we shouldn't look at her when she's —" I trailed off, uncertain how to finish.

Yes, you can draw the sheet up over her face.

"I was holding her hand. After she died. I was touching her. Is that all right?"

I had walked out of the room for a few minutes to make a phone call and all of a sudden Candis called me back sharply. "Sarah!" It sounded like a bark. I knew exactly what it meant, though I'd never heard that tone before. I slammed down the phone and ran, and when I got there...

"Mommy!" The moaning arose suddenly, from somewhere in the depths.

"Mommy!"

My mother's eyes, fully open now, expressed gentle consternation and a calm astonishment, not fear, and without any sound her lips were slowly opening and closing, opening and closing. She seemed to be trying to get air. Tenderly cupping my mother's face in my hands, frantically trying to stop this. "Mommy! Poor Mommy!" My cries sounded to my ears like the sorrowing, dissonant bellows of a cow for her calf. "I wasn't here! I wasn't here! Why wasn't I here!" I was really wondering, how could this have happened? So brutally unfair! "Why wasn't I here?"

I felt my sister's arm encircling me.

After all these years, needing desperately to be there for her! I'd been determined. After these months, these days, after these hours of waiting by her bed! And of not waiting!

"Sarah."

Of guilt when I'd go out to get coffee, and guilt when I'd get restless and stay away for a few hours, and guilt while I was rushing back, because every single labored breath for days on end had looked as if it must be her last, but in the end, when the moment came, I hadn't been there! No! "Why wasn't I here?" It was like some kind of trick. Cruel! The knowledge of having missed her departure was tearing me. It's what must be meant by a broken heart.

"Sarah," said Candis. I felt her face near mine and turned to look. "You are here." It struck me, how her cheeks were wet in the afternoon light. Then, very quietly: "It's happening now."

I was going to reject this information, then thought, What do you know, I am here. I heard my voice crying, "Mommy! No!" Frantically smoothing the hair away from her forehead, trying to tenderly soothe her brow. "Poor Mommy!" Stroking her hand madly, almost violently, pressing her hand in mine, kissing her forehead, her face. My sister's hands and mine. "Mommy! Sweet Mommy! No!" As if from a distance, I could hear my sister's voice crying in mine.

Mommy's hand, infinitely familiar, was warm to the touch, just as if she were Mommy.

She was leaving us now.

It was the eyes that informed me. In the fraction of time between one second and another, they had changed.

They looked horrible to me. Those were not her eyes.

Eyes without light.

My sister gave a single nod, the slightest of possible nods, which without sound declared: Yes.

Our mother's light... on unseen wings it had been borne away.

She'd flown.

Rabbi Eidelitz said it was all right. He asked if I'd already informed the *chevra kadisha.*

"I spoke to them a few days ago. I gave them all the information."

He told me to call them now, and that they would remove the body from the house and take care of everything. He told me to dump out any liquids that might have been in the room where she died, such as a glass of water, or anything in a pitcher, and not to eat or drink anything in the room, so as not to recite *berachos*, which could cause pain to her *neshamah*. It would be like flaunting our aliveness. "The *neshamah* is present and awake," he said. "The *neshamah* sees and hears everything clearly and understands. More so, in fact, than the person saw and understood in life, because the perception is no longer clouded. So if there is anything you would like to say to your mother, this is the time to do so. If there is anything you would like to ask *mechilah* for, now is the time."

❧ ❧

My mother was telling me that a few years ago (did she say it was after Daddy died or before?) she had been in Robinson's/May one time and had seen a pair of jade earrings in the jewelry department.

She'd always liked jade, she said. (Now that she mentioned it, I remembered that yes, she'd always liked jade.) And it was a beautiful pair of earrings.

She looked at them and she looked at them, she told me. It was a beautiful pair of earrings. But they were very expensive, two-hundred something dollars.

Finally, the man behind the counter asked her if she was interested in trying them on.

She tried them on.

And they were beautiful.

Should she? Shouldn't she? She couldn't make up her mind. She knew the salesman was watching. Finally after a long time he said, "Sometimes you have to know when to give yourself something."

My mother looked at me.

"So what happened?" (Knowing her, surely I guessed.) "Did you get them?"

"Oh, no."

"Oh, Mommy."

"Yes. I think I should have. Later on I regretted it. I learned from that." She wanted me to benefit from her mistake. She was passing on the lesson. "I think the salesman was right. Sometimes you have to know when to give yourself something."

"Maybe we can go back!"

"Oh, no. I don't need them. And they're not there anyway. One time I was there and I went to the jewelry department just to see if they were still there."

"And they weren't?"

"No." She almost smiled. Not that she'd ever give it any thought, but her whole life she'd denied herself things. That's simply how she lived. Orphaned at ten, when her father had died; her mother had to support the family as a seamstress and my mother had to serve as a second mother to her siblings. Childhood poverty — though she said that it had never once occurred to her, when she was a child, that her family was poor — had trained her from the earliest age not to question Spartan self-denial; it never occurred to her that self-denial was something to regret. That was simply the behavior she permitted herself.

"So let's take a trip over there! Let's drive over there today!"

"Oh, no. I don't think so."

I tried to convince her but she wasn't going to be convinced, so I got an idea: I'd surprise her. What a wonderful, wonderful surprise it would be, the best present anyone could give her, and I'd be the one who had thought of it. She'd always given me things, my whole life, but ever since first grade — when I'd sewn her an apron which refused to become an apron — I'd never known what to give her. I knew she never expected anything, or wanted anything from me. But now I finally knew exactly what to get her, and it would be the perfect gift. I got excited just think-ing about it. Daddy would have been proud.

There must not have been enough time on that visit, or... I didn't make time. On my next visit to Los Angeles, I went to Robinson's/May and they had one pair, for about three hundred dollars. Out of the question, and besides, Mommy wouldn't have wanted it. If Daddy got her something like that, that was differ-ent, otherwise, she wouldn't be able to stomach having that kind of money spent buying her jewelry.

The next visit, I forgot about it. When I got back to Jerusalem, I remembered, and resolved to take care of it the next time.

The next time I was back in L.A., the man at the jewelry counter said they were getting in a shipment of jade in three weeks, but by then I'd be back in Israel. (Why didn't I try Macy's? I do remember being in some other store in the Nordstrom's Mall one time, and they did have a few things in jade, but nothing good.)

On my next visit, I don't remember what happened, but in any case I didn't make it over to Robinson's/May.

The time after that, they had several pairs, and they were all on sale for $19.95. Nothing extraordinary but that was all they had in jade, so after much deliberation I made my choice.

Standing there watching as the woman removed the price tag, trying to assess whether or not Mommy would like them... They weren't very special but they were pretty good, actually. Maybe they were even beautiful, in a way. Two small pendants, pale, un-even green, to match Mommy's eyes. I asked the woman to gift-wrap it, please, and she said gift-wrapping was up on eighth. I took the elevator up and the clerk said she had three other pack-ages to do first. It was a half-hour after Mommy's lunchtime. I'd have to make lunch right away, as soon as I got home. "I have somebody not well at home," I said.

"Sorry, madam, these people were here before you."

I stood on line muttering under my breath, clucking my tongue, staring pointedly at the wall clock over the woman's head. She finally finished, I drove back fast, pulled into the driveway, slammed the door of the station wagon and threw open the front door.

There she was, on her black chair, chin slightly uplifted, hands clasped upon her lap. It was unnerving, seeing her like that, not doing anything. It still seemed unlike her. Was she peaceful, or bored? The New York Times was on the end-table, still in its plastic wrapper from the morning delivery.

I strode up to her, smiling, and presented her with the box. For an extra $5.00 I'd had them do it up with a rather artistic gold and pink floral paper, and a special ribbon entwined with a stiff, pale pink insertion that could possibly suggest a bird taking flight. Not her taste, exactly (nor mine either, for that matter); she wasn't one to spend money on special wrapping.

"What's this?" she asked.

"A present."

"A present?"

I nodded, expectant.

She very slowly removed the bird wings, or whatever that was, and the exquisite paper, and put it on the little round table next to her chair, where along with the Times, she kept her magnifying glass, and a glass of water, and miscellaneous papers and letters and whatever biography she was reading at the time. The biography sitting there now (hey, it occurs to me as I write this, sitting here in a Jerusalem coffee shop five months later: I did get her presents, after all; maybe I'm too hard on myself) was one I'd given her quite some time ago, of an artist whose stark, lonely images of buildings in blocks of sunlight had always been among her favorites. She had found the book disillusioning, however, even depressing; the artist was supposedly quite a brute. At least that's what his ex-wife said. My mother had wondered aloud how such beauty could have come from a man capable of that kind of cruelty.

She lifted the lid from the small blue box, now, and set it aside.

The earrings were lying inside atop a square of cotton. I waited for her to try them on.

"How nice," she said. "They're lovely. Thank you." She looked up at me with a soft smile.

"Mommy, remember how one time you wanted a pair of expensive jade earrings and the man behind the counter told you that sometimes you have to know when to get yourself something?"

"Oh, yes. I remember. Were these very expensive?"

"No, not at all. They were on sale."

"Oh, good."

She carefully picked up one of them off of the cotton and held it up between thumb and forefinger. "Oh, yes, it's really quite lovely."

"You see how they're not the same color exactly, Mommy? And the shape of them isn't the same?" I took out the other earring and compared it to the one she was dangling. "This one's a little lighter. See? And this one's a little longer. The woman told me that's because they're real."

I handed her the earring and waited.

She put the two earrings, one after the other, back into the box, then she closed the lid and put the closed box on the table. "That's really so nice," she said. "Thank you."

All of a sudden it was as if my eyes opened: She's too weak to put them on.

Not only physically but emotionally.

Certainly too weak to get up and look at them in the mirror. And where would she go with them anyway? To her bedroom? She can hardly get up and walk to the kitchen, much less go out anywhere.

I realized: Mommy is now too weak to enjoy a pair of jade earrings.

That was also when it hit me — hit me like a brick in the head — that about a year must have passed since she told me that story about Robinson's/May. It could have been more than a year. Maybe two.

"Thank you," she said again. "They're beautiful."

❧❧

My mother was sitting on her chair. I was next to her on the black leather footrest, and had gotten a phone call from a friend in Manhattan.

My friend, who liked my mother very much, said, "Tell your mother that if I believed in G-d, I'd get down on my hands and knees and pray for her."

In a few more minutes I got off the phone and gave my mother the message. Her eyes filled with tears.

Wondering if it was the sincerity of my friend's goodwill that had touched her, I asked my mother why the message had made her cry.

"Oh, well, I —" She fell quiet.

"What, Mommy?"

"I feel so sorry for her."

"You do? Why?"

"Because if you get to a time in life, if something difficult happens and you don't have that, I think it will be very difficult."

"You mean, G-d?"

She nodded.

❧❧

We'd been sitting around her kitchen table on Friday night, Dovie and Mommy and I, and out of the blue my mother had started talking about her childhood. I had noticed her looking at him intently, oddly, while he was saying Kiddush.

"I didn't learn about Judaism when I was growing up," she said — not to me but to him; I already knew this story. "My mother came to America all alone when she was fifteen, and worked to save money to bring over her family from Russia. And she did. That little fifteen-year-old girl earned enough money to buy tickets for her entire family. That's my mother. She was a remarkable woman.

"Mama lived on Hester Street in the Lower East Side. She worked in one of those factories they had then for immigrant workers. Have you ever heard of the Triangle Factory, Dovie?

You know what that is, don't you? That's where there was a big fire, and many of the young women jumped to their deaths. There was a big uproar about the working conditions."

"Yes, yes, I know about that. Sure," he said.

"Well, my mother got married to Papa very young, but then Papa got sick and the doctor told them that if they didn't move to a better climate, Papa would die a young man. So they got on the train to California — this was about 1912, probably. Maybe they had one baby by then. Maybe two. Gladice and Sabina. The train stopped at all the stations along the way across country and the passengers would get out to stretch their legs, and when the train stopped at the Salt Lake City station, Mama and Papa got out to walk around and they were just bowled over. The air was so clean and wonderful. There were snow-covered mountains in the distance. The streets were wide and clean, and in the gutters running alongside all the streets — the streets were broad wide boulevards — there were streams of clear fresh cold spring water rushing down, from high up in the mountains. They'd never seen anything like it. They were flabbergasted. Papa decided then and there they should stay right there, and Mama said fine.

"Papa and Mama both came from religious families in Russia but in Utah we were the only Jews in town. There were just Mormons and Methodists and gypsies. In retrospect, I think one of the reasons Papa was so angry at me all of the time — it's only now that I realize this — is that I used to go around singing the Christian hymns. I heard them and I liked them, so I would sing them. And now I realize, here was Papa, from an Orthodox family, and it must have made him furious. But I didn't know that, then. I just thought he hated me.

"There was no synagogue in Price. Though I do remember that when Papa died — he died on Yom Kippur, did you know that, Dovie?"

Dovie said he wasn't sure; it sounded familiar but he wasn't sure he'd heard that before.

"I remember that the funeral did take place at a synagogue, so there must have been one in that area. When Papa died — he died a young man, anyway, in spite of the climate, and Mama was a very young widow with no money — we moved to San Francisco. I was about eleven then, so my Aunt Anita — she and my Uncle Harry belonged to the big new Reform Temple — had me enrolled in the Confirmation Class. She wanted me to marry a Jewish boy. I felt shy at first, because the other girls were from rich families. All the girls used to wear all kinds of very expensive outfits, and I only had one dress for the class, that I used to wash every time. But I forgot about that after a few weeks and it was all right. I enjoyed it. I had a very good time.

"My mother and Aunt Anita used to go every Friday night to listen to Rabbi Neiman speak at the Temple. Everybody thought the world of Rabbi Neiman. Everyone said he was an intellectual and that he used to give the most interesting talks. Each Friday he would review a different book. I didn't understand everything he was talking about a lot of the time, but he was tall and elegant. He wore pince-nez glasses and always had on a beautiful suit, and he was very intelligent and dignified. To me, he looked just like Papa. I was in awe of him.

"One day I was in the Temple and I don't know why, I just got it into my head after class to go talk to Rabbi Neiman. So I went over and knocked on his door.

"I heard him from inside his office asking who was there, so I said, it's Eleanor Kopf, and I heard him say, 'Come in.'

"I came in and he said, 'Well, miss, what can I do for you?'"

"I just stood there looking at him. I didn't know what to say.

"He asked me again. I was speechless. I had no idea what had made me knock on his door. He said, 'What's the matter?' Now it sounded as if he were getting mad and before I knew what hit me I started crying.

"That just threw him for a loop, he didn't know what to make of it. He raised his voice at me. He said, 'What are you crying about?'

"That just made me cry harder. The last thing in the world I wanted was to be crying in Rabbi Neiman's office, but I couldn't stop. I heard him asking it again, 'What are you crying about?' He was yelling, or at least that's what I thought, I was so petrified. I stood there with my head bowed, too scared to look up at him. I knew my nose was running. I was sobbing, these great big sobs, trying to get my breath. I was a mess. I knew he thought I was an idiot."

"Why didn't you tell him that he reminded you of your father, Mommy? And that your father had just died?" This was for Dovie's benefit. I already knew the answer.

"Oh, I couldn't say that to Rabbi Neiman. I was as scared of him as I'd been of Papa. I can imagine how astounded he must have been. This child whom he doesn't know comes into his office and starts bawling her head off. Finally he just got up out of his chair and opened the door for me and said, 'Get out of here, right now! Out of my office!'"

My mother still looked baffled by this story. After a lifetime, the wound was fresh. We'd never found a way out. And as on other occasions when I'd heard it, my anger twisted up inside me like a snake. In my opinion, to some extent it was thanks to Rabbi Neiman's great kindness that from then on (for the next fifty years) my mother would think twice before striking up any more friendly conversations with rabbis — any kind of rabbis. "Mommy, I wish I could tell Rabbi Neiman what he did to you. How that affected the rest of your life."

"Yes, I know, he had no idea. Well, he's long gone."

"I know he is. But still. I hate him."

I then made my other usual remarks on the subject, which I won't record for posterity.

"Did you ever tell your mother about it? Or Aunt Anita?" This, too, I probably knew the answer to. It was Dovie I had in mind.

"No. That didn't occur to me. I was too ashamed of myself, and I knew what people would say, anyway, if they found out. 'What in the world do you think you're doing, going into Rabbi Neiman's office! How could you do such a stupid thing!'"

"Oh, Mommy!"

"Oh, well. Don't worry about it."

The Shabbos candles — two of mine and two of Mommy's — were flickering. I'd gotten chicken soup with matzah balls, from Glatt Hut, and on the table, in aluminum take-out pans from Nissim's, were the remains of our spinach kugel and roasted potatoes, the chicken in wine sauce, the chicken with mushrooms. My mother was sitting with hands folded, and she looked over at me with a smile, about to say something, then didn't.

"What, Mommy?"

"Oh, it's something I just thought of, about Daddy." This was my father, not hers.

"What?"

"He never liked it when I'd say, 'Oh, well.' He'd always say, 'Don't say that!'"

"Yes, Daddy was the opposite of 'Oh, well.' He didn't like resignation. Though you mean it more as acceptance, right?"

"Yes, I think you're right about that."

As usual while I was at her house, we were eating with plastic utensils, on plastic dishes I'd gotten at Ralph's Supermarket, and my mother had been working her way through her tiny portions. Even those, she'd tried to block my hand from serving. "No, no, that's too much. You're giving me too much." She'd been doing her best, though. She still strove with all her strength to finish everything on her plate, because that's what her father had taught his children: not to waste food.

"I think we kids were always scared to have people know we were Jewish when we were growing up," she said, looking again at Dovie. *"I don't know why I was scared like that. I'm not proud of that. It's not very admirable."*

"There was a lot of anti-Semitism in America then, wasn't there, Mommy?" I said. "After the First World War? That whole non-religious generation of Jews was scared."

"Yes, I guess so."

"I was scared, too. In Connecticut. You know that, don't you?"

We had talked about this on many occasions, but I could see she was considering it all over again, as if for the first time.

"And nobody ever said anything anti-Semitic to me. It wasn't anything outright like that. It was just something I sensed. Not from most people but from a few. By the way, Mommy, remember Mary Dickson? From fifth grade? She just wrote to me on my e-mail. She found my e-mail address."

"Really! Isn't that amazing. What an amazing thing computers are. It's something that's just beyond me." She gave a small wave of her hand, a gesture that took in the whole 20th century. "You girls had a lot of good friends in New Canaan, though, didn't you? Nancy Hutchinson still sends me New Year cards every year. All those babies she adopted! Five babies, I think. I think that's very admirable."

"The last I heard, they'd adopted two more, another set of twins. So now they have seven."

"My goodness. I don't know how she does it."

"Oh! And Mommy! Remember Susan Fletcher? That pretty little girl with blonde hair and a ponytail? I got an e-mail from her, too, just a little while ago. She does cancer research." I didn't say that Susan had written her mother had died, of cancer. "I used to sit behind her in fourth grade and I remember sitting there one time trying to imitate everything she did. She'd put her elbows on her desk, like this — and I'd put my elbows on my desk. She'd push her bangs out of her eyes, I'd push my bangs out of my eyes. I thought if I just did everything just the way she did it, then I'd be popular."

My mother bit her lip in wonder. "Really. Isn't that amazing. Why? I thought you were very popular."

"Mommy. I was popular until sixth grade. That was when I realized there was something going on about my being Jewish, and I started feeling scared."

"Yes, I know you've told me that."

"There was something in the air. A child feels it. That's what you felt, too. So don't blame yourself. You knew enough to be

scared. And for me, Mommy, I think it's partly because I had a Jewish name."

She shook her head, amazed. "Isn't that remarkable. Well, I think it's a beautiful name. Daddy liked it. Because of his mother."

"Oh, I love my name. I'm so glad I got a Jewish name! It affected my whole life! You know what they say, Mommy." I grinned. "Anti-Semitism is G-d's gift to the Jews, to make us remember who we are."

She looked solemnly over at my son. "Dovie," she said, "you don't feel scared like that, do you?"

He looked startled. "Not at all. I feel great to be Jewish."

She peered at him intently, intrigued. "Well, I guess you were brought up in it, and you grew up in Israel."

He nodded. "Uh hmm. Right. Yeah, I feel just great."

"When your mother got interested in Judaism, it was as if a window just opened up in front of me. It was a whole new world I'd never known was there. I've never been a religiously observant person. But now I've come to understand why your father was in a yeshivah for so many years, studying the Torah all day long. And why Orthodox people pray so many times each day. It's because that's really the most important thing in life." She looked over at me. "I didn't understand that before." Then, in a small voice, she said, "I'd like to learn more about the Torah now."

My heart constricted, then expanded, with a pure thrill of joy. The words I'd been waiting for. I felt I should say something. Then I felt I should stay silent. Not to jump on her. Not to scare her off.

On Sunday I drove down to the 613 Judaica Store and got her Rabbi Pliskin's new book called Patience. I read some of it aloud to her and she said, "Isn't that remarkable. I never thought of patience as being something that can transform your life." But I was hesitant, and... lazy. There was another week or so left on this trip, but she was too weak to read to herself and I'd never particularly liked reading aloud. And especially now that her hearing aid had gotten lost, it was a strain. That was another thing I had to do, I had to go with her to get her a new hearing aid.

I resolved that the next time I came, I'd bring along some other books. Gesher HaChaim, by Rabbi Tucazinsky. The Two-Way-Channel, By Rabbi Avraham Baharan. Rabbi Pliskin's Gateway to Happiness, The Sabbath, by Rabbi Grunfeld. That would be perfect. And we'd get the new hearing aid.

On September 11th, I was on board a Delta flight to Kennedy Airport when we were diverted mid-flight to London. "For security reasons," the pilot explained amiably over the cabin loudspeaker.

As one of the stewardesses hurried past me down the aisle, I asked if there had been a warning of a terrorist attack on the plane. "No," she said, "It's something in America."

No planes were allowed in or out of the country. Finally, six days later, El Al was permitted to run a flight back to Tel Aviv on Motzaei Shabbos. One seat remained. I took it.

Rosh Hashanah came and went.

A few days before Yom Kippur, there was an unexpected call from my sister. I should come back to L.A. as soon as possible.

"Today?"

"No, it doesn't have to be today. But the sooner the better."

I got a reservation for that night. Before leaving for the airport, I rushed over to the bookcase. What should I bring? I didn't see any of the books I'd thought of.

There was no time to look. I had to run. I'd buy some books in L.A.

But in L.A., The Bridge of Life didn't even come to mind. Gateway to...? That gate had shut.

And as for the hearing clinic, forget it.

◈◈

I turned off the Fisher-Price Nursery Intercom, so no one in the kitchen would hear.

"Mommy?" I leaned down close to the pillow. "Mommy, it's Sarah. Can you hear me?"

Andrea had installed the intercom the week before, so that whoever was in the kitchen could keep track of Mommy's breathing, and so that Mommy could let people know when she needed something. I'd been surprised, speaking to my sister over long distance, that my mother had agreed to such a thing. She couldn't possibly have resigned herself to not getting up and going to her own kitchen. On the contrary, said Andrea, she liked it, she thought it was great. And there'd been some joking around, some funny repartee. Mommy saying, "Hi, deh!" from the bedroom, and the two of them singing our favorite old songs as she made dinner.

When the red, red robin comes bob, bob bobbin' along, along!

There'll be no more sobbin' when he starts throbbin' his OL', sweet song!

WAKE up, wake up, you sleepyhead! GET up, get up, get outta bed!

CHEER up, cheer up, the sun is red! Live, love, laugh and be happy!

What if I was blue, now I'm walking through fields of flowers!

Rain may glisten but still I listen for hours, and hours!

I'm just a kid again, doin' what I did again, singin' a song,

when the red red robin comes bob bob bobbin' a, bob bob bob bob bob bobbin' aLONG!"

There was also a wheelchair in the bedroom now, Andrea warned me. They'd gotten it from the hospice program at Cedars-Sinai Hospital. "A wheelchair?" I had protested. "Really? Mommy agreed to it?"

"Sarah, dear. When was the last time you saw her?"

"I don't know, a few weeks ago."

"Well. I think you'll find there have been some big changes."

By the time I arrived, Mommy speaking over the intercom was a thing of the past. The wheelchair had been pushed over against a wall, out of the way, until the hospice people could come get it.

Now my lips were close to my mother's ear, and her hand was warm in mine.

"Mommy?"

No answer.

"Mommy? Do you hear me?"

A sound in her throat.

"Mommy, it's Sarah."

No answer.

"Mommy, I'm going to ask you something. Can you say, 'Shema Yisrael'?"

I waited. "Mommy, can you? Shema."

About five seconds went by, then, from deep in her throat, a loose dangling slur. "Zssssmmm."

"Yisrael."

Another long pause, then: "Zz—llll."

I squeezed her hand.

About five seconds passed, then: "Wuuu… zaaa?"

Not a brick, this time, but a boulder. "It's what Jews say when we wake up and when we go to sleep. We say it three times a day. It means, 'Listen, Israel.'"

How many years had I been observant, thirty? And I'd been too careful, too scared of alienating her to give over that much? So reluctant to pressure her that I'd never found an opportunity to mention the Shema?

Or had it just been laziness?

Laziness, most likely.

Her eyes were closed. An arrhythmic muscle in her neck was twitching, then fluttering.

Twitching. Fluttering.

From her throat came a thick gurgling.
I turned the intercom back on and walked out.

⧯⧯

After calling the *chevra kadisha* I went back into the bedroom. Candis and Dovie were sitting there next to the bed. I told them everything Rabbi Eidelitz had said.

My mother's tall yellow rose bush hovered outside the bedroom, pressing its many soft faces up against the sliding glass door, each velvety blossom a lavish expansion of gentleness. I slid open the door and walked out, holding the silver pitcher and glass of water, that had been on the bureau by her bed.

The air was so mild, so still, there was hardly a breeze.

I went over and dumped out the water under one of her orange bushes, then stood there, looking around at the Los Angeles hills. Dovie came out to join me. He stood looking around, too, hands in his pockets. "Everything out here..." he said, "It's amazing. I don't know, everything's the same." He shook his head, once. "Life goes on."

I knew what he meant. A few weeks ago I had thought: *the amazing thing is that life goes on,* then had corrected myself: *The amazing thing is that death goes on.* For all we knew, the world was about to come to an end. The War of Gog and Magog seemed just around the corner. But inside our own walls, we in our own little family persisted in our lives. Far away, buildings had crashed, economies and planes had crashed; back home in Israel, on the network of highways surrounding our home, people were being shot at daily. More and more children were becoming orphans all the time. But my mother's dying carried on steadily, relentlessly; we were totally absorbed.

Inside, on the bed a few feet away, Mommy was lying under a sheet.

"You want to talk with her, Dovie?"

He nodded.

Candis was taping pillowcases over the mirrors. She and I left the bedroom and I shut the door behind me. After some time, Dovie came out and Candis went in.

Then it was my turn.

I shut the door and went over to the bed. I felt hollow. *This is the time... If you have anything to ask mechilah for...*

What was wrong with me? This was the opportunity of a life-time. I certainly had a lot to say.

I stood there next to her bed, trying stiffly to apologize for something, then stumbled awkwardly into silence. It seemed utterly inadequate. I would have liked to cry, but was made of emptiness. I was nothing. The inner weather was utterly still, and arid. Finally I sat down, embarrassed, and looked out the glass door at my mother's pale sky. Some long tendrils of floating cloud hung weightlessly in the blue... not moving.

My eyes fell on the ancient framed photograph of my parents as newlyweds, hand in hand in a field of flowers. There they were, back before time and history began, eternally laughing and running toward me, as usual, eternally unaware of my presence. That picture had hung in their room for as long as I could re-member, but it momentarily seized me anew, for obvious reasons. The supreme drama of my looking at it as my mother lay a few feet away from me, under a sheet, was the stuff of literature, or Hollywood. It was such a blatant crossroads in my journey, and demanded of me such a meaningful response, that nothing I could summon up right now seemed equal to this bizarre moment. Here I was in my own real-life theatre, I was actor and audience both, and all that was happening was that I'd drawn a blank. I had no script. It was like spending a lifetime climbing to the top of the highest mountain in the world, and wondering, once you arrive, if your odd mood comes from tiredness. What do you think you're doing, all the way up there on top of the world, walking around in thin air?

Something I didn't bother putting my finger on prompted me to look at the photograph more closely. And with mild surprise I noticed, for the first time, that actually, there were no flowers in the picture. All my life I must have imagined them. It was just a field, with high grass.

I looked again. It was true. The field of flowers had no flowers.

I don't know how long I sat there.

Candis knocked, and said in a low voice through the door that the rabbis from the *chevra kadisha* had arrived, and could I come out to talk to them.

Hmm. That's a mighty important job, now, isn't it, for the baby in the family. I walked into the living room.

The two rabbis and I discussed various alternatives regarding travel plans. My mother was going to be buried alongside my father, in the family plot at Mt. Lebanon Jewish Cemetery in New Jersey; the funeral service was going to be in Edison. We had to get reservations to the East Coast as fast as possible, for everyone in the family, so as not to delay the funeral, but due to security problems since September 11th, there were unavoidable delays with the carrier he regularly used for transport of caskets. If I wanted, we could wait two days, and then travel all together. American had seats available on Wednesday.

The information wasn't holding together. "You mean, with my mother?"

"Yes."

"But we can't wait two days. She has to be buried within twenty-four hours, doesn't she?"

"That would be best. So there's a flight tonight at eleven, on Delta, that can take caskets. Ordinarily the casket would go directly to New York but because of the security situation, the direct flights are not operating, and there will be a stopover."

"A stopover? Where?"

"I don't know yet but I can get back to you on that. Now, that flight is full but the family can use another airline."

"But doesn't somebody have to stay with the casket?"

I sounded incredibly matter-of-fact to my own ears. It occurred to me that these rabbis must think this woman didn't care that much about her mother.

"Well, under unavoidable circumstances such as these, we can assume that on board the flight there will be at least one Jewish passenger, who can serve as a *shomer*."

"Really? *Frum* people do that?"

"If necessary, yes. Some people do it."

"Is that valid even if that Jewish passenger doesn't know he's a *shomer*?"

I can't recall his answer. I didn't want to hear it.

"How about if we all just go on the same flight as my mother's?"

"As I said, that flight is full."

I wanted to stop thinking, wanted to... I wanted him to take over.

So he did.

And when they wheeled her out of the bedroom on their gurney, and into the living room, when we stood off to the side as they steered her out the front door onto the driveway and passed us by — one tiny little mound rising under the sheet — and slid her into their van, my feeling was not at all unlike that of a mother who has just given birth.

The nurses are going to clean up the baby. They'll take care of everything. You can turn your head to the side, now. And close your eyes.

Didn't somebody say that they give the babies sugar water when the nursing mothers aren't looking, to keep the nursery under control? Even if you've given them instructions to the contrary?

Later. I'll think about it later.

"*Your* job, *geveret*," chirps the nurse, "is to get some rest! Don't you worry, you'll see Baby soon enough! Once you're back home (ha ha!) she'll be keeping you up all night!"

OK, sounds good to me! (Go away, everybody.) L'hitraot!

Bye-bye, baby, see you tomorrow!

Say bye-bye, baby!
Bye-bye!

❦ ❦

That afternoon and evening, after my mother had been taken away, I took care of everything that needed taking care of. I felt proud of myself. At long last, a convincing grown-up! I drove over to pick up the plane tickets at the travel agency, and stopped off at the mortuary to pay for everything with my mother's credit card: the "basic fee," and the casket, and the *taharah.* (In the mortuary office, waiting to sign all the papers, looking around at the sample gravestones that covered his wall, I said to one of the clerks, "It must be good in a way, to work here. It must make you very aware of life and death." The person shrugged. "No, it's not so good. It sort of has the opposite effect." "Oh, you mean, it desensitizes you?" "Well, I wouldn't say that, but I get used to it.") The funeral was all set for Wednesday at 12. Andrea was informing all the relatives.

I was proud, and felt like a traitor. I felt horrible, and relieved, and baffled by the airy formality of my demeanor. It was as if I'd gone out to lunch and left myself behind, as if I'd vacated the premises. *Well, I suppose I was prepared. There were so many warning signs posted all along the route. This Way, Death. Continue On, Straight Ahead. Caution, Death! Right Around the Bend.*

In any case, I was doing all right. It was going to be easier this time around.

I was finally ready to call. I sat down in my mother's black chair, leaned back, and dialed.

❦ ❦

It was 1975, about a year before I moved to Israel, and I was with my parents for the weekend, at our house in Connecticut. On Sunday morning when we awoke, the world had turned into a dream, a shining fairyland. Outside the windows, sky and earth were one. A luminous land was the soft sky above and upside down was the sky beneath. All the trees everywhere had turned into exquisite black lacework and intricate tracery etched upon the white air, every inch of black line accentuated by its precise double in white trimming. All the world was purest light, and brighter than white. The world was new. It had just been created.

"Let's go for a walk!" said my parents. They bounded out into the cold. They were running. I followed, trying to keep up but purposefully lagging behind, too. I was photographing them in my mind. I knew... I would need this picture of them one day. "That's my parents," I was thinking. "This is the essence of them."

They were both sixty, then.

They were holding hands and laughing.

I was running along behind.

They ran through the opening in the tall pine hedge, where a path through the woods led into an open field, but they then stopped short. The way was blocked. A great, long, branch of pine had drooped down over the path under its tremendous white load, all the way to the ground.

For a moment the two of them stood there. Had the limb snapped under the weight? What a pity. My mother said, "Wait, maybe it's not broken. Maybe if I just shake it off —"

My father and I stood watching as she stepped up to the branch and tried to shake it. It was so heavy, it hardly budged.

"Well, maybe —" She tried again. My father joined her. Trying, trying. The branch lifted up off the ground a little. They kept going, the snow was falling off in clumps. The two of them were shaking it, and more and more snow was dropping off. The dark brown bark had appeared, the dark green needles. More snow falling off, more snow... Suddenly — swoosh! — the tree came alive, leaping up high over our heads and showering us with white! The big, long heavy branch! Liberated! My mother and fa-

*ther laughed! The way was cleared. They caught hands and start-
ed running again along the path.*

I followed.

∽∾

*It was unusual, my father asking me to come for Thanksgiving.
I was happy, and surprised, and wanted very much to see everyone, but felt uncomfortable with the national holiday's
quasi-Christian overtones, and with the associations it had for me.
This was in spite of the fact that in our family, Thanksgiving had always served simply as the largest Jewish get-together of the year.*

*Such discomfort wouldn't stop me nowadays, after what hap-
pened. But at the time, I didn't know whether to deal with it or
skip it, so I asked a sheilah.*

*"So maybe," replied Rabbi Scheinberg, "you can tell your fa-
ther you'll come a little later."*

That's what I did. I reserved tickets for December 7th.

*On Thanksgiving Day I called to say hello. A cousin answered.
"Can I speak to my father? Is he around?" No, he said, he was
out taking a walk with Andrea.*

"Can you tell him I called?"

"Sure, no problem."

*My father never called back. I was sad. I wondered if he was
mad at me for not coming.*

He died the following week.

*Turned out that the relative who picked up the phone had for-
gotten to give him the message, but I only learned about that a
few months later.*

∽∾

*A friend of my parents offered us the use of her private cor-
porate jet, at no cost to us, to transport my father's body, along
with our whole family, from L.A. to New York.*

It was an adorable, sleek little plane. The cabin was luxurious, smiling pilot and crisply attired staff were part of the package, and the cute oval portholes were sparkling clean. Outside, all the way across the continent, the city of clouds and adjacent kingdom of blue sky soared all around at our command, magisterial and at peace. It was a treat. We laughed. "Daddy would have enjoyed this," said my mother. "He'd be tickled pink."

As America slipped by at our fingertips, far below, I asked my sister about that walk they'd taken. Andrea told me that at one point Daddy had said to her, out of the blue, "You know, Pigeon, before Mom and Pop died —" (that was his parents, Sarah and Sam,) "I thought that if anything ever happened to them, I wouldn't be able to go on."

"Really? Pigeon! So he must have known! What did you say when he said that?"

"Nothing. I was so surprised, I just looked at him. I wondered why he was telling me this."

"Did he say anything else?"

"Yes. He looked me in the eye and said, 'But I did go on.'"

"No! Really!" I started crying. "Then what?"

"Nothing. I wish I'd said something like, 'Daddy, why are you telling me this?' or 'So tell me! What's the trick? How did you go on?' But I didn't."

Shortly thereafter, at some point during the flight, I noticed the little door at the back of the cabin and suspected maybe that was the cargo room. When nobody was looking, I opened the door, tentatively. A whoosh of chilled air and tremendous engine noise rushed out at me.

There it was on the floor. I'd never seen a body bag before but knew it when I saw it. It looked like one of his golf bags.

I slipped into the semi-darkness and shut the door behind me.
"Daddy!"
I knelt down on the metal floor.
"Daddy!"

So cold for him!

So dark!

Daddy!

A whole lifetime poured out like a river.

Thank you, Daddy! Thank you! For everything! You were so wonderful!

I'm so sorry I didn't come!

Who knows how much time passed. With all the racket from the engine, I didn't have to worry about the noise I was making. That sublimely silent passenger cabin was soundproof. Everyone must have realized I was in there — maybe somebody had opened the door and peeked in, and I hadn't noticed — but nobody bothered me.

I told him everything. Everything. Until there was no more to say.

When I returned to the others, and took my seat, I thought: That's good. I got the major mourning all out of me at one time.

≈≈

I was prodding my mother for some more stories. There were a lot of them.

"Did you ever hear about the time he was in an army plane during World War II?"

"No. What was that?"

"Well, Daddy had a job as an Army journalist during the war and he was on a plane that was transporting soldiers to Europe. After the plane took off, Daddy noticed that across from him — in those army planes, the soldiers didn't sit facing front the way people do in commercial airliners; they all sat with their backs to the windows, facing in — Daddy noticed after takeoff that across the aisle from him, one of the young soldiers was crying. He was crying for quite some time, and Daddy unbuckled and got up out of his seat and went over and kneeled down in front of the young soldier to ask him if there was anything he could do to help, and just then there was a big popping sound. The window behind Daddy's seat had cracked and the seat he'd been sitting in had been sucked right out of the plane."

"No!"

"Yes. Well, that's what happened."

"That's a metaphor for his whole life, isn't it, Mommy? What about that time you and Daddy were in New York and his overcoat got stolen?"

"His overcoat got stolen?"

"Remember? The overcoat, and the man who was in jail."

"Oh, that. Well, Daddy and I were in New York City and he found a parking spot somewhere near his office — I think that was when the Saturday Review was on West 45th St. We went out and did whatever we had to do and when we came back somebody had broken into the car and had taken his briefcase, and his overcoat, and maybe some other things, I don't remember. So we went to the police to report a theft and they took down all the information and we left. I don't remember where we went after that, but in any case, it wasn't very long before the police contacted us to say they'd caught the thief and had recovered the items and we could come get them. So we went back to the police station and Daddy was just delighted. There was his briefcase — none of his papers were missing, they'd found it in a garbage can — and his overcoat. It was Daddy's favorite overcoat, it was very nice and warm. Daddy liked it. So he was just delighted and after the police finished the paperwork they said we could go home. But Daddy asked them, where's the man who broke into the car? And they said there was nothing to worry about, they had him right there at the station. He was already behind bars. So Daddy said that if it would be all right with them, he'd like to meet him.

"Well, Daddy went back into the jail to meet him and the man was a very poor man. He told Daddy his whole life story. They talked for quite a long time and in the course of conversation, Daddy found out that the overcoat had fit the man perfectly, it was just his size. So Daddy took it off and gave it to him."

"Then the court?"

"Oh, so Daddy found out when the man's case was coming up in court, and Daddy went to testify on the man's behalf. He said that if they would let the man out of jail, he'd assume legal responsibility for him. And the judge agreed. Daddy got the man a job, and he did pretty well at it, if I remember correctly. It was something to do with printing, I think."

❧

At the sound of his voice, the sky broke.

"Hello, Yaacov?" The rain started falling. A whole history with our parents that we shared. Rain, rain. We cried and cried. All the way across the ocean, the vast expanse between two telephones of a thousand tiny gray waves, turning, and churning, over and over, rolling over and over and over, white and gray and gray and white and white and gray and gray and white, turning, and weaving, turning in and out of themselves under the thousand silent tiny drops. From thousands of miles above in the high grey sky, the rain was falling down everywhere into the waves, gentle, insistent, returning to the sea.

Our parents had died and we were alive. Alive, after all.

❧

Who needs such crying? You keep thinking that if you just do enough of it, you'll get over some kind of hump and get to the other side. But it just keeps on going, on and on with no let up, ad nauseum, and at the end of it, all you get is more of the same. It's exhausting. It depletes you. Been there, done that! Like waves coming in from an ocean. Endless! You never get to the bottom of it! What good is it?

Sometimes it's scary. Is this ever going to stop? Will I ever get back to normal?

After a while, though, eventually it happens that a few days go by and you realize with a start that you haven't been crying.

Somebody mentions his name and you don't dissolve, or crumble, or want to get down under the floorboards and sink. You think, "What do you know, it's over." You've finally gotten there. You've come to the end, the end of the tears, where you wanted to be.

You're glad.

It feels strange.

After a little while, relief turns into something else, a faint apprehension. There's an emptiness, something large, that's kind of creeping up on you, and a fear. You feel as if you're forgetting him, abandoning him. Or — is this worse? — that he's abandoning you. Is he letting go? Like a big balloon, floating off over the trees?

You're alone.

A few hours later, something makes you think of him and tears spring into your eyes. Daddy! Hello!

He's with you again!

〜〜

We'd arrived in New York, Dovie, Candis, Shigeko and I, and were just finishing our dessert at a kosher restaurant.

Shigeko, my adopted Japanese sister, had been maimed by the Hiroshima Bomb as a teenager. In the early 1950's, she and about thirty other young girls had been brought by my father's magazine to the United States for plastic surgery, and Shigeko had stayed with us. She became part of our family; she called herself "Jewpanese." Mommy had been a mother to her. Shigeko, now in her sixties, is a registered nurse.

A few days previously, my mother had been in a coma. Candis and I were sleeping in her room and some dream about my mother woke me up about 4 a.m.

I looked over anxiously at the hospital bed. A small light was on. Shigeko, standing with her back to me, was manually siphoning mucous from my mother's mouth to prevent her from choking. She'd been doing it all night.

Now, in the restaurant, we were all talking. I didn't want to admit it, but a great weight had been lifted off all of us. Suddenly, Dovie looked over at me and said, "Where is Mom now?"

Where is Mom now?

I got a strange kind of seasick feeling. "I don't know. I guess she's in flight, on her way here."

"Mommy," he said, "you don't know?"

It was as if I'd been fast asleep. Signing papers in the mortuary, I had inwardly joked to myself in silence that maybe I should forge her signature for the credit card, but to wonder if she was lying in an adjacent room, on the other side of the office wall, had not even occurred to me.

Where was she?

And the *shomer!* She didn't have a *shomer!* She was alone.

Now Candis was looking at me intently. She had depended on me for this part of the process. "Sarah, didn't the *chevra kadisha* rabbi tell you they were going to put her on a flight last night? When does she arrive in New York?"

We paid and rushed out. In the hotel room, I plunged down onto the couch, grabbing the phone. *Crazy hotel! These stupid buttons! They don't even say which ones are for long distance!*

Finally, there was Debby on the other end. "Debby! I don't know where my mother is! Is Rabbi Eidelitz there?" He wasn't. I told her the whole story.

"Now I'm sure it will be all right, the airlines generally take very good care of these things. Do you know what airline she's on?"

"Delta!"

"And do you know where the connecting flight was going?"

"No! I don't!"

"All right, now don't worry, I'm going to call my husband right now and I'm sure he'll be able to figure it out. It's just a question of the *chevra kadisha* being closed now, probably, and how long it will take him to reach the director. Just stay right there until he calls. It shouldn't be a problem."

The Eidelitzes' kindness... Hashem's *chessed* made manifest. Twenty minutes later the director of the Los Angeles *chevra kadisha* had called our New York hotel room with the number of the flight, the phone number of the Delta Airlines Cargo Terminal in Atlanta, Georgia, and the phone number of that city's *chevra kadisha*. I was now on the line with a Delta representative in Atlanta who heard my story and had just put me on hold, whereupon we were promptly disconnected.

I dialed again, madly, furiously. "Idiot!" I was shouting. "He disconnected me!" Candis and Dovie were looking on. Shigeko, subdued and taken aback, was doing something in the hotel kitchenette, going quietly about her business.

This time I got a recorded announcement. All Delta representatives were presently busy now with other callers. The voice asked me to please hold the line and await my turn, and a representative would be with me shortly. My call was very important to them. If I would like information about Delta's Caribbean Holiday Package, please press 1. If I would... Suddenly somebody real came on. "How can I help you?"

Unlike the soothingly earnest robot who had just been addressing me, this frosty young lady sounded cheerily insincere. I fought my way past her, back to the other clerk. "Yes, ma'am, sorry about that. We were cut off. It seems there were a number of caskets on that Los Angeles flight and they're all being held in a separate room."

"A separate room? You mean just for caskets?'

"Yes, ma'am."

"Is it locked? Is the room locked?"

"No, ma'am, we are not allowed to block access to the cargo rooms."

"Oh, no! Then how do you know people aren't breaking in there?"

"Ma'am, no one is going to break into the casket room, I can assure you."

"When is the connecting flight?" I was trying to keep my voice down.

"That flight is due to depart at... Just a moment and I'll check... 8 a.m."

"She's going to be there all *night?*"

"You mean your mother."

"Yes! My mother! She can't be alone all night!"

Silence.

"Sir, are you there? She can't be there alone all night!" *I need some human kindness! Put the recording back on!*

"May I ask why?"

"It has to do with something from Judaism. It's Jewish law. I don't think I can explain it in just a few sentences, there are a number of different explanations, some of them practical and some for spiritual reasons but the main thing — you know, I'm really not sure it's pertinent to go into all that right now. Unless you think it would be helpful."

"Ma'am, what is it you would like us to do?"

"What I'd like to do, sir, is arrange for a member of the Jewish Burial Society in Atlanta — I have the number, I can call them right now and they'd be delighted to do it, this is just the kind of thing they're there for — I need to have someone from that organization come sit with the casket."

"In the cargo area, you mean."

There was hope! "Yes."

"I'm sorry, Federal regulations do not permit non-airline employees inside the cargo area."

"Can't you make an exception? I can't tell you how important it is."

"I'd like to help you, ma'am, we're more than happy to accommodate the religious customs of all Delta passengers. But I'm not prepared to violate Federal regulations."

"Please, sir, can I speak to your supervisor?"

"I am the supervisor."

"Oh." I wilted — a cartoon flower keeling over. "I see." *Dear G-d. Please. Help me.*

"Ma'am, you can rest assured that your mother's casket is being well taken care of."

"I understand. But I don't know what to do. The casket has to be guarded."

"There is a guard."

"There is?" The flower popped right back up.

"Yes, ma'am."

"There's a guard?"

"That's what I said."

"Can I speak to him?"

"It's a her."

"What? That would be wonderful if I could do that. May I ask his name?"

"Suzy, ma'am."

"Suzy? The guard's name is Suzy?"

"That's right."

"Can I speak to her, please?"

"Well — "

"*Sir. Please.*"

"Just a minute. I'll see if I can transfer you."

Several seconds went by. *Maybe her name is Suzy Rabinowitz! Or Suzy Gross! Who knows!* There were a few clicks, then the tone changed. "Oh no! I don't believe it! He disconnected me again! I can't stand it! I'm going to have to start all over again!" I was about to hang up when a woman's soft Southern accent said, "Hello?"

"Hello! Is this Suzy?"

"Yes, it is. Can I help you?" She sounded nice! I loved Southern accents!

"Suzy! I'm so glad to talk to you! Are you the guard for the casket room?"

"Yes, I am."

"I'm the daughter of one of the people in the caskets. It's my mother, Eleanor Cousins. Can you check to see if she's all right?"

Silence.

"Oh, I don't mean to open it up! I just mean to look at it! Hello?"

"Yes, ma'am, I'm here."

"Can you do that? It's the casket of Eleanor Cousins."

"Eleanor who?"

"Cousins! Like relatives!"

"Just a minute."

I heard the phone being set down, and remarkably, heard the click of Suzy's heels echoing in the cargo room in Atlanta, Georgia.

"Yes. I see the casket."

"You do, Suzy? You see the casket?"

"I'm looking right at it."

"You are?" My heart, my mind, my hands, my feet — all together now we flooded with exultation. "Are you sure that's the right one? How do you know?"

"Her name is Eleanor Cousins? The name's on the box."

"Oh! How wonderful! Suzy, thank you!"

"You're very welcome."

"Suzy, can you do something for me?"

"I can try."

"Look, I know that none of us can say what goes on after death, but what I'd like to ask of you is, on the chance that the soul is aware and that she could hear you, do you think you could just go over to my mother and tell her something for me?"

"Certainly."

"Oh, thank you! Could you tell her that her daughter Sarah called, to tell her that she's in the airport in Atlanta, Georgia, on her way to New York, and that she's going to be buried right next to her husband, in the cemetery in New Jersey? Can you tell her that?"

"Will do."

"Oh, that's so wonderful! And can you tell her that we all love her and that we're all in New York, waiting for her?"

"I certainly will. I'll do that right now."

"Suzy. Thank you."

"I'm happy to do it. I'm sorry for your loss. You take care of yourself."

Ki le'olam chasdo. His kindness endures forever.

⬿⬾

It's a facial expression I have almost no hope of describing.

She had been in a coma for three days; she was no longer with us. Every labored breath seemed it would be the last; for three days and three nights, I was scared to leave the room. "This is it! Oh G-d!" How many times did I think that? A hundred times. A thousand times. Ten thousand times. When I was alone with her, I'd turn off the intercom so no one would hear me. I knew it was crazy for me to be doing it but I'd cry, "Mommy! Do you hear me? Mommy! Do you hear me? Mommy!"

No answer.

No answer. "Mommy! Please!" No answer. She was still breathing. "Mommy!"

It was Saturday night. We had been standing around her bed, all of us. It reminded me of the scene from the Chumash of Yaacov and his children, except that Yaacov hadn't been in a coma; he'd been able to speak. (Mommy! Give me a blessing! Give me a blessing, Mommy! Please!) Her beloved baby brother, aged eighty, and her sister-in-law, and her grandson, and her daughters, and Shigeko and Shigeko's son and his wife, and his baby girl. We were all there, around the bed. We'd been there for hours. Hours and hours, hours upon hours. She was breathing.

All of a sudden, one of us yelped. I can't even remember if it was me or someone else.

"Look!" We all jumped. "Her eyes!"

"She's looking at us!"

"She's looking at us!" All of a sudden, a mighty chorus! We were all screaming, hooting, clapping our hands, we were crying, we were laughing.

"Eleanor!"

"Mommy!"

"Mom!"

"Mother!"

"Ellen!"

"Mommy!"

Laughing, crying. "Mommy! Mommy!"

Rubbing her hands! Pressing her hands in ours. "Mommy!" Stroking her face! Shouts! Laughter! Crying! "Mommy! Mommy!"

What was it we had seen in her eyes that was the difference between absence and presence, awareness and unawareness? Impossible to define and impossible to miss. It was unmistakable. She was here again! "Mommy!"

And then…

(This is what I almost give up trying to describe here, before I even start.)

On Motzaei Shabbos, the 3rd of Cheshvan, 5762, October 20th, 2001, my mother, Eleanor Cousins, Eleanor Esther, born 1914 in Price, Utah, third daughter of Feigel (nee Goldberg) and Adolf Kopf, newly immigrated from Russia:

This Eleanor underwent something that transformed her.

She was, I suppose, still recognizably my mother, whom I had known my whole life, but the expression on her face was something I'd never seen before, neither on her nor on anyone else. I despair of doing it justice, but for your information I'll give it a try.

She wasn't looking at us, though for a few moments she had indeed been with us again. She was focused now, with the singularity of her whole being and with what looked as if it must be painful intensity and concentration, at something above us, something that was obviously not as far away from her as it was from us. For she herself was in another realm from ours, a realm hermetically sealed off and far removed from ours. Whatever she saw was above us, behind us to our right, but way higher than the ceiling, way out beyond the house. She was up close to it, beneath it, and looking up at it, at a steep angle. She was looking at something quite specifically and pointedly; for her it was immediate and real, more real than anything she'd ever seen down here. Nothing had ever elicited from her that kind of attention. The quality of her attention was something new. She was right up close to something terrifying, yet something that evoked, too, her total, deepest trust. Her face was made of love. Her mouth was no longer hanging open. Her lips were pursed gently shut, with respect and determination. Between her eyebrows a single deeply chiseled cleft had appeared.

It was the face of a very young child.

It was a child who feels chastised, but a child possessed of complete understanding. She has been reprimanded, not by way of a reprimand but by having been granted a view of something.

Her face was utterly focused, determined, and... angry.

And one aspect of what that look declared (and forgive me, Mommy, for being unable to convey a meaning that was so obvious, lucid and unambiguous) was:

"I DIDN'T KNOW." Or maybe it can be better conveyed by: "BUT YOU DIDN'T SAY."

Don't ask how this communicated itself. Please, don't dare ask me how I could read that look even though it had no words, just as if it were a caption that was being printed out in Teletype, underneath her chin. Don't ask, but don't doubt it, either. She was looking up, up, up. Something had been revealed, a veil uplifted, a curtain had been drawn aside, for her. And whatever it was that she saw, shocked her to her core.

Her face was made of shock, anger, and pure obedience. She had inhabited her face so potently and fully that she had become perfectly herself, and in so doing, had become somebody else.

She was looking at something that was evoking the purest possible fear and the purest possible courage. She was afraid but not at all cowering, or cringing. I had never imagined that expression or visualized it on a face, or seen a picture of it, but when I saw it, there was no failing to recognize it. And it was clear as day what she was looking at.

She was a child looking up at her Father.

Not her earthly father, who for unknown reasons had been plucked from her before she ever really knew him, or he her, in earliest childhood, but her incorporeal Father.

Her face was that of a little girl standing at the footstool of Hashem. And if you don't believe it, sorry.

It was now self-evident that all those apparently aimless days spent drifting in and out of consciousness, drifting farther and farther out, had never been aimless, after all. On the contrary, she'd been traveling, all that time. She'd been completing a long, long journey.

She had been on her way here, to this place, not only for the last four years, but ever since the day, in 1914, that she was born. All the suffering she had ever gone through, not only during this illness but in her life, and there was much, much — every fragment of her suffering, not only in this illness but everything else, too — had been making her ready, for this. She was ready now. A split second earlier would have been too soon. Shehechiyanu vekiyemanu vehigiyanu la'zeman hazeh.

My mother's face... I'd always assumed, of course, that I knew what she looked like. But that was merely her "personality," which had been dropped, now, along the way, like so much excess baggage.

As for jade earrings, she'd let go of them long ago.

We were being granted a glimpse of my mother's unadorned soul, and it was the most terrifying, the most beautiful thing I'd ever seen in my life.

She was the mother I loved, but it was her Father, alone, Who could hold that child in His arms.

~~~

My husband told me that the first few times he said *kaddish* for my mother, an odd thing happened. Each time, as he began, a vivid image would appear in his mind's eye, of my parents holding hands and running in a meadow. "They were so happy," he said. "They were smiling, and laughing, and the meadow was full of flowers. It was so clear, I just kept seeing it, again and again. It was hard to concentrate on my *davening*." This happened for three days, he said, then subsided.

"Yaacov," I asked, "did you ever see that picture of my parents running in a field?"

"No. What picture?"

But he wasn't there.

After all that emotion, over the crest of the next hill, he wasn't there, after all, waiting for you with an answer. She won't be either.

Can't go through that again, that's for sure. Who needs it?

It was my first morning back home in Jerusalem, my fifth day of sitting *shivah*. My daughter Yehudit told me she had dreamed that she met Mom and asked her how she was. Mom was laughing and smiling and didn't answer. "How is it for you, Mom?" My mother just kept smiling. In the dream, Yehudit hadn't wanted to say anything about her having died; she didn't know if Mom knew.

I'd propped up some pictures of my parents on our piano and as I glanced over at them, now, my throat tightened. *Don't start. What good is it.* I'd had those photographs for years. Why couldn't they have been infused with that kind of significance, why couldn't they have given off that kind of electricity when there was something I could have done about it? When I could have picked up the phone and called them? Why must it be that it's only in the backward glance that the people you love are this vivid? Why must it be only when a person vanishes that he acquires such visibility in one's mind; only losing a person absolutely which brings him fully to life?

It's true, even, of objects. Even of objects I dislike. I never liked the Twin Towers. Other then to mock them for their crass pretentiousness, I'd almost never given them a thought. Yet once they had vanished, once their destruction had lent them a poignant vulnerability, my eyes opened to the role they had played. It was only their absence which revealed to me the significance of their presence.

My daughters were asking if I wanted them to tell the neighbors. I said no.

I went through all that already, with Daddy. Thank you very much. This time I'll pass.

"Are you sure, Mommy? Daddy said to be sure to tell people before we leave the house, so you won't be alone today. You don't want anybody? What about Esther Linder?"

No. No. I shook my head.

"Are you sure? Malka Adler called to ask. What about Pam?"

No, no. I have to be alone. I can't relate to anyone.

So, everyone left. I was sitting on the cushions, re-reading the L.A.Times obituary notice that my sister Candis had clipped for me. *Could it be? I'm in our living room having a cup of coffee and reading my mother's obituary.* I was confused by the sense I had of being suspended nowhere at all. Was I depressed? Was I depressed that I wasn't depressed? To feel or not to feel, that was the question. Was I stopping myself from feeling, was that my problem? Wasn't it better to stay where I was, on shore, where at least there was land beneath my feet?

I went back to the *halachos* of mourning. The book, Maurice Lamm's *The Jewish Way in Death and Mourning,* was split along the binding, from my frenzied use of it eleven years earlier.

> *From the moment of death until burial, the deceased may not be left alone. Therefore, the family must arrange for a person called a shomer (watcher) to be at his side at all times. While it is preferable for the watcher to be a member of the family or a personal friend, this is not always possible. In such cases, a person must be engaged to watch the body and recite from the Book of Psalms... The mourner should ascertain clearly whether the watcher is reliable, for he must remain awake and should recite Psalms all through the night.*

...The onen is a person in deep distress, a person yanked out of normal life and abruptly catapulted into the midst of inexpressible grief. He is disoriented, his attitudes are disarranged, his emotions out of gear. The shock of death paralyzes his consciousness and blocks out all regular patterns of orderly thinking. "The deceased lies before him," as the sages said, and psychologically, he is reliving the moment of death every instant during this period. In this state of mind, unfortunately, the mourner must make detailed and final arrangements with the funeral director, burial society, cemetery and rabbi. He must also notify friends and family. Yet inwardly, his primary...

Just then, like lightning, something struck a live nerve: *that roll of wallpaper.* One day a few years ago, my mother had helped me choose it, in a store on Ventura Blvd. It was do-it-yourself wallpaper, multicolored flowers in pastels, and in the end it hadn't matched our kitchen. It must be sitting, real and actual, in one of our closets.

That she had ever been alive at all struck me now as something unbelievable, as unbelievable as the notion that she had died.

...his primary concern is with his own loss ... Often at this time, he is burdened with guilt for the moments of unhappiness he may have caused the deceased ... The bereaved searches the time before the death for evidence of failure to do right by the loved one. He accuses himself of negligence and exaggerates minor omissions.

...The Burial Kaddish is a prayer affirming that G-d, in His good time, will create the world anew..., and that the deceased will be raised up to everlasting life...

The purpose of the visitor's presence and speech during the shivah should not be designed to distract the bereaved... The visitor should, by all means, be sensitive to the mourner's feelings. There is a time for all things, the Bible tells us, and surely there is a time for leaving the house of the bereaved. Visits should never be unduly prolonged, in the mistaken belief that one's presence brings an unusual degree of relief...

An hour or so passed. The sky outside was bright enough, but darkness had entered my mind. *I'm alone.*

Inner twilight speeded up into night. The darkness was getting darker, fast. *Nobody loves me.*

Another half-hour or so passed. *So this is the truth, when it comes right down to it. Everybody's ignoring me. My mother has died and nobody cares. I'm all alone.*

I put down the book and got up to check my e-mail, finding, to my delight, a letter of condolence from Paula Van Gelder, a writer and friend of mine in Los Angeles.

> *...At the time that my Grandma died, in 1993, she was 108 years old, close to 109. I know that we were granted a great blessing in her longevity. Yet when she died, we cried bitter tears — her children, grandchildren and great-grandchildren. I remember how devastated my mother was. She even said, "Every year after 100, it seemed that she would go on forever." I know that we never truly accepted her mortality. Around the same time, a young man in the community died suddenly of a heart attack. A local woman, herself suffering from a terminal illness, was not trying to be mean or cruel. Yet, when she heard about my Grandma, she said: I cry for [the young man]. I don't cry for your grandmother." I know what she meant. I understand it rationally, but it hurt then and it still stings now. We can never compare.*

I went back to my cushion on the floor. Being visited by Paula had been wonderful.

I got an idea. *Mrs. Striegler.* I looked up at our living room wall.

We hardly know each other, she and I, though we've shared that wall for fifteen years, and we sometimes hear her grandchildren playing the piano. But one day, years ago, I'd been in line at the grocery store when I realized Mrs. Striegler, also in line, was looking over at me with a questioning intensity. I glanced around — maybe it was somebody else, someone behind me, maybe, whom she was staring at?

She had then come over to me, and asked, to my surprise, why I hadn't come to visit her during her *shivah* for her mother. I explained that I hadn't known. She said, "But there were signs up. You didn't see them? There were signs on the building. There was one in your entrance."

I was shocked. "No, I didn't notice. I'm so sorry, I often don't read signs when they're in Hebrew." Her eyes filled with tears, and I thought, *Is this what's in store for me with Mommy?* My eyes filled with tears and we hugged each other.

We'd never visited each other after that incident, and hadn't had anything further to do with each other in our daily lives, but ever since, I had felt a love between us.

The front door opened now. It was my son. "Yehudah! Could you do me a favor? Go to Mrs. Striegler and tell her I'm sitting *shivah* for my mother."

"You mean the people who live —"

"Mrs. Striegler! From Mexico. On the other side of our wall, in *knissah bet*."

"O.K., but Mommy, they don't even —"

"Just go! She'll understand."

He left. I waited. The bitter darkness was expanding. There was a possibility that maybe she wasn't home. She probably wasn't home. In about three minutes, my son was holding the door open and in she stepped, looking around, hesitant.

"Mrs. Striegler!" I jumped to my feet, she opened her arms, and I flew into her embrace. We cried.

I felt much better after that and later on, told my family about it. I had imagined I knew better than the *halachah*, I said. I had been sure that I knew best what was best for me: that it would be difficult, having to deal with visitors.

My family apparently took this in, and before I knew it, the people started coming. The Ingbers, and the Sales. My niece Becky, and Esther. My cousins the Cowans, my cousins the Talents. Dena and Sara, Arlene and Esther. Naomi, Lyndon, Drora, Rica,

Shoshana. Uriela and Brachah. My daughters' friends Shani, who spread the word to her mother Rochel, and my daughters' friends Nechama and Shiri, Chany and Avigal, Batsheva, Leebie, Laiky, Riki, Pnina, Miriami. The Israels came, and the Lubans, Mr. Poupko and Hani, Mr. Greenblatt and Dr. Lampner, Dr. Slater and Shifra, the Garbians and Breini. Bonnie, Miriam, Chava, Rebbetzin Bulman. Happy, Chaia, Goldie… The door kept opening, and opening. They were coming in on waves.

I was still by myself, but was surrounded by a constantly changing circle of faces, and was being buoyed and kept afloat by their presence. As *halachah* prescribes, they didn't speak unless I initiated conversation. I had neither to rise when they entered nor make conversation when they sat; there was no obligation to thank them when they got up to leave, nor to say goodbye when they walked out. I didn't have to acknowledge anyone; they knew what the instructions were. They knew what it was like, losing a parent, or — if their own hour hadn't yet arrived — knew that they, too, would one day be kept company from afar.

For twelve months, I would be held in place by the *halachic* structure, a building designed to endure all turbulence and rough weather. Eventually I'd be able to bear the unbearable thought of my mother as she had been in life; one day she would begin to reemerge, as my father had, and in the wake of their deaths, I, too, would start coming back to life, detail by detail by detail.

In a world full of orphans, to feel the loss of your own parents is to travel to that lonely place, out on the dark ocean at night, alone, where nobody ever wants to go.

But it's there you can find the only Father Who never leaves.

Ha'Makom yenachem eschem b'soch she'ar aveilei Tziyon vi'Yerushalayim. May you be comforted among the other mourners of Zion and Jerusalem.

I was surrounded by friends but was alone with G-d, as night became day under my stormy skies.